QUESTIONS OF CONTEXT

Reading a Century of German Mission Theology

JOHN G. FLETT *and*
HENNING WROGEMANN

An imprint of InterVarsity Press
Downers Grove, Illinois

InterVarsity Press
P.O. Box 1400, Downers Grove, IL 60515-1426
ivpress.com
email@ivpress.com

©2020 by John G. Flett and Henning Wrogemann

All rights reserved. No part of this book may be reproduced in any form without written permission from InterVarsity Press.

InterVarsity Press® is the book-publishing division of InterVarsity Christian Fellowship/USA®, a movement of students and faculty active on campus at hundreds of universities, colleges, and schools of nursing in the United States of America, and a member movement of the International Fellowship of Evangelical Students. For information about local and regional activities, visit intervarsity.org.

All Scripture quotations, unless otherwise indicated, are taken from The Holy Bible, New International Version®, NIV®. Copyright © 1973, 1978, 1984, 2011 by Biblica, Inc.™ Used by permission of Zondervan. All rights reserved worldwide. www.zondervan.com. The "NIV" and "New International Version" are trademarks registered in the United States Patent and Trademark Office by Biblica, Inc.™

Christine Lienemann-Perrin (b. 1946), "Mission in the Turn of Eras" / "Mission in der Zeitenwende," in Das Christentum an der Schwelle zum 3. Jahrtausend. Erfahrungsgehalte der jüdisch-christlichen Tradition angesichts von Schwellensituationen und Jahrtausendwechseln, ed. Albrecht Grözinger, and Ekkehard Stegemann (Stuttgart: Verlag W. Kohlhammer, 2002), 151-66 (2232). Used by permission of Christine Lienemann.

Henning Wrogemann, "Intercultural Theology—On the Definition and Field of Study of the Sixth Discipline of the Faculty of Theology" / "Interkulturelle Theologie—Zu Definition und Gegenstandsbereich des sechsten Faches der Theologischen Fakultät," Berliner Theologische Zeitschrift 32 (2015), 219-39. Used by permission of Henning Wrogemann.

Andreas Feldtkeller, "Mission und Religionsfreiheit," Zeitschrift für Mission 28 (2002), 261-75. Used by permission of Andreas Feldtkeller.

Richard Friedli, "Kultur und kulturelle Vielfalt: Bemerkungen zur interkulturellen Übersetzung von Ex 3,14" in Die Begegnung mit dem Anderen: Plädoyers für eine interkulturelle Hermeneutik, ed. Theo Sundermeier (Gütersloh: Gütersloher Verlaghaus Gerd Mohn, 1991), 29-38. Used by permission of Richard Friedli.

Theo Sundermeier, "Erwägungen zu einer Hermeneutik interkulturellen Verstehens," in Die Begegnung mit dem Anderen: Plädoyers für eine interkulturelle Hermeneutik, ed. Theo Sundermeier (Gütersloh: Gütersloher Verlaghaus Gerd Mohn, 1991), 13-18. Used by permission of Theo Sundermeier.

Heike Walz, "Kritik der europäischen Vernunft? Herausforderungen für die Interkulturelle Theologie aus Lateinamerika und Afrika." Interkulturelle Theologie 42, no. 2-3 (2015): 261–83. Used by permission of Heike Walz.

Cover design and image composite: David Fassett
Interior design: Daniel van Loon and Beth McGill
Images: multicolored circles: © MirageC / Moment Collection / Getty Images

ISBN 978-0-8308-5108-9 (print)
ISBN 978-0-8308-2745-9 (digital)

Library of Congress Cataloging-in-Publication Data
A catalog record for this book is available from the Library of Congress.

P	25	24	23	22	21	20	19	18	17	16	15	14	13	12	11	10	9	8	7	6	5	4	3	2	1
Y	41	40	39	38	37	36	35	34	33	32	31	30	29	28	27	26	25	24	23	22	21	20			

"All through the twentieth century, German missiologists made important contributions to missiological reflections on culture and contextualization. Studying these contributions is crucial for anyone who seeks to understand contemporary missiological debates. In this very accessible yet thorough volume, Flett and Wrogemann present the foundational texts of German missiology, demonstrating beyond doubt that these texts cannot be ignored. Its structure renders it very suitable for use in academic teaching, while professional missiologists and students of world Christianity will benefit from the lucid introductions and analytical sections. Warmly recommended!"

Stefan Paas, J. H. Bavinck Professor of Missiology and Intercultural Theology at Vrije Universiteit Amsterdam, the Netherlands, professor of missiology at Theologische Universiteit Kampen, the Netherlands

"Flett and Wroggemann provide for the first time to English readers not only access to landmark essays but also an insightful analysis of developments in German missiology from the twentieth century to the present. These discussions have followed a somewhat different path than in Anglo-American missiology. Thus, even to those who disagree with the authors' conclusions, this volume opens up new horizons for framing the issues."

Craig Ott, professor of mission and intercultural studies, Trinity Evangelical Divinity School

"This interrogation of 'culture' in German missiology is long overdue in the English-speaking world, which has appropriated the concept of peoples being wedded to cultures without regard for its complicity with Nazism. Constructively, this careful historical and documentary approach explains the important development in continental Europe of missiology as intercultural theology. A must-read for the sake of world Christianity."

Kirsteen Kim, professor of theology and world Christianity, associate dean for the Center for Missiological Research at Fuller Theological Seminary

"With this work Flett and Wrogemann have built a solid bridge between English-language and German-language missiology. They right away make mission theologians, who thought and wrote missiology in German, walk this bridge; they send them off in pairs or small groups; they create vivid discussions on mission. On the other side of the bridge they hand them over to the reader, each time with a brief yet sharp analysis, and then off they are, these men and two women on their way to further engage with the reader. This book challenges the reader to rethink histories and mission histories of the last century—with its two world wars and intensified intercultural encounters—through mission theology. This book is an invitation to design courses on missiology written in other languages than English! It is a book of excellent missiological engagement and exchange."

Dorottya Nagy, professor of missiology, Protestantse Theologische Universiteit, Amsterdam

"The discipline of missiology has been one of the major drivers of the growing awareness of the need for intercultural theological exchange. At the same time, missiology has in other respects become more monochrome because of the dominance of the English language. Flett and Wrogemann have done us a great favor by making a selection of insightful German missiological contributions available in English and placing them in context with their careful introductions and conclusions. In the mirror of this missiological tradition we discover that understandings of mission and contextualization are themselves also shaped by their particular contexts. Their contextual limitations or even distortions remain hidden unless we engage in intercultural conversations about contextualization itself."

Benno van den Toren, professor of intercultural theology at the Protestant Theological University, Groningen, the Netherlands

"Flett and Wrogemann offer a guided tour through insightful analysis and primary documents (translated to English) that demonstrate and analyze the changing thought patterns and approaches taken by German missiology during a century that ranged from the triumphal World Missionary Conference (1910) through the horrors of two world wars (including the rise of the Third Reich) and the demise of colonialism and colonialist missiological thought and practice. The century concluded with the initial development of intercultural theology as the best approach to engage the increasingly polycentric and pluriform nature of church and mission. In its contemporary manifestation, intercultural theology is posited as the best path forward for both the theory and praxis of mission today. In sum, *Questions of Context* offers an accessible, concise, and enlightening tour of mission thinking and practice through the eyes of German missiology over the course of the twentieth century."

A. Scott Moreau, professor of intercultural studies and dean, Wheaton College Graduate School

Contents

Acknowledgments	vii
Introduction: Is It Possible to Abandon Contextualization?	1
1 At the Beginning of German Mission Theory	15
2 Grounded in the Orders of Creation	45
3 Eschatology and Agency	70
4 The Widening of Horizons	104
5 Hermeneutics, Communication, and Translation	136
6 Intercultural Theology	175
Conclusion: The Proper Complexity of Context	213
Bibliography	225

Acknowledgments

It is always difficult to give due credit to all the people who assist over the course of a multiyear project. Foremost it is necessary to thank Dr. Karl E. Böhmer for the translation of most of the German texts. Second, we are indebted to the institutions that have and continue to support our research: Pilgrim Theological College, the University of Divinity, the Uniting Church in Australia, and the Kirchliche Hochschule Wuppertal/Bethel. Without them providing the necessary time, space, and resources, this work would not have been possible. Nor would it be possible without the Dalton McCaughey and the Kirchliche Hochschule libraries and the librarians who work within them. John is especially indebted to Pilgrim Theological College for sabbatical leave and the opportunity to work on this text as a visiting scholar at the United Theological College, Bangalore, India, and in the Netherlands as a researcher-in-residence of the Theology and Religious Studies faculty at the Vrije Universiteit, Amsterdam. We are also indebted to Rev. Nigel Hanscamp and Cristy Tice, who kindly read parts of this text for its communicability. Our thanks to the editors at IVP Academic: to David Congdon who commissioned the text, to Dan Reid for forgiving us our multiple delays, and to Jon Boyd for seeing the whole to completion. We also acknowledge all of the authors, for their work over multiple years and in multiple contexts, upon whom this text relies.

■ ■ ■

As an editorial note, the selected texts have been shortened with the purpose of emphasizing their main argument. This has included the deletion of some references. Only references that are direct citations have been included.

Introduction

Is It Possible to Abandon Contextualization?

The idea for this book developed out of a request—could I supply a bibliography of German language texts dealing with the theme of contextualization? Though the question first seemed straightforward, it proved very difficult to fulfill. Where English language texts often deal with theories of contextualization, few German language texts address the subject, and those that do refer back to the standard English language treatments.[1] Given its general importance within missiological discourse, an evident question follows: Why are theories of contextualization largely absent from German missiology?

To begin, this question requires a couple of qualifications. First, contemporary German mission studies has a great interest in different contexts: the institutions, art, customs, ethics, signs and symbols, and all of the historical, religious, economic, and political forces that have shaped and continue to shape each context. It uses a range of social science research methodologies to understand and speak about these contexts. Second, German mission studies is interested in how these contexts form the faith in terms of the resulting institutional, liturgical, ritual, and structural variety and in the contextual theologies that develop. It is interested in how the Christian faith takes root and is embodied differently in different times and places. Third,

---

[1] Stefan Schweyer, *Kontextuelle Kirchentheorie: Eine kritisch konstruktive Auseinandersetzung mit dem Kirchenverständnis neuerer praktisch-theologischer Entwürfe* (Zurich: TVZ Theologischer Verlag, 2007), 239-98. See also Notger Slenczka, "Kontext und Theologie: Ein kritischer Versuch zum Programm einer 'kontextuellen Theologie,'" *Neue Zeitschrift für systematische Theologie und Religionsphilosophie* 35 (1993): 303-31; Norbert Schmidt, "Kontextualisierung und Ethnotheologie: Gedanken aus der Perspektive eines missionierten Landes," *Theologische Beiträge* 28 (1997): 103-14; Heinrich Balz, *Der Anfang des Glaubens: Theologie der Mission und der jungen Kirchen* (Neuendettelsau: Erlanger Verlag für Mission und Ökumene, 2010), 240-60.

in the early part of the twentieth century, German mission *did* develop a quite profound account of how the gospel works in and through local contexts and an accompanying account of missionary practice. However, German missiology abandoned this approach by the mid-twentieth century and has not developed any formal theory of contextualization in its place. To understand why this occurred it is necessary to look to this past and how it has shaped the contemporary debate.

To this point, the term *contextualization* has remained undefined. This is part of the concern: the concept is fluid and often determined by a great variety of factors that remain assumed rather than identified and examined. At its most simple, contextualization concerns the expression of the gospel within particular localities in a way that is faithful both to the gospel and to the context. This follows a theological axiom—it belongs to the gospel to become and be local. There is no single cultural expression of the gospel, one form and language to which all peoples must conform. The gospel can be spoken using local languages, embodied in different ways, and addressed to different sets of questions.

While this axiom may be clear enough, matters quickly become complicated. Even if there is no singular cultural expression of the faith, are there proper limits? Is it possible to become a Christian and, for example, to retain Hindu community forms and imagery? We might be happy to talk of Jesus Christ as "ancestor," but what of the title "witch-doctor"?[2] He is the Lamb, but is he also the "pig of God"?[3] Can the church simply appropriate local rituals into its liturgical life?[4] The fear these questions encourage is that culture has some form of priority over the gospel. But does that not assume a certain form for the gospel that cannot be contextualized? Where do we find the standard? We might say the Bible is that standard, but what role does our own cultural norms play in interpreting that message and so in establishing a particular embodiment of the gospel as the "biblical" one?[5]

---

[2] Aylward Shorter, *Jesus and the Witchdoctor: Approach to Healing and Wholeness* (Maryknoll, NY: Orbis Books, 1985).
[3] Ama'amalele Tofaeono, "Behold the Pig of God: Mystery of Christ's Sacrifice in the Context of Melanesia—Oceania," *Pacific Journal of Theology* 33 (2005): 82-101.
[4] Luvuyo Ntombana, "The Trajectories of Christianity and African Ritual Practices: The Public Silence and the Dilemma of Mainline or Mission Churches," *Acta Theologica* 35 (2015): 104-19.
[5] Tinyiko Sam Maluleke, "Christ in Africa: The Influence of Multi-culturity on the Experience of Christ," *Journal of Black Theology in South Africa* 8 (1994): 49-64.

Such questions go to the heart of "belonging," which often means, to quote Claudio Carvalhaes, learning "a religious language, an ethical code, a mode of being, a certain cultural category deeply attached to the gospel of Jesus Christ and its ways of belief, prayers and practices."[6] As one consequence of this, "what derives from other parts of the world cannot be considered tradition but mission and missionary work, merely an addendum to tradition."[7] The associated embodied forms of worship reify "the notion that one set of people holds the proper way, while all others must learn about it to *become proper*."[8] This is no theoretical abstraction; it comes out of the lived experience of many within world Christianity.[9]

This leads to the question of becoming overcontextualized, of confusing the gospel message with its local form to the extent that one ceases to hear the gospel. While it is evident that this occurs, discussion of the problem tends to highlight where it occurs in other places and times—not our own. Only infrequently might a community acknowledge that it has confused its own embodiment of the gospel with the gospel itself. One indicator of the problem is the assertion of one's own community as being in the right over against other Christian communions. This can lead to a defensive posture (we are to protect what we have received), to a closing of that community to different voices, and to a type of missionary activity that demands conversion into this particular expression of the faith. Not only do we become deaf to the critical voice of the world Christian communion, we become the ones who are "true" and have the unique responsibility to preserve this gospel and advance it via a particular mission to this other world.

It is often stated that when the gospel is embodied in different ways in different times and places, the Christian church learns more about the gospel itself. But, in becoming local, in taking on different form, does the gospel itself change in some way? Does something happen to the gospel? This question does not refer to the history of Jesus Christ as recorded in the

---

[6] Claudio Carvalhaes, "Communitas: Liturgy and Identity," *International Review of Mission* 100 (2011): 40.
[7] Carvalhaes, "Communitas," 40.
[8] Carvalhaes, "Communitas," 40.
[9] Bernard Ukwuegbu, "'Neither Jew nor Greek': The Church in Africa and the Quest for Self-Understanding in the Light of the Pauline Vision and Today's Context of Cultural Pluralism," *International Journal for the Study of the Christian Church* 8 (2008): 305-18.

New Testament. It refers to the interpretation and embodiment of that story through time and in culture. The gospel is a story of God's relationship to human beings. It is the story of a first-century Jew, meaning that the gospel was never without context. It was never a disembodied message that might take on different form as though it were a naked idea taking on different cultural clothing. It belongs to the gospel that it exists only in context, as it is embodied in Christian communities. If the gospel is gospel only in its embodiment, and if the form of this embodiment is informed by each context and the questions asked in these contexts, might the gospel become a different word in different times and places? And what might the church learn from this difference? This radical position is, for Lesslie Newbigin, the lesson that comes from the conversion of Peter in his encounter with Cornelius (Acts 10:1-48). In relation to this pagan servant of the empire, Peter learned anew who God in Christ was, and this would inform the events of the Jerusalem Council concerning the Gentiles and the law. In this event, Newbigin argues, "'Christianity' was changed."[10] Nor, Newbigin continues, is it a task of the church to make demands as to what commitment to Christ might mean for these new believers in different cultural contexts. It is for the church to "learn from them new lessons about its own obedience."[11] This applies not simply to matters of precise theological interpretation, but to the big questions of human life: to those of power, governance, politics, economy, gender and race relations, social hierarchies, and sexuality, to name but a few examples.

These are difficult questions and the answers vary depending on a range of associated concepts. First, how might one understand culture? While generic definitions abound, it is a notoriously difficult concept to define. Culture can refer to a whole way of life, one necessary to our being as social creatures. This includes, among other things, beliefs, rituals, symbols, law, education, government, mores, customary ways of behaving, taboos. It gives us ideas about the nature of a human being and how human beings should relate to one another. Culture can refer to "high culture," a body of art, literature, architecture, and intellectual commentary. Culture can refer to a

---

[10] J. E. Lesslie Newbigin, *The Open Secret: An Introduction to the Theology of Mission* (Grand Rapids, MI: Eerdmans, 1995), 182.
[11] Newbigin, *Open Secret*, 140.

"cultured person," one educated in a certain style and body of knowledge, a social elite. Culture is also a young concept. Johann Gottfried Herder was the first to theorize the diversity of cultures, and to develop a formal concept that is familiar today.[12] Around the same time, the term *culture* appeared in 1871 in Edward Tylor's *Definition of Culture*.[13] Prior to that, a so-called classicist view of culture prevailed. This assumed that only one culture existed and it was in contrast to simple people, natives, and barbarians. This approach informed earlier ideas of civilization and imperialism, and its legacy continues today especially in establishing evaluative measures by which cultures different from our own are judged. It finds expression in terms such as the *developing world*, which indicates parts of the world that are expected to attain a standard of economic and technological production. But where does this set of values come from? Should all cultures be valued the same? If not, what is the standard of judgment and who creates and applies it? Is a "better culture" one that maintains a just and free community in relation to those within it, but also to those outside its borders, and to the whole of creation? Or is it one that results in the strongest economy and greatest military capacities? One challenge with conceiving the nature of culture, in other words, lies in what we ourselves value and so what we expect to find in other cultures. Our culture, by this measure, becomes the highest and the best. How we describe culture can ignore differing and perhaps even competing accounts that are normative in other places.

Second, how might we understand the range of interactions between cultures? A number of terms developed within the social sciences explore the nature and consequences of cultural interaction. *Acculturation*, used in its contemporary sense in the early 1880s, refers to the encounter of cultures and the psychological and cultural changes this encounter generates, with a particular focus on one culture taking on the aspects of another more dominant culture.[14] *Transculturation*, coined in 1947 by Fernando Ortiz, stresses more the unidirectional movement of cultural elements, and this includes

---

[12]Johann Gottfried Herder, *Sämmtliche Werke*, ed. B. Suphan, 33 vols. (Berlin: Weidmannsche Buchhandlung, 1877-1913), 14:228.
[13]Edward Burnett Tylor, *Primitive Culture: Researches into the Development of Mythology, Philosophy, Religion, Art, and Custom* (J. Murray, 1871), 1:1.
[14]Robert Redfield, Ralph Linton, and Melville J. Herskovits, "Memorandum for the Study of Acculturation," *American Anthropologist* 38 (1936): 149.

deculturation (the loss of cultural forms), and neoculturation (the development of new forms).[15] *Enculturation*, first used by Melville Herskovits in 1948, is the process of learning a culture, its language, values, norms, and rituals, the process by which one grows into and is part of a culture.[16] It appears quite often today in theological discussions concerning entrance into the Christian community and growth in the faith, especially in a particular understanding of how liturgies, rituals, practices, and traditions form a people. This is only a brief snapshot of three complex approaches, and it fails to mention a range of other concerns such as, for example, domination, gender, postcoloniality, and hybridity. The point, however, is clear: there are multiple complex ways of naming the interaction between cultures and what occurs in and as a consequence of that interaction.

Third, how might we understand the relationship of the gospel to culture? Along with the above three terms that have been appropriated by theology as ways of describing the interaction between the gospel and cultures, a number of theological terms have developed.[17] *Indigenization*, or *indigeneity*, is another term from the nineteenth century that looks to encourage forms of the gospel's embodiment in terms of traditional culture, rather than importing forms from the outside. While a good first step, it was ultimately rejected because of its anachronistic and paternalistic tendency to reinforce a static picture of traditional local culture.[18] In 1973, Shoki Coe introduced the idea of *contextualization*: a way of being involved in the *missio Dei* (mission of God) in a particular context and through which a local theological reflection develops as a necessary consequence.[19] The emphasis here is less on the church as a given body, and more on the pilgrim people of God

---

[15]Fernando Ortiz, *Cuban Counterpoint: Tobacco and Sugar* (Durham, NC: Duke University Press, 1995), 97; Jossianna Arroyo, "Transculturation, Syncretism, and Hybridity Critical Terms," in *Caribbean and Latin American Thought: Historical and Institutional Trajectories*, ed. Yolanda Martínez-San Miguel, Ben Sifuentes-Jáuregui, and Marisa Belausteguigoitia (New York: Palgrave Macmillan US, 2016), 133-44.
[16]Melville J. Herskovits, *Man and His Works: The Science of Cultural Anthropology* (New York: Knopf, 1948), 39-48; Margaret Mead, "Socialization and Enculturation," *Current Anthropology* 4 (1963): 184-88.
[17]Aylward Shorter, *Towards a Theology of Inculturation* (Maryknoll, NY: Orbis Books, 1988), 3-16.
[18]W. A. Visser 't Hooft, "Accommodation—True and False," *South East Asia Journal of Theology* 8 (1967): 5.
[19]Shoki Coe, "In Search of Renewal in Theological Education," *Theological Education* 9 (1973): 241-42.

becoming the new creation. A similar debate developed among Roman Catholics, leading to the idea of *inculturation*.[20] This indicates a mutual process whereby, in the words of John Paul II, "the Church makes the Gospel incarnate in different cultures and at the same time introduces peoples, together with their cultures, into her own community. She transmits to them her own values, at the same time taking the good elements that already exist in them and renewing them from within."[21] With this definition, evangelization includes not simply individuals, but cultures—the gospel is to remake cultures as part of the new creation.[22] More recently, Benedict XVI has criticized inculturation because, in his opinion, religion is the "determining core" of any culture, and culture is an interpretation of the world according to its understanding of the divine. Given this tie between a religion and a culture, it is a nonsense to suggest that a religion might enter another culture. Benedict argues instead for *interculturality*. The "faith is itself culture. . . . Faith is its own subject, a living and cultural community we call the 'people of God,'" one that has "matured through a long history and through intercultural mingling."[23] The faith enters a culture as itself another culture and appropriates other cultural values into itself.

With this range of theological accounts, it is evident that no single understanding of the relationship of gospel to culture exists. Every position includes not simply an account of culture and of the interactions between cultures, but a range of theological commitments regarding the nature of the church, of how the gospel can be and is embodied, and of mission. It is possible to identify significant and fundamental theological assumptions that, in turn, lead to different Catholic and Protestant approaches to contextualization.[24] Even the very idea of contextualization itself is not neutral—it developed out of a particular problem: that of theology and the church

---

[20]Pedro Arrupe, "Letter to the Whole Society on Inculturation," *Studies in the International Apostolate of Jesuits* 7 (1978): 1-9.
[21]John Paul II, *Redemptoris Missio: On the Permanent Validity of the Church's Missionary Mandate* (Washington, DC: United States Catholic Conference, 1990), §52.
[22]Gerald A. Arbuckle, *Culture, Inculturation, and Theologians: A Postmodern Critique* (Collegeville, MN: Liturgical Press, 2010), 167.
[23]Ratzinger, Joseph, "In the Encounter of Christianity and Religions, Syncretism Is Not the Goal," *L'Osservatore Romano* (weekly edition), April 26, 1995, 6.
[24]Robert J. Schreiter, "Contextualization from a World Perspective," *Journal of Theology* (United Theological Seminary) 97 (1993): 63-86.

finding their place in "non-Western" contexts. These origins often frame the discussion in terms of a dominant and normative theology located within a Western tradition and secondary and derivative theologies from other parts of the world. So framed, it often overlooks already existing contextualized forms of the gospel.

To return to Benedict XVI, his critique rests on the complex question of the relationship between religion and culture. A cascade of questions follows this critique: Is religion the basis of every culture? Do different religions produce a different account of culture and so lead to culture structured in different ways? Can culture develop separately from a religion? Alternately, one might ask whether there is such a thing as religion. Talal Asad, by way of example, argues that the concept of religion is itself a product of modern Western discourse.[25] One might question whether cultures can indeed express the gospel. Can one "find" the gospel in culture? Does the gospel work "through" culture? Some argue that the gospel creates culture and this spills out from the church to inform wider society. If, by extension, some cultures might be understood as creatures of the gospel itself (to whatever degree), are certain cultures more open to the gospel, while others are more closed? If this is a determining factor, what role for the acting of God? Are cultures and places "sanctified through time"? Is a nation "made holy" by generations of exposure to the gospel—forming what is often called a "Christian nation"? If some cultures by virtue of this secular process of sanctification are closer to the gospel, who is to make that judgement and using what criteria? If one culture is privileged in this way, and its people "a special people," does this not create a hierarchy and an expectation that others should grow to look like us (though they can never be us)? If we understand culture to be one of the main ways through which God acts, is mission the cultivation of a Christian culture? How might we understand conversion and related missionary strategies within this definition?

The key affirmation across all these questions is that it belongs to the gospel to be spoken by every tribe, tongue, and nation (Rev. 7:9). Though this is a theological promise, the above makes clear that there is no given form of relationship between the gospel and culture, and every suggested

---

[25]Talal Asad, *Genealogies of Religion: Discipline and Reasons of Power in Christianity and Islam* (Baltimore: The Johns Hopkins University Press, 1993), 27-54.

approach includes a range of additional philosophical and theological commitments concerning the nature of the church and of mission. Most of these commitments remain submerged and unexamined as part of our view of the Christian faith embodied in communities and so in cultures. More often than not these commitments privilege the view of the world out of which we come. Nor, as we shall see, is this privileging benign. Contextualization is not a simple good that resists all critique. One challenge lies in identifying where our accounts of contextualization actually reinforce our own improper accommodation of the gospel. This is difficult because we lack the necessary distance from our own contexts and the associated theologies and embodied forms. Yet it is important because how one approaches the relationship of the gospel to culture informs how one understands mission and the embodiment of the faith in communities.

This leads us back to the question of the absence of theories of contextualization within German missiology. *There is a reason for this.* It can be argued that German missiology at the beginning of the twentieth century had a much greater interest in context and local appropriation than its English-language cousins. Indeed, contemporary theories affirm many of these early German insights concerning the significance of local custom and institution. German theory was rooted in missionary practice, in engaged crosscultural experiences, was supported by a robust theological argument, and treated the local cultures with utmost seriousness and respect. But it also drew on philosophical traditions and cultural memories that informed a mythos of German self-identity. The most sophisticated theological account of contextualization had a remarkable downside: it would align quite naturally with the rise of Hitler and National Socialism.

As a way of exploring the multiple considerations that feed into the discussion of contextualization, this text engages in a longitudinal study of how these questions were approached over a century of German missiology. Evident distance exists between English- and German-language missiology. This is, by no means, a hard distinction: through the twentieth century, a number of translators crossed the language border. Nevertheless, a distance exists—one that is historic, dating from the late nineteenth century, bound with the geopolitical events of the twentieth century, rooted in differences in language, culture, and history, and includes material differences in the understanding of mission. For this present study, the distance is important. But so is the similarity of experience. Germany as did the rest of Europe engaged in the colonial mission enterprise. Both the German and the so-called Anglo-American traditions encountered the same set of questions concerning the transmission of the gospel and the establishment of believing communities in contexts foreign to Western culture. The distance between the German and the Anglo-American traditions is both close enough to speak to similar contemporary experiences and far enough apart to permit a critical reading of those experiences. Indeed, the value of this present study lies in the significant mistakes German missiology made, in the theological positions it constructed in support of these mistakes, and in the direction it has taken in reaction to these mistakes and the widening recognition of world Christianity.

This book is a translation of sorts. It introduces a range of texts across the decades of the twentieth century that illustrate the changing understanding of the relationship of gospel, culture, and the embodiment of the faith within German mission discourse, and, by extension, the changing definitions of missionary activity. The seven chapters are heuristic divisions, but each indicates a differing approach.

The first chapter begins with an exchange between Gustav Warneck, the father of contemporary missiology, and Ernst Troeltsch, the famous advocate of cultural Protestantism. For Troeltsch, the power and content of Christian mission rests in Western civilization. Mission takes the form of the export of this culture for the purposes of Westernizing other cultures. Because the Protestant religion was the beating heart of this culture, becoming Christian belonged to the civilizing process. Different mission strategies were needed because each local culture was at a different stage of development relative to the highest level of Western civilization. Warneck opposed this approach because every ethnic culture is an expression of God's orders of creation. As such, the gospel needs to be translated into every different cultural form so as to purify the primal ties with God that exist within every culture. Warneck, as a consequence of this position, rejected every form of colonization. He also regarded this temptation to confuse the process of Christianization with that of Europeanization or Americanization as a particular problem of the Anglo-American approach to missions.

German missions, by contrast, and due to its own interest in culture, was able to enter into local cultures and to meet them were they were.

During the first part of the twentieth century, Warneck's insights regarding God's working though culture and the missionary forms that correspond to this account of God's working were further developed by Bruno Gutmann. His approach to "primal ties," examined in chapter two, represents the high point of this cultural theory within German missiology. Much of his work is complex and may sound odd to contemporary ears, but it is notable for two reasons. First, his work developed out of many years of missionary praxis and is a sophisticated and sensitive approach. Gutmann sought to protect local cultures against what he saw as the acids of modern life: a rampant individualism that maintains only a transactional relationship to other people. God reveals Godself primarily through social relationships, and it was the necessary missionary task to protect and nurture these relationships. Second, though Gutmann opposed the fundamental modern mechanisms at the heart of National Socialism, his account of indigenization nevertheless found support from theorists of that political ideology. Indeed, as the reading from Siegfried Knak makes clear, via this missionary account Hitler can be seen as an evangelist who was working to bring the German people back to its culture and so back to God. As God works through cultural ties, so Christianity would grow with the rediscovery of German culture. Nor is this simply a cautionary tale: one can draw firm connections between this approach to indigenization and more recent accounts of mission within English-language discourse.

As the various liaisons between German missions and National Socialism became apparent, it became necessary to reorient mission theory. The key here was constructing a theological account of mission detached from the anthropological starting point of the earlier theories. Chapter three follows Karl Hartenstein and Walter Freytag in setting mission within an eschatological horizon. The church lives "between the times," in this period between the resurrection of Jesus Christ and the final parousia. All of history needs to be viewed through this eschatological lens, meaning that the time now is the time of mission. This account of history withdraws every accidental motivation for mission: mission results not from the discovery of new lands, nor from falling numbers; it strives not for the ennoblement of cultures, nor is directed by primal orders, nor exists for the expansion of Christendom. Mission is the form of the in-breaking kingdom of God, and the church is by nature missionary. The community itself—not politics, culture, or ethnicity—is the agent of mission.

However, while this theological approach succeeded in deidentifying mission from key themes within German culture and identity, the question of how a Christian community is established, the form it takes as a living people, remained. As a consequence, while the orders of creation could no longer be stressed as they were during the Nazi period, they did not simply disappear. For Hans-Werner Gensichen, the theory of indigenization advanced by German missions constituted the "how" of embodying the gospel. Gensichen illustrates how readings of contextualization speak not simply to the entrance of the gospel, but envision the very nature of the gospel's embodiment—they reflect what we understand the substance of a community to be. To criticize this particular account of contextualization was to deny the church a body. As a consequence, Gensichen argues that it was necessary to retain some modified account of the German approach to maintain the possibility of establishing the church.

Chapter four looks at the developments through the 1950s and '60s. This was the period when the reality of colonization and its fallout began to be felt within Western missions. Dutch missiologist Johannes Christiaan Hoekendijk, based on his critique of German mission theory, extended the eschatological approach of Hartenstein and Freytag and, with this, a missionary understanding of the church. Church structures were necessary because there is no such thing as a community without structures. But they are provisional and develop in service to the church's witness to the world. As part of this critique, Hoekendijk focused on the "world." The world had its own proper life that was not destined to be consumed by the church. This was a significant shift because it broke open the closed circle of gospel, culture, and church. Where the eschatological approach of Hartenstein and Freytag set all of history under the sign of judgment, Hoekendijk opens that history to eschatological creativity. While this was a positive theoretical advance, it was soon subsumed by critiques focused on the impossibility of establishing the church as a body.

While both Hans Jochen Margull and Walter Hollenweger were significant voices in this 1960s discussion of "the church for others," which itself draws on Hoekendijk's thinking, the reality of the Christian faith beyond the horizon of the West came to inform their thinking about mission and culture. This reality expanded the discussion field by demonstrating how many of the ideas governing Christian experience were by no means necessary. A plurality of Christian expression, for example, is not a deficit, not destructive of unity, but is a proper part of the Christian faith and present also in the New Testament. Nor is a local church something that can be shaped by outside influences. To continue to expect that Christian communities in other places look like "us" is to maintain the path of Western arrogance evident during the colonial period.

Shoki Coe's coining of the language and theory of "contextualization" occurred in 1973. Contextualization theory never takes ground within German mission theology. Living with the lessons of World War II, the direction within German missiology shifted away from active theories of indigenization and toward a passive and mutual ground in hermeneutics. Chapter five looks to this hermeneutical approach to mission as it first appears in the work of Theo Sundermeier. Sundermeier, drawing on Latin American liberation theology, developed the notion of "convivence" to formulate how the Christian might positively witness in the context of cultural diversity. Understanding and living together with the stranger becomes the key theme. The process is less one of an acting subject bringing a message to a passive object, than it is one of mutual speaking and hearing and together becoming something new. In concrete terms, Richard Friedli illustrates how even translating the Bible into local languages introduces new concepts, in this example concepts from another religious heritage, into Christianity itself. While this hermeneutical direction may appear for many too passive in relation to more activistic accounts of missionary activity, Christine Lienemann illustrates how this movement "toward the other" is essential to the faith as such. This approach is by no means less active; it is instead the activity of the whole community and not a select minority. It is the community opening itself up to difference as the form of missionary witness.

Though Hollenweger coined the term *intercultural theology* during the 1970s with his work on Pentecostalism and non-Western Christianity, not until the 2000s did it become the field-defining concept it is today within Germany. Because Christianity has become a polycentric phenomenon (having many centers), it needs to account not only for visible cultural variations, but deep cultural difference concerning such things as the nature of truth, the nature and form of community, and the nature of time and the community's relationship to the past and the future. Chapter six looks at the developing method of "intercultural theology." Hermeneutics now dominates German missiology as the framing method for understanding the phenomena of world Christianity. The essays by Henning Wrogemann and Heike Walz look at key methodological considerations within the field. One ongoing question is whether intercultural theology, even with its hermeneutical focus, fails to broaden its account of culture beyond that of the West. Walz answers this question with "maybe, yes." A second question concerns the ongoing relationship of mission to intercultural theology: Is intercultural theology a replacement mission studies? The answer, as Andreas Feldtkeller demonstrates, is no. The question itself, however, reflects the ongoing challenge of honoring difference within the worldwide Christian community in a way that does not destroy it, but encourages our participation in that difference.

There is no single answer to the question of context and so no single answer to the question of the establishment of local Christian communities witnessing to the gospel of Jesus Christ. Mission theology is itself a located enterprise. With an eye to world Christianity, different strategies of mission, such as exorcism and healing services, indicate how our understanding of mission is a reflection of our deepest theological interests. The neglect of mission within theological reflection, by extension, only results in fundamental errors within our theological systems, no matter how established they might be. This points both to the complexity of context and its necessity in our missionary witness, theological discourses, and in the embodiment of the faith.

1

At the Beginning of German Mission Theory

INTRODUCTION

Though perhaps often overlooked in contemporary discussions, it is nevertheless the case that globalization helped shape the nineteenth century. Continents, regions, and countries were drawn together through the activities of European colonial powers. 1856 saw the complete annexation of the Indian subcontinent by British troops. India became a crown colony of Great Britain. Other occupations followed. At the so-called Berlin Conference, which took place at the turn of 1884/1885, representatives of fourteen European countries agreed on the partitioning of the African continent. In following decades, this resulted in the occupation of nearly every African territory. This was the era of imperialism, marking the attempt of colonial powers to gain as much territory as possible.

The military expansion of European powers soon affected the endeavors of Christian missions, missions that had been at work in different African regions long before the advent of imperialism and the arrival of the colonial powers. During that earlier period, and whatever might be said concerning the relationship between missions and trading companies, it was not uncommon for Christian missions to coexist peacefully with local ethnic groups with permission of their chiefs. These missions were an outcome of the great awakenings that took place in the late eighteenth and the early nineteenth century. The awakenings started in North America, spread to Great Britain, and had a strong impact on different regions in central Europe. During the Second Great Awakening (1787–1825), many Christians felt called to share the faith with other peoples. At the conclusion of the eighteenth century, a number of mission societies were founded to work among people in different continents. To give a few examples: In 1792, the Baptist Missionary Society was established, followed by the London Missionary Society (1795), and the Church Missionary Society (1799). On the European continent, the Basel Mission came into being in 1815, followed by the Berlin Mission (1824) and the Rhenish Mission (1828). The number of Protestant missionaries increased during the nineteenth century significantly, counted first in hundreds but very soon in thousands.

This encounter with cultural and religious difference stimulated missiological reflection on questions of mission, religion, and culture. What was the motivation for and justification of Christian mission? What goals arise from that justification? What forms of organization and work best help achieve these goals? How should the European or North American Christian missions relate to the local cultures and social customs? What was the ongoing significance of local religions in relation to the Christian message? What theological significance did Christian missions have, and what meaning did the claim that Jesus Christ was the Savior of all creation have for these different cultures?

We enter these questions through the work of Gustav Warneck, rightly known as the father of German missiology, and the discussion that ensued between him and Ernst Troeltsch, a classic theologian in the liberal tradition and well-known advocate of "cultural Protestantism."

Gustav Warneck (1834–1910) was a Lutheran minister who, after entering the ministry in 1862 and completing his PhD in 1871, served between 1871 and 1874 as the theological advisor and preacher for the Rhenish Mission Society located in Barmen.[1] Here he developed much of his thinking concerning the theology and practice of mission. In 1874, Warneck become the pastor of a Lutheran mainline church in Germany, where he served for twenty-two years. Also in 1874, he founded the journal *Allgemeine Missions-Zeitschrift*, and in his opening editorial noted the limits of previous approaches and their inability to bring the study of mission to a proper academic level. He sought to draw on mission history, along with studies in geography, linguistics, anthropology, ethnology, cultural history, and

---

[1]For greater biographical detail, see Hans Kasdorf, "The Legacy of Gustav Warneck," *International Bulletin of Mission Research* 4 (1980): 102-7.

religious history.² This became the most important missiological journal of Protestant German mission studies. In 1896, Warneck was appointed to the first chair of missiology in Germany at the University of Halle, and between 1892 and 1903 he authored his three-volume magnum opus, the *Evangelische Missionslehre* (*The Protestant Doctrine of Mission*).³ This work became the most influential textbook on missiology for the next fifty years both in Germany and Scandinavia.

According to Warneck's theology of mission, individual conversion was an undeniable goal of mission, but this was to be embedded in the broader and final goal of establishing a church, or, more precisely, the establishment of a local *Volk* church (*Volkskirche*). This German term *Volk* is notoriously difficult to translate into English. Such difficulty is important to note here because it points to the conceptual and value systems that themselves frame any thinking on contextualization. The idea of the *Volk* stemmed from German Romanticism, an intellectual movement of the late eighteenth century. Johann Gottfried Herder (1744–1803) developed the idea of the *Volk* in terms of a consistent ethnic group, unified by kinship bonds, a common region of settlement, and a common language and religion. In his concise definition, German missiologist Hans-Werner Gensichen, names *Volk* as "the sum total of social and environmental relationships, constituted both by ties of blood and by the sharing of common ground, by blood [*Blut*] and soil [*Boden*]."⁴ *Volk* was an enduring and organic entity ("organological," naturally grown community in unity). The culture of a *Volk* existed at its inception in a pure form, a cultural matrix that constantly reproduced the same features. This framing idea informed how one understood the basic relationships within cultures, how one saw the gospel working within a culture, and how one envisioned the formation of the church and its structures. German missionaries applied this understanding of social unity (consciously or subconsciously) to the regions and peoples they were working with.

---

²Gustav Warneck, "Die cur hie? Unser Programm," *Allgemeine Missions-Zeitschrift* 1 (1874): 7.
³Gustav Warneck, *Evangelische Missionslehre*, 3 vols. (Gotha: Friedrich Andreas Perthes, 1892–1903).
⁴Hans-Werner Gensichen, "German Protestant Missions," in *Missionary Ideologies in the Imperialist Era, 1880–1920*, ed. Torben Christensen and William R. Hutchison (Århus, Denmark: Aros, 1982), 187.

As a first concern, it looks not to political institutions, but to people who belong to the same ethnic group, live in the same region, and speak the same language. This understanding mirrors a widespread tradition in European lands: for a thousand years the state churches were the dominant institutions in almost every country. After the Reformation period, German territories held to the principle of *cuius region eius religio* ("whose realm, his religion"), meaning that the subjects of a certain political entity (like a kingdom or princedom) had to follow the creed of their ruler (Protestant or Catholic). Nor had the German territories ever been politically unified. During the seventeenth and eighteenth centuries, today's Germany was divided into more than three hundred political entities. The only unifying factor was the German language, though in a number of different dialects. Only in 1871 did a German nation state come into being. *Volk* provided the underlying unity and so was stronger than any national identity.

The first text is taken from the first chapter of Warneck's three volume *Evangelischen Missionslehre* (*The Protestant Doctrine of Mission*). In volume one, he deals with the "ground" of the Christian mission (*Die Begründung der Sendung*), and in volume two with the "organs" of mission (*Die Organe der Sendung*), that is missionaries, mission societies, mission schools, and so on. Volume three examines the "praxis" of mission (*Der Betrieb der Sendung*). The selected excerpt constitutes Warneck's theological definition. Mission is first conceived in *geographical terms*: it is confined to territories without or with only a small number of Christians, congregations, or churches. Mission takes place outside Christian Europe (*corpus christianum*) and North America. Second, mission is *transconfessional* and *ecclesiocentric*: the goal for all Christian confessions is to establish a church where no church existed before. The addressees are non-Christians, and so mission is not proselytism, or the attempt to convert Christians from other confessions (e.g., Catholic, Orthodox) to one's own tradition (e.g., Lutheran, Baptist). Third, mission is *temporary*: once a local and independent church had come into being, the mission had come to a successful conclusion. And without the need of an ongoing foreign mission, this local church had become responsible for its own mission activity. Fourth, mission is a *commission*: while missionaries were the visible acting agents of mission, the actual subject behind the human mission endeavor was the risen Christ himself. Fifth, mission is a *pragmatic activity*: mission is an ordered exercise; it is to be planned and the plan implemented. This approach can be contrasted with that advanced by Count Nikolaus von Zinzendorf (1700–1760), the founder of the Moravian Brotherhood and the Moravian mission. For him, like the mission undertaken by Jesus himself, missions were to be spontaneous. The Herrnhut mission, as the earliest Protestant mission movement from European soil, based its method within this spontaneity with some significant success. Warneck was of a different opinion. Mission needs to be accompanied by academic missiological research. Mission studies at universities were necessary for "science is nothing but praxis that reflects upon itself, reasons with itself, judges itself and describes itself. Science systematizes praxis and clarifies it, deepens it and thereby supports it; but praxis, life itself, is the great provider of material for science."[5] Though subject to a good deal of critique and revision through the twentieth century, much of Warneck's definition remains intact in popular contemporary understandings. This makes him a good place to start, especially on the question of how definitions of mission develop and how they inform expectations of how the gospel ought to interact with culture.

The systematic theologian **Ernst Troeltsch** (1865–1923) remains one of the most prominent representatives of cultural Protestantism (*Kulturprotestantismus*).[6] He held the chair for systematic theology at the University of Bonn and later at the University of Heidelberg and, in 1915, became professor for the philosophy of religion, social affairs, and history and Christian history of religion (*Religions-, Sozial- und Geschichts-Philosophie und christliche Religionsgeschichte*) at the University of Berlin. Troeltsch's own position was influenced by the philosophy of Georg Friedrich Wilhelm Hegel (1770–1831). In simple terms, the entire human history was the sphere of God's or, more generally, divine activity. History, by extension, was also the history of revelation, even though in different times and places such revelation would occur in differing degrees. Sin refers not to original sin as found within traditional Protestant Christian teaching but is the stimulus of a process of evolution. Salvation—like revelation—is gradual, meaning

---

[5]Warneck, *Evangelische Missionslehre*, 1:9.
[6]For an in-depth biography, see Hans-Georg Drescher, *Ernst Troeltsch: His Life and Work* (Minneapolis: Fortress Press, 1993).

that it can be more or less present within a particular culture or religion. But if truth, revelation, and salvation appear within different cultures and religions to differing degrees, what is the basis for their discernment? For Troeltsch, the answer lay in scientific and comparative method. Using these means it was possible to identify the highest and purest expression of revelation.

Freedom and justice are two criteria within this process of discernment. Troeltsch traced the richness of Europe's (and North America's) Christian culture to its roots in the Protestant understanding of faith. This culture was scientific, free, developable, and ethical. The Protestant emphasis on God as the Creator allowed Protestantism to conceive the world as mere creation and not as inhabited by spirits. This allowed it to be examined *scientifically*. Protestant believers felt accountable only to God and their own consciences, with the consequence that they felt free toward authorities (priests and religious hierarchies) and rigid traditions (unchangeable religious laws). This strengthened the sense of *self-reliance* and allowed for *social developments*. The belief in the God proclaimed by Jesus Christ, a God of love and justice, established the Christian *ethic and philanthropy*. Based on this, Troeltsch regarded the Protestant Christianity found in Europe and North America as the current highpoint in the history of religion and culture. It had brought into being the best culture and forms of civilization, and, on this basis, it was the most appropriate to spread throughout the world.

Herewith lies both the basic motivation and the associated method for mission within Troeltsch: Christian faith is to be transmitted *through the medium of this particular European Christian culture*. The faith does not exist without this cultural medium, and there is no culture if not based on this foundation of faith. The proper missionary goal for Troeltsch is not the establishment of a local church, but the creation of a Christian culture. There exists no particular obligation to conduct missions; mission work is to be conducted where the cultural conditions demand it. The content of the message is not necessarily the gospel of the Christ crucified but a broad Christian worldview and Christian values. Mission is the spread of this worldview, these values, and this culture.

With Protestant Europe the standard, other cultures were judged relative to this norm. Tribal cultures, for instance, occupied the lowest level of culture. Developed cultures like Islam assumed the middle level. Older Asian cultures like India or China represented a high level, though one still below that of European Christianity. Troeltsch develops a universal understanding of culture, one that establishes norms for judging every particular culture. In terms of mission method, this causes Troeltsch to focus less on preaching, and building congregations and churches as the means and goal of mission. He is more interested in the institutions of civilization: education, science, schools, and other institutions of higher learning.

Gustav Warneck

The Protestant Doctrine of Mission
~1897~

BY THE TERM *Christian mission* we mean the sum total of Christian activity directed at planting and organizing the Christian church among *non-Christians*.[7] This activity bears the name *mission* because it is based on a *mission directive* issued by the head of the Christian church, because it is carried out by *emissaries* (apostles, missionaries), and because its goal is achieved once the mission is no longer necessary.

To be sure, the word *mission* is sometimes used in a very broad sense to designate the carrying out of an assignment given by some higher authority. When Jesus says, "As the Father has sent me, I am sending you" (Jn 20:21), and Paul writes, "We are therefore Christ's ambassadors" (2 Cor 5:20), then this is a canonical mission given to all who are "servants of Christ" and "entrusted with the mysteries God has revealed" (1 Cor 4:1). However, in common parlance this broader sense has been narrowed down to those assignments referring to a *mission* in the actual sense of the word. For instance, we do not refer to a minister or a president or a judge as a "royal emissary"; this title is usually reserved for the kind of representative of a prince or state who serves in a political capacity outside of his country of origin. In the same way, we do not refer to pastors serving in their home country or to persons serving in church governance as missionaries; rather, we reserve

---

[7]Warneck, *Evangelische Missionslehre*, 1:1-7.

this title for those ambassadors of Christ who are sent out in the actual sense to cross the boundaries of Christianity in order to spread the kingdom of God among non-Christians beyond these boundaries. It is in this specific and limited sense that we speak here of mission.

(1) Accordingly, the *object* of mission is not Christianity, but rather the entire non-Christian world inasmuch as it consists of Jews, Mohammedans, and heathens. Thus it does not include proselytizing among adherents of other Christian denominations or branches of the church, nor does it include the multifaceted work of salvation lumped together under the umbrella term "inner mission" [*Innere Mission*], which is carried out within the church.

By delimiting the term *mission* in this way, we reject, first of all, the concept of mission officially held by the *Roman* Church, according to which all those Christian lands where the Roman Church does not predominate are designated as "mission territories," such as the United States, Great Britain, Scandinavia, and so forth.

Unfortunately, a number of *Protestant* denominations operate with a concept of mission that is just as confusing, not to mention disrespectful. This refers primarily to the Methodists and Baptists. Thus the Roman Church is by no means the only one to refer to the activity of proselytizing as mission; certain Protestant branches of the church do exactly the same. Mission refers to the work of Christianization; for this reason, those people groups that already bear the name Christian, which have been received by baptism into the fold of Christianity in general, and are therefore no longer non-Christian, cannot count as objects of mission, no matter how deficient their Christianity is seen to be by one or the other church body.

It follows that what is commonly known in America and England as "home mission" or "domestic mission," as well as those enterprises usually labeled "colonial mission" and "continental mission" should not be subsumed under the term *mission*. The same goes for our own so-called urban mission here in Germany . . . and for the church's efforts to care for German countrymen in America, Australia, or some German colony.

We Germans find it a little difficult to understand the concept of "*home* mission." It should not be confused with our own so-called inner mission. Home mission encompasses everything done by churches, especially in

North America, to reach those unaffiliated with any religion, as well as members of other denominations. Its particular concern is to win over people who have not yet joined any Christian church body and who are designated in America as "unclassified." It also seeks to make proselytes of members of other church bodies.

"*Domestic* mission" refers to church work done among members of one's own denomination, especially those who live in remote places or have strayed from the church.

Strictly speaking, it is incorrect when some in the United States refer also to mission efforts among the Indians or among the Chinese as home mission, since it lumps work done among Christians and non-Christians in the same category. Since there are actual heathens living in North America, people should distinguish between "mission at home" and "mission in foreign lands." By contrast, the distinction between home mission and foreign mission is based on a nebulous definition of the concept of mission. The work of Christianization among Indians and Chinese in North America is mission in the actual sense of the word, since its object is non-Christians. Church work among Christians does not become mission when they live abroad; in the same way, church work among non-Christians does not cease being mission when they live in the same country as the church in mission.

In England, the term "*colonial* mission" does not refer to, say, the work of Christianization among non-Christians in England's own colonial territories, the way we in Germany speak of colonial mission these days. Rather, it refers to English church bodies caring for their Christian countrymen living in the colonies.

The same goes for "*continental* mission," which generally refers to pastoral care given to Britons living in the European continent, usually only temporarily.

Finally, the so-called *inner mission* is also incorrectly labeled as mission. It would be far more correct to refer to all of the salvation work and charity efforts carried out for the purpose of addressing religious, moral, and social wrongs within Christianity itself as the *service of mercy* (*diakonia*).

To be sure, this concept was originally so broad that it could mean anything the church does (Jn 12:26; Acts 6:4; 26:16; Rom 15:16; 1 Cor 3:5;

4:1; 12:5; Eph 3:7; Col 4:17; etc.); in fact, Jesus even refers to himself as a servant (Lk 22:27; Mt 20:28; Mk 10:45). But it did not take long for the service of mercy to be defined more narrowly, so that it came to mean specifically aid efforts rendered in caring for the poor, the sick, and the congregation as a whole (Acts 6:2; Rom 12:7; 16:1-2; 1 Tim 5:10; 3:8, 12). This service was coordinated with and subordinated to that of the apostles, and later that of the presbyters and bishops. In this sense, the "inner mission" also serves to assist the ministry of the church, and therefore its manifold work should also be referred to as the service of mercy. Such mercy work is also done in the mission to the heathens, for example nursing care. When nursing care is extended to non-Christians, then it may be counted among the indirect means of mission, since it serves to open the door for the Christian faith.

(2) The task of Christian mission is to spread Christianity, that is, to plant the Christian church throughout the entire world. Church planting may not take place merely in the form of an incidental and sporadic proclamation of the saving truth of Christianity to individual souls. Rather, it calls for a coordinated approach, one that aims at the establishment, nurture, and organization of an ethnic body politic that is Christian—a church.

That being said, mission has always been carried out by individuals as well, and this is still true today. This kind of mission work is done apart from any organized society, partly by simple Christians (civil servants, merchants, colonists, soldiers, etc.), and partly by so-called independent missionaries [*Freimissionare*]; but this work is always somewhat preparatory in nature and needs to be supplemented by organized mission efforts. The very fact that mission is based on a directive and therefore constitutes an authorized ministry characterizes the merely occasional, incidental, and individual spreading of Christianity as a deficient form of mission work. At the same time, it would be wrong to label it an aberration, since every believing Christian is called to bear witness to his faith. Naturally, the first task of mission is to win over individual souls for Christ and to gather them in little congregations; but the mission task is accomplished once a church has been established—a church that is not only firmly rooted in the foreign soil but also, God willing, gradually absorbs the people group as a whole.

There has never been a lack of trials threatening to make this task difficult. When it first began, Protestant mission was in danger of becoming overly *restricted* in that in good pietistic fashion, the focus was on the conversion of individuals and on gathering little congregations of the elect. There can be no doubt that this pietistic limitation proved in many ways to be detrimental to the mission of our time, but . . . the blessing of God's wise guidance far outweighs this damage.

Far greater yet is the temptation to *broaden* the mission task by supplanting it with a purely external churchification of the masses or with an attempt merely to civilize them. . . . When the promulgation of "Christian culture" is labeled as the actual task of mission, mission itself is in mortal danger, since its *religious* task is thereby altered and displaced by a foreign element. Now of course Christian culture is a consequence of the work of Christian conversion; but if people mistake this consequence of mission for its actual task, then they substitute a kingdom-of-God purpose with a worldly one. There is a strong tendency at present to *secularize* Christian mission in this way. This tendency has been fueled by the economic interests and national jealousies of the most recent colonial politics, and it has revived the medieval misuse of mission in the interests of the secular powers. In the face of this danger that threatens the heart and soul of Christian mission, the most urgent need is to clarify its religious task.

(3) The task of Christianizing the nations can only be accomplished through *sending out* faith messengers (ἀποστολή, *missio*). This aspect of sending is so essential for the work of Christianization that it has given its name to the endeavor: *mission*. This sending refers to the mandated and systematic propagation of the message of salvation throughout the entire world by called messengers (ἀπόστολοι, *missionarii*). While the work of Christianizing the nations would not necessarily come to a complete standstill without this sending, it would certainly become haphazard and thus no longer truly missionary in nature, since it would lack the firm basis of a commitment to implementation.

The *modus operandi* of mission work, just like its systematic organization, is principally determined by the nature of the sending. Faith messengers differ from soldiers, colonists, merchants, and so on in that they propagate God's message of salvation throughout the world in a professional capacity. From the character of their profession and of their message, it follows that their task is to convince non-Christians to accept the Christian faith not by physical violence, training people to do industrialized work, or merely outwardly familiarizing them in church customs, but by witness and persuasion.

The sending of faith messengers is preceded by a *call* and by *professional education*. It is also governed by an organized *administration* and supported by the active participation of a sending church, which is also in charge of *caring* for the livelihood of the missionaries.

Coworkers are solicited from the local population as soon as possible to work alongside the faith messengers from the older form of Christianity. When it becomes possible to entrust the entire care and leadership of organized church bodies of heathen Christians to native church structures, then *the sending ceases*, since the mission has achieved its goal.

(4) Ultimately, the subject of the sending is the *Lord Jesus Christ* himself. He imparted a *universal* character to the salvation he won for sinners. He issued a fixed *decree* instructing that the sending take place, and by the Holy Spirit he ensured that *faith messengers will continue to be called*. The missionaries are therefore emissaries of *Jesus Christ*.

Humanly speaking, the sending entity is the *Christian congregation* that the Holy Spirit has reminded of the Great Commission and is inspired by a desire to be obedient in faith, to bear witness, and to show love to Jesus and their fellow human beings. Ideally, this congregation is to be identical with the organized church, and it is supposed to initiate the sending and exercise leadership over the missionaries in this capacity. However, except for a few small independent church bodies, this ideal has never corresponded to the reality, and it never will. For this reason, *faithful cell groups within the church* need to become bearers of the mission. These cell groups must organize themselves as *independent societies*, and they must conduct the sending and oversee the emissaries with their own structures. Since the time of the apostles, mission has been conducted in a spirit of *volunteerism*. The problem of how to combine this with a certain measure of oversight on the part of the official church structures has not yet been satisfactorily solved.

Ernst Troeltsch

"Mission in the Modern World"
~1906~

EVERY SPIRITUAL POWER has an innate drive to expand and to communicate, either by way of personal communication or impersonally by way of literature published for a universal audience.[8] ... The churches ... are a spiritual power and can exercise an inordinate amount of social and political influence as a result of their significance in the eyes of the masses. ...

This brings us to the most important point, namely to our contemporary view of non-Christian religions as shaped by the modern discipline of religious studies, the newest among the modern sciences. This discipline has discredited the fiction that when religion first began, people had a perfect knowledge of God; that "heathenism," the non-Christian religions, is a consequence of the fall into sin and the corruption of original knowledge; and that without the converting light of the gospel, all idolaters stand condemned forever. Instead, a completely different picture emerges. We have no knowledge of the beginning; what we later perceive by the light of history is a multifaceted development that is, by and large, progressive; though marred by terrible malformations and degeneration, we also find in it diverse religions with extraordinarily rich and profound morality and piety. Even if we consider Christianity to be the high point of this development, extra-Christian religion also features true and profound religious life, and its inner life often produces marvelous fruit. ... This however puts paid even to the most elementary and urgent impetus for mission, namely the duty to be merciful and to save. It is not about saving, but about uplifting others to something greater, not about conversion as such, but about ennobling. ... But then the question should be whether and when mission has the right to interfere in the religious life of others. ... Another question is whether it is even possible to communicate Christianity to all developmental stages of civilization, and whether there might not perhaps be people groups who are and were meant to be totally incompatible with Christianity. ... In other words, the mission task is certainly not absolutely imperative, nor is it always

---

[8]Ernst Troeltsch, "Die Mission in der modernen Welt," *Die christliche Welt* 20 (1906): 8-12.

uniform. It depends on circumstances and situations and can hardly set itself the task of Christianizing all of humanity at all costs.

But does recognizing the mission task as conditional not mean calling the mission task into doubt and paralyzing its vigor? At any rate, the mission activity of our time, or rather the interest people have in mission today faces some serious questions and difficulties.... At the same time, when religious people ponder the issue, they clearly recognize that they are obligated to engage in mission.... But there is yet another reason that compels us to do so. Struggle and expansion are necessary for our own inner development and progress. That which does not grow, perishes. It perishes not just as a result of resignation and the decision not to grow, but as a result of not using its powers, of impoverishment, and of shriveling up. In addition, the Christianity of the Christian nations in the European-American cultural circle has become intricately interlaced with all kinds of historically contingent idiosyncrasies arising from their particular circumstances. Its churches are established, it has absorbed both ancient and modern scientific ideas, and it has been formed by social and political contexts. It has been dulled by these things in many areas, and its basic ideas have become corrupted. Before being transferred into new contexts, it must first recall its true essence, unfold its own full potential, revisit its association with the variable elements of culture, and strengthen and internalize its connection to the perpetual elements of culture.... Christianity needs to grow and to disengage itself from its rusty European forms. Yet new growth only occurs when prompted by new stimuli and new influences....

A third reason goes beyond this boundary. We spoke earlier of the community of all civilized nations.... The modern world takes the diversity among the nations and states for granted and associates them with each other only on the basis of a shared spirit and culture. This spirit however is based on the Christian idea of the community of humanity, which is independent of the incidental uniquenesses of the individual and of the individual countries.... Now if a new system of nations were to come into being in the Far East, ... [it would be impossible] to establish unity with this new system ... on the basis of technology, natural sciences, cannons, military instructors, machines, or trade. Unity can only be created by finding common ground in religion and the innermost spiritual development....

Now mission is indispensable in this regard. For without Christianity, the elements of the Western spirit are incomprehensible and it is impossible to establish genuine community with the West. . . .

Thus there still is a need for mission. Christian nations owe it to their faith, to themselves, and to their fellow human beings to engage in mission. Mission is the shared concern of European-American culture, the importance of which even those must acknowledge who have broken with the ecclesiastical form of Christianity. . . .

Mission today is not the same thing as the mission of the ancient Christians . . . , as the mission of the Middle Ages . . . , as the mission of the Pietists. . . . Mission today is the expansion of the European-American world of religious ideas, closely correlated to the expansion of the European sphere of influence. . . . For this reason, it associates mission especially with schools and the area of education, and among the savages also with instilling a work ethic and with cultural education. . . .

Mission is then always obligated to take into account the particular religious circumstances of non-Christians. . . . This leads us to the important conclusion that it is not necessary to engage in mission everywhere, but only where there is a reason and a need for it, where the internal circumstances themselves call for mission. This will apply in all those instances where European civilization and colonization obliterate the traditional living conditions of individuals, directly or indirectly destroy their morals and culture, and expose them to the effects of a civilization that will prove to be destructive to them unless their moral, religious, and intellectual capacity improves. . . .

A reason of a different kind is found wherever the local religious development of the ancient civilized nations leads to disintegration and decay, as is the case in Japan today and probably soon will be in China. . . . And it will not help to import European philosophy; its best and most profound creations were influenced by Christianity and require the nations to be Christian in order to understand and apply them. . . .

It is a matter of helping these nations and people groups to identify a new religious basis for their existence, and to solicit their cooperation in attaining to the spiritual community of civilized humanity. . . . But we remain confident that in its combination with the heritage of European-American civilization, the Christian religion continues to be the highest form and power of spiritual life, despite all the weaknesses, contradictions, and impurities of our civilization. For this reason, we feel obligated to intervene and justified in introducing our more advanced heritage wherever people are trying to or have to develop something better and more advanced.

....

GUSTAV WARNECK

"The Motive for and Mandate of Mission According to the History of Religion School"
~1907~

NOW IF THE MODERN HISTORY of religion school is to make a positive contribution to mission, then it must earnestly attempt to avoid the above-mentioned dangers by portraying the foreign religions in a truly objective manner.[9] What makes this task rather complicated is that this school is not without bias itself. For this school of thought, researching non-Christian religions is not an end in itself, but rather a means to a different end; this is not a purely historical discipline, but a dogmatic one. Ultimately, its aim is to prove its two basic hypotheses: that all religions, including the Christian religion, are relative, and that Christianity is undergoing continuous development. [It] dismisses ... any possibility of supernatural divine revelation and translates such revelation into mere historical development. This shows that its point of departure is that Christianity is not the absolute religion. Granted, this school of thought currently believes that Christianity is the most developed religion, but the expectation is that we will eventually come up with an even more developed one in future. We will do so by way of some marvelous syncretism, or by way of compromising with or rather crystallizing out the very best aspects the most advanced non-Christian religions have to offer. The idea is that this will happen either when these religions embrace aspects of what we today refer to as the "essence of Christianity," when Christianity assimilates the elements of truth present in the

[9]Gustav Warneck, "Missionsmotiv und Missionsaufgabe nach der modernen religionsgeschichtlichen Schule," *Allgemeine Missions-Zeitschrift* 34 (1907): 3-15, 49-61, 105-22.

non-Christian religions, or both apply. This fantastic universal-ideal religion of the future, of which Max Müller poetically dreams, will naturally only be available to the educated. In the modern history of religion school, this ideal is still obscured, more or less hovering in the background; nevertheless, that is the consequence, the abstract goal of the discipline that sets its pace and determines its direction. . . .

Even so, the history of religion school does not discard mission entirely, as Troeltsch in particular remarks in his three-part article "Die Mission in der modernen Welt" ["Mission in the modern world"]. He wants mission to be carried out, and complains about the lack of passionate interest in mission, discussing the reasons why not all people share this interest. That being said, he modernizes mission, he supplies a different motive for it, he sets a different goal for it, and allocates only a limited right and a limited scope to it. . . . But whether the new motive for mission will prove to be a stronger impetus for mission or even merely comparable to the old one, and whether the new mission task will lead to greater or even to merely comparable mission results—that is a different question altogether. . . .

Among the old school missionaries, and in each of the Asian mission areas in particular, there are many men whose academic education is fully equal to that of the few proponents of the new school. Troeltsch restricts the former to working among "simple circumstances and the lower classes" and proposes that the latter address themselves to "the educated classes." This amounts to a both insulting and audacious distinction between first-class and second-class missionaries, not to mention between plebeian missionaries and aristocratic ones, one I will refrain from criticizing lest I become insulting. It is true, we do go to the "lower classes," and we are not ashamed of it at all, for in so doing we follow Jesus who preached the gospel to the poor. Even so, we have been daring enough to include "the educated classes" in our scope of activities as well, and certainly not without effect. And we will continue to do so, despite Troeltsch's unfriendly distinction. However, we do not have a twofold gospel, a first-class one for the wise and a second-class one for the simple. Nor is the gospel that we proclaim quite as dogmatic as Troeltsch supposes. The tremendous linguistic difficulties in and of themselves urge us to proceed with the greatest simplicity. Quite apart from that, we are also privileged over the missionaries of the history of religion school in that our gospel is all about the great things God has done for our salvation, whereas they try to liberate Christianity from its so-called mythical elements and to propagate only a "world of religious ideas." As a result, our proclamation is much simpler than theirs, which is all about "a Christianity based on historical education and tinged with philosophy."

I mention that only in passing. My point is—and I need to emphasize this—that the section to which I refer, and, in fact, the entire article, does not clearly stipulate the content of the faith that is to be promulgated in mission. After all, concepts like a "Christian idea," a "European-American world of religious ideas," a "Christianity based on historical education and tinged with philosophy," "an ethical and religious worldview"—these are all very vague. They can mean all kinds of things, and for many people they are in fact nothing more than catchwords and phrases. It is surprising that a man like Troeltsch . . . can fall prey to the illusion that they contain powerful impetuses to mission comparable to the content of the apostolic faith that has overcome the world up to this day. . . .

Even after we have been enriched by this gift, we remain convinced that we have something to give to the non-Christian world it does not have, something not even the most advanced non-Christian religions were able to give and that they will continue to be incapable of giving in future, no matter how much they progress on their own accord. And we also remain convinced that imparting this gift is worth every sacrifice.

The basis of justification, the motive, the task, and the promise of Christian mission is that Christianity possesses by way of revelation a guarantee for the objective truth of its faith. Because of this revelation accomplished in the sanctified person of Jesus Christ, the Christian religion differs from all others not just in degree, but also in kind: first, because instead of merely subjective human conceptualizations about God, it possesses the objectively true knowledge of God; and, second, because instead of human attempts at self-redemption, it teaches the divine act of redemption. If God's self-revelation (in the biblical sense) and the divine act of redemption are eliminated from the Christian religion because some believe that sin is not "very sinful at all" and that a world without a savior is not lost and dead in its sins, but able to recognize God as he is and to save itself by its own strength—why bother people with mission? But Scripture says, and our experience to date clamorously agrees, that there is no distinction, that all people have sinned and fall short of the glory of God, that they are unable to save themselves by their own strength and therefore in need of a redeemer, of salvation given by grace, that we must all first become works of God before we can do the works of God. And if this is so, then the grace we have received, God's redemptive act that we have experienced, places us in debt to both God and people, to both the wise and the simple; and that is a motive for mission filled with mission power. Furthermore, in God's act of redemption, which is central to the Christian faith, we possess what no non-Christian religion possesses: a knowledge of the love of God that surpasses all human understanding; comfort greater than all suffering; the peace the world can neither give nor take away; the living hope of eternal life; and the power needed to satisfy the greatest ethical requirements, which not even the most moral of non-Christian religions is able to give. All of this strengthens the impetus to mission to such an extent that we have made it our own. Even Troeltsch will have to admit that if mission is salvation because it imparts the gospel of the Savior, then its motivation is incomparably clearer, deeper, more internalized, and more powerful than the history of religion school's rationalization of the obligation to mission. . . .

But before I address the new mission method envisioned by Troeltsch, it will be helpful to take cognizance of the consequences he draws from it. The first is that he limits the area of mission extensively and abolishes the universality of Christianity. To wit, Troeltsch insists that it is unnecessary to engage in mission in all places at all, but that it is necessary only in those places where there are a reason and a need for it.

It goes without saying that our own preference also is to go where the internal circumstances themselves call for mission, but we do not limit ourselves to such places. We believe that there are "a reason and a need" everywhere, namely because all people at all times and in all places need what the gospel of Jesus Christ and only this gospel offers, and because this gospel contains within itself the saving will of God, which is part of its essence and which is universal. Because there is no distinction between people in that they are all sinners without exception, and because they all can be justified only by God's grace, without any merit of their own, through the redemption given in Jesus Christ, we hold that the area of mission cannot be limited. This is the basic difference that separates us from Troeltsch: because he does not believe that sin is "very sinful at all," and because in his view not every human being is in need of saving grace, he does not recognize the absolute imperative to engage in mission. Having drawn attention to this, we ask, Where in his view are there "a reason and a need" for mission? . . .

In the case of so-called indigenous peoples "who as a result of their natural development are not or not yet ready for or in need of Christian mission," Troeltsch comes straight out and says that "no universal Christian duty and no public interest exist."

Now what if we saved some individuals from the people groups at issue here—is the soul of an individual not infinitely valuable to God? Did Jesus not begin by saving the souls of individuals? And does the process of founding congregations and Christianizing whole people groups not begin with the conversion of some? And if "we were to introduce . . . conflict and disunity"—what of it? Has there ever been mission without struggle? Does the history of religion school not introduce "conflict and disunity" itself? It is simply not true that mission only introduces conflict and disunity to the people groups in question; on the contrary, mission serves as a powerful peacemaker among them. Nor is it true that we "convert only a handful of individuals": we can point to compact Christianities numbering in the tens and hundreds of thousands, even in the millions. . . . And there is no "lack of results" in the mission among these people groups, neither quantitatively, nor qualitatively; there are many individuals whose Christianity must be labeled as vibrant, even if it is elementary. Besides, the religious, ethical, spiritual, and social changes the mission has produced on the whole are striking compared to what would have happened otherwise. . . .

It certainly does not accord with the mission experiences of the present nor with those of the Middle Ages that a low level of culture makes people "impervious" to the message of the gospel. Troeltsch and others far overestimate the significance of culture for religious faith and life. He argues that the Christian mission should not become active among non-Christian religions in which "the driving force of a culture capable of development is present"—as if culture makes Christianity superfluous! It is just as evident that the high point of culture certainly never equates to the high point of religious faith and ethical life; all too often, the exact opposite is true. In the same way, a low level of culture is often associated with tremendous heartfelt piety and with a sober sense of ethics. True, a low level of culture may make it difficult for people to understand the message of the gospel. However, since the content of the message is simple and essentially historical, at least initially, people groups with a low level of culture are perfectly able not only rationally to grasp the simple content of the gospel, but also to assent to it in faith, simply because they have common sense and a natural affinity for religion....

Troeltsch entirely excludes Islam, Judaism, and Brahmanism from the scope of Christian mission....

As long as Christian mission has existed, it has believed its task to be making disciples of non-Christians for Jesus, that is, to move them to exchange their paternal faith along with the associated way of life they inherited from their fathers with the Christian faith and the new way of life to which it leads. This task often led to controversy, depending on whether the observers focused only on its individualistic aspect, its church founding aspect, or its Christianizing of nations aspect, or whether they differed about the plethora of issues each of these aspects raises. But the basic task of converting non-Christians into Christians has been the same at all times and in all places, and this coherent view according to which the task of mission is the task of conversion is, at any rate, clearly defined.

The same cannot be said about Troeltsch's treatment of the task of mission. ... To be sure, in the past, developments in the history of religion did not actually take place as hypothesized by perspicacious academics, nor, it may be supposed, will they take place in the future the way some scholars prognosticate from the comfort of their offices. But in order for us to make a sound judgment about [that], ... Troeltsch should at least have provided us with a few basic examples to illustrate for us his idea of how the process of development propels non-Christian religions onward and upward. But about this key point of his he tells us nothing.

He also says nothing about what "Christian mission can learn from the varying progression and purity of (non-Christian) formations," or about which "new ideas Christianity will adopt from its encounter and interaction with Buddhism (and probably with other non-Christian religions as well), which is related to Christianity on so many levels." Surely he should have submitted some of these ideas, in order to allow his readers to ascertain whether they are in fact able to improve Christianity by way of their religious and moral content which is so much greater, more profound, more sincere, and truer than that of Christianity. But Troeltsch leaves us with nothing but the catchwords currently trending in the history of religion school.

....

Ernst Troeltsch

"The Motive for Mission, the Task of Mission, and Contemporary Humanitarian Christianity"
~1907~

ON THE WHOLE, however, the position is too firmly established on broad fundamental convictions for me to change it.[10] It is simply the standpoint of a Christianity answering to the modern world of ideas and being permeated by it. It is difficult to come up with a name for this form of Christianity without people twisting it into a noose with which to hang me. I would like to designate it the Christianity of modern humanity. I use the word *modern* in a purely chronological sense to mean that this Christianity addresses itself to certain basic features of the modern world that seem irrefutable to me. The word is certainly not meant to convey the notion that modernity is a completely uniform school of thought that is to be accepted en bloc....

So this is not a matter of aristocratic versus plebeian missionaries, but of different tasks. It goes without saying that my intention was not to disparage the intelligence or the academic education of the missionaries of the old school. I do not need to know strict Catholics of the highest intelligence and with an excellent academic education, or subscribers to the doctrines of social democracy who are highly intelligent and well-educated, to consider a rigid confessional subscription to be irreconcilable with intelligence and academic education in the case of members of my own denomination. But intelligence and education are not the same thing as an *academic frame of mind*, as inclination and the resolve to make your worldview and religious ideas contingent on general considerations and to sacrifice your confessional allegiance to any knowledge gain that may contradict it....

---

[10]Ernst Troeltsch, "Missionsmotiv, Missionsaufgabe und neuzeitliches Humanitätschristentum," *Zeitschrift für Missions und Religionswissenschaft* 22 (1907): 129-39, 161-66.

However, all you need is an obligation to the truth you recognize and to humanity, reverence to God's truth, and love for all people. That does not mean that you need categorically to establish absolute religious unity among all people and to save those condemned by their heathenism. You can be convinced of the duty to spread Christianity without having to disseminate it all over the place and without making any distinctions regarding the feasibility and urgency of Christianization; you can see Christianization as inward advancement and, in many cases, as healing humanity, without thinking of it as saving people from condemnation and hell. Granted, for direct mission work, the idea of saving people from condemnation, the idea that there is a need for a Christianness that will win over all people, and the idea of Christianity's absolute and completely unique authority and ability to save, on which the first two ideas are based, undoubtedly make for a stronger psychological motive for mission. For this reason, in general, those of the old school will be the ones in the limelight for mission work.. . .

Without a doubt, both struggle and progress take place in the domain of religiosity. That being said, religiosity is never just about the doctrines of faith. Religiosity refers to the sum total of life and action it covers and embodies, and this alone is what truly matters. A truly valuable mission will therefore focus on practical issues and on the sum total, and for this reason it will proceed not simply by way of a conversion of faith, but by way of inward education building on the religiosity which is already present. And we will consider it to be valuable and promising to the extent that it does and accomplishes this—despite or because of its old school position.

This brings us to the simple benchmarks for our position on the mission communities I mentioned in my article. We will prefer these benchmarks to the extent that missionaries do not merely save and convert people by getting them to assent to the faith that redeems them from condemnation and hell, but to the extent that they impart faith as something that elevates and transforms people's entire state of life, that they instill a work ethic, offer cultural education, and aim at establishing independent churches among the heathens. It goes without saying that the conversion from sin is as self-explanatory in the case of the heathens as it is in ours; it is just that their sin does not consist in their having-been-heathens. This brings us to our second point, namely, that such mission is particularly urgent wherever things are at a particular religious low point, or where there is religious disintegration and a need for new structures. This is especially the case where we ourselves are busy destroying the religious world with our colonization and are therefore obligated to find a replacement. Conversely, mission is a lot less urgent wherever an advanced and strong religiosity already exists, at least potentially, and where there is a great deal of reluctance toward a mission coming in and raising a claim to salvation or advancement, and thus standing little chance of direct mission successes. We will therefore prefer mission enterprises working in a place where it is easy to recognize that mission is justified and where it has good prospects. It is from this point of view that the three groups emerge to which I refer in my article: the group where there is a clear obligation to mission—that of colonial territories and the areas in eastern Asia where there is a world-historical crisis of religion occasioned by the interaction with European culture; the group where we should refrain from engaging in mission—which in my view definitely includes Judaism and Islam . . . ; and, finally, the group where there is uncertainty—people groups devoid of civilization who are peaceful and undisturbed in and of themselves, where it is difficult to say whether they truly are in need of Christianity and whether they have the prerequisites for receiving it. Warneck alerts me to the fact that if I include the colonial territories while excluding the untouched savages, then the colonial powers are left with nothing, since they have divided the world among themselves. But there is a big difference between those territories that may well be nominally occupied but in actual fact experience little or nothing of the influence of European culture, and those territories touched to the core by their experience of proper rule and genuine coexistence. Naturally, the former fall under the third group.

Analysis

The first thing of note in Warneck's position is his use of the same guiding biblical texts as found in contemporary missiology: John 20:21 and 2 Corinthians 5:20. Sending and the establishment of reconciling communities is the basis and end of the missionary task. Sending he also located within the doctrine of God: "in the certainty that the origin of mission lies in *God*, is rooted not only in all subjective missionary obedience, but the whole objective *existence* of mission."[11] Jesus Christ is the primary subject of mission, and the gift of the Spirit draws people into that mission. Much Warneck wrote matches the theological lines of argument marshaled even today in some missiological quarters.

Second, Warneck's own construction of mission appears rather straight forward: trained missionaries are to proclaim the gospel to non-Christians. While it would be quite natural to interpret this definition in ways familiar to English-language missiology, to do so would be an error. This definition is driven by Warneck's understanding of the relationship between gospel and culture, meaning that it is necessary to locate Warneck over-against the missiological developments then taking place within the English language world. There existed significant tension between "continental" mission theorists (Scandinavian, German, Dutch) and the "Anglo-Americans." The latter, in Warneck's estimation, stood guilty of producing an imperial mission theory and method.

As early as 1889, in a statement read to the Ecumenical Conference on Foreign Missions, Warneck issued a sharp assessment of the prevailing Anglo-American approach.[12] His critique focused on the activism and related superficiality of mission planning and implementation. Participation in missions were being motivated through the use of "rhetorically dazzling . . . catchwords" such as "expansion," "diffusion," and the "evangelization of the world in this generation."[13] By contrast, Warneck asserts that the "mission command bids us '*go*' into all the world, not '*fly*,'" and this concern

---

[11]Warneck, *Evangelische Missionslehre*, 1:66.

[12]On the reception of this report, see William R. Hutchison, *Errand to the World: American Protestant Thought and Foreign Missions* (Chicago: University of Chicago, 1987), 133-35. For Hutchinson, American missions displayed "an overwhelming sense of the rightness, glory and providentiality of their own Christian civilization [that] made it nearly impossible for these American theorists to stifle the cultural and national elements in their message. As theory, and even as a kind of 'proclamation,' American activism was surely a reality." William R. Hutchison, "American Missionary Ideologies: 'Activism' as Theory, Practice and Stereotype," in *Continuity and Discontinuity in Church History*, ed. F. Forrester Church and Timothy George (Leiden: Brill, 1979), 355.

[13]Gustav Warneck, "Thoughts on the Missionary Century," *Missionary Review of the World* 23 (1900): 414, 415.

with haste and diffusion over concentration he describes as "dangerous."[14] In an article titled "The Modern Theory of World Evangelization," Warneck observes how the phrase *the evangelization of the world in this generation* shapes the mission task by supplying a particular missionary motivation and a corresponding method. The missionary task is foremost the verbal proclamation of the gospel. Such a task, though it would include "leavening influences" such as schools and hospitals, is a matter for each individual Christian. To cover the whole world in this generation would demand missionary numbers in the hundreds of thousands.[15] As an ancillary effect, this would diminish the work of established missionaries through the removal of resources and its negative effect on any coordination between missions. This approach stresses the urgency of proclamation—it needs to occur now where there has been no prior witness. But such urgency would result in missionaries insufficiently trained in theology, in the local language, and in the tools needed to understand the local culture and religion.[16] Indeed, there is no sense that the missionary would be committed to a particular people, for once the gospel has been proclaimed in that region, the missionary task is completed. In terms of the *three-self movement* as an important Anglo-American reflection on indigenization, Warneck welcomes the intention to form "independent churches of native Christians," but judges that it suffers from "too much haste and unwise impatience."[17] The haste, which itself derives from an activist culture, succeeds only in forcing foreign forms of thinking and a foreign language on the people. As to language, Warneck counters that "the missionary command does not say: *Go ye and teach English to all nations*. Not more, but *less English* in the missions; that should be the watchword of the great missionary problem to be solved."[18] In contrast to such haste, mission of necessity takes time and requires well educated

---

[14] Warneck, "Thoughts on the Missionary Century," 415.
[15] Gustav Warneck, "Die moderne Weltevangelismus-theorie," *Allgemeine Missions-Zeitschrift* 24 (1897): 308.
[16] Warneck, "Die moderne Weltevangelismus-theorie," 309-11.
[17] Warneck, "Thoughts on the Missionary Century," 416, 417. Warneck nowhere examines the three-self-movement in detail and while he congratulates Rufus Anderson for his "energetic advocacy" of the three-self approach, he critiques him for "the 'doctrinaire' haste" which failed to educate the missionaries being sent. Gustav Warneck, *Outline of a History of Protestant Missions from the Reformation to the Present Time* (New York: Fleming H. Revell, 1906), 108.
[18] Warneck, "Thoughts on the Missionary Century," 416.

missionaries (those with a thorough knowledge of the local religion, history, culture and language). Mission requires a different approach, one based in concentration, one that rejects denationalization and affirms the fostering of local language.

Warneck's own constructive approach understands "the greatest of all mission problems" to be "the implantation of Christianity into the foreign soil of heathen nations in such a way that it takes root like a native plant and grows to be a native tree."[19] An independent Christianity will only grow where the faith has become naturalized. This process requires the Christianization of the local language, customs, and social ties. If the "national and popular customs" are destroyed, "Christianity will never become a national and social power."[20] Warneck sees this danger lying in three approaches: first, the concern with individual conversion as one finds it in the Pietists (because this removes people from their local culture and needs to accommodate them within Western culture); second, in a "mere outward *ecclesiasticization*, in the mass-baptism of the unprepared, in the mere mechanical adaptation to ecclesiastical customs";[21] and third, from a conscious or unconscious amalgamation of Christianization and Europeanization (Anglicanization, Germanization, etc.) and even of Christianization and civilization itself.[22] Mission is much more than making non-Christians Christian—it is the process of Christianization, of turning the entire culture and its structures Christian.

For this reason, Warneck is at pains to distinguish *mission* from other terms like "home," "domestic," "colonial," "continental," or "inner" missions. Mission is the Christianization of a *Volk*, of a people. It is a holistic process that attends not to social or class segments, but to the cultural whole. He develops this position within an extended treatment of the "Great Commission" found in Matthew 28:16-20.[23] The Great Commission, in Warneck's estimation, contains a complete mission program: Christianize (disciple) the peoples. Though individual conversion is important to the establishment

---

[19]Warneck, "Thoughts on the Missionary Century," 416.
[20]Warneck, "Thoughts on the Missionary Century," 416.
[21]Warneck, *Evangelische Missionslehre*, 1:25.
[22]Warneck, *Evangelische Missionslehre*, 1:279.
[23]Gustav Warneck, "Der Missionsbefehl als Missionsinstruction," *Allgemeine Missions-Zeitschrift* 1 (1897): 41-49, 89-92, 137-51, 185-94, 233-39, 281-90, 377-92.

of congregations, the terms "heathen" and *Völker* (peoples) are collective concepts. The field of mission is "the heathen world in its organized embodiment."[24] The peoples are to embody the gospel. In a remarkable reflection on language, Warneck notes that every language is capable of speaking the gospel, and in the process of translation new religious and moral concepts can come into being.[25] Translation takes time, but it can so occur because Christianity is a history, and it believes in actions in history. On this same basis, the peoples can organize the gospel as they will. Jesus instituted no final form of the church, nor any social or political orders. Christianity "possesses a universal adaptability. As it may not be identified with a particular state form (such as the monarchy) or a political party direction (such as conservatism), so it is not bound to a specific cultural level or specific form of society."[26] This gives the processes of Christianization a positive shape. To affirm that "the forms that this communal life bears in the church and civil society should retain the national color and can change with the needs of the times," means that the gospel is nowhere foreign and is capable of assimilating local forms even as it is also assimilated within these forms.[27] Christianization is not achieved through haste. It is a long-term process led by the Spirit. In this lies the importance of baptism and the need to seek the meaning of baptism reflected in life. For Warneck, the missionary task is complete when the gospel is embodied in the new life of a people.

Turning to the debate between Troeltsch and Warneck, note first that, even at the turn of the twentieth century, there prevailed very different accounts of culture and its relation to religion and so of mission's basis, strategies, and goals. The differences between the two are evident: where Warneck sees the gospel as a religious message for every culture, Troeltsch looks to the particular cultural expression of the faith as found within European and American culture. It is this which is to be carried through the world. Christianization is, for both, the goal, but Troeltsch understands this mission in terms of expanding Western cultural influence and so associates it with education and the processes of civilization. Because Troeltsch conceives

---

[24] Warneck, "Der Missionsbefehl als Missionsinstruction," 142.
[25] Warneck, *Evangelische Missionslehre*, 1:285-95.
[26] Warneck, *Evangelische Missionslehre*, 1:279.
[27] Warneck, *Evangelische Missionslehre*, 1:282.

culture in terms of a sliding scale, even those cultures and religions deemed to be at the lowest stage, nonetheless, contain important truths.

Warneck's response is clear. Christianity is not a cultural message, and such a "secularization" of mission continues the misuse of mission by secular authorities as was evident during the medieval period and exists today in the colonial period. As is typical of the time, the discussion focuses on the motive, means, and goal of mission. How one conceives these defines mission method. The key terms are those of *sin, salvation, conversion,* and *Christianization.* Troeltsch denies any need for salvation because sin is not the loss of a perfect knowledge of God. Mission, by extension, concerns not conversion but builds on the religious sentiment already present. This undercuts motivations for mission based in a notion of salvation. Mission is a matter of "ennobling" or civilizing a people. Not all cultures can or should be so civilized, so the work of Christianizing is relative to context. The key consideration is whether mission as the expansion of Western cultural ideals might damage the existing local culture because this lacks a sufficient moral, religious, or intellectual standard to interact with more advanced cultural forms. Where religious disintegration has already occurred through colonization, it is necessary to create new structures. This results in a clear missionary obligation toward the colonial territories and anywhere that the encounter with the West has prompted a religious crisis.

With the message of Christianity now described using terms like the "European-American world of religious ideas" and "an ethical and religious worldview," Warneck questions the content of mission. His response is a basic retelling of doctrinal points dealing with sin, salvation, and conversion, and a reaffirmation of the need for every culture to hear and respond to the gospel. Troeltsch acknowledges that while much mission is motivated by saving people from condemnation, an idea related to the idea of Christianity's unique authority to bring salvation, this no longer constituted the key benchmark for mission. Salvation and conversion exist to the extent that missionaries "impart faith as something that elevates and transforms people's entire state of life, that they instill a work ethic, offer cultural education, and aim at establishing independent churches among the heathens." The content of mission, in other words, was not the Christian faith as a range of theological commitments or even rituals. It was a Christian worldview, and its corresponding values and cultural forms (such as, for example, freedom, democracy). The point is significant: first, how one conceives the motive, method, and goal of mission develops, not incidental to, but within a whole theological system; second, this mutual relationship between mission and theology is itself located within a particular understanding of the gospel's embodiment and its expression within a cultural and historical location.

While the tragic realities of colonization may warn against expressly cultural forms of mission such as the one forwarded by Troeltsch, his approach builds on the idea that the gospel leavens culture. The longer the gospel has worked within a culture, by extension, the greater the justice and freedom of that culture. This permits also the relative evaluation of cultures, with some deemed closer to the gospel and some further away. Such ideas are not unknown today and related to the notion of sanctifying of time and place.

As to Warneck, it would be difficult to overstate his importance as an intellectual figure within the history of mission studies. He widened the field to include social science forms of knowledge and methods. He was interdisciplinary and empirical, but also developed significant theological grounding. His understanding of the importance of language and structure for the local appropriation of the gospel remains remarkably contemporary. He opposed any attempt to link the transmission of the faith with the processes of civilization or colonization. And yet, as we see in the next chapter, his approach is grounded in and expresses his own cultural heritage and this was subject to significant abuse.

2

Grounded in the Orders of Creation

INTRODUCTION

Renowned Yale historian Kenneth Scott Latourette once described the nineteenth century as "the great century."[1] This was a time of the expansion of the Christian religion, both through missionary effort and as part of Western imperialism. A great number of pioneer missions founded congregations and churches in most parts of Africa and Asia. Within the colonial territories, far reaching social, cultural, and economic changes took place due to the military conquest and the subsequent administrative and economic penetration. Though the degree varied depending on place, traditional forms of communal structures and economies disappeared. Theologians like Ernst Troeltsch welcomed these cultural and social changes as indicators of human development. Other thinkers regarded the same phenomena with more critical eyes and accused the European and North American colonial powers of destroying long-established cultural customs and laws. German missiologists like Bruno Gutmann and Christian Keysser, on the basis of Christian missions, sought the preservation of these local cultures. For them, the industrial societies of the West did not represent progress in human civilization. Quite the opposite, the West represented the disintegration of culture, leading to human isolation and the impoverishment and atrophy of human beings. Both missiologists regarded the local cultures of Africa and Asia as lying close to the primordial orders of creation. These God-given orders still existed and afforded the best opportunity to live a full human existence.

From its earliest beginnings, Protestant missions focused on the *conversion of individual believers*. The German Herrnhuter Brüdergemeine

---

[1]Kenneth Scott Latourette, *A History of Christianity* (New York: Harper & Brothers, 1953), 1063.

(Moravian church) started its mission in 1735 concentrating on the conversion of a small selection of "real" Christian believers, on "winning souls for the Lamb." After the increasing successes of mission endeavors during the nineteenth century, whole groups of people started to convert to Christianity. The notion of group conversion (*Volksbekehrung*) became a controversial topic of discussion. Was it theologically appropriate to baptize entire groups of people if one was not sure whether they understood the Christian faith and were ready to act and behave as Christians? The famous German missionary **Bruno Gutmann** (1876–1966), who from 1902 to 1938 worked among the Chagga tribe in the Kilimanjaro-region of what today is Tanzania, advocated for the model of group conversion.[2]

In order to understand Gutmann, it is necessary to understand his early years. Raised in the industrial German city of Dresden, Gutmann observed the miserable life conditions of poor workers. This experience imprinted on him a particular judgment of the world: life in the modern cities with mass societies meant cultural decay, whereas life in rural areas and villages expressed the real and authentic culture of the people (*Volkskultur*). This perspective took on theological significance as Gutmann came to regard every ethnic group as a distinct entity that follows an inherent order (*Ordnung*) given by God as the Creator. These orders of creation (*Schöpfungsordnungen*) consist of social and kinship relations and rites. Though it was possible, to some degree, to effect these orders, human sin did not and could destroy them. Original sin effects people living within these orders of creation, but the orders themselves, because they are established by God the Creator, are neutral or even positive. Authentic life may blossom only within these orders. From the viewpoint of European-Christian missions, tribal or ethnic peoples were not to be regarded as occupying the lowest level of human culture, as Troeltsch had postulated. Quite the contrary, they were closest to the orders of creation. For Gutmann, European "civilization" was lost because it eroded and destroyed these very orders through modernization, industrialization, and urbanization. It was a key task of Christian missions

---

[2]For greater biographical detail, see Ernst Jäschke, "Bruno Gutmann 1876–1966: Building on Clan, Neighborhood and Age Groups," in *Mission Legacies: Biographical Studies of Leaders of the Modern Missionary Movement*, ed. Gerald H. Anderson et al. (Maryknoll, NY: Orbis Books, 1994), 173-80.

to resist the destructive forces of Western civilization and to maintain these orders of creation among ethnic groups and other people.

Since social orders were preserved through kinship bonds, neighbor relations, and so forth, Gutmann opted for the conversion of entire kinship groups. There were rules. The people of a village should be baptized, but only after the majority had already embraced the Christian faith, otherwise isolated individuals would die a "social death" or the social structures would disappear. After the formal conversion of the people, a church should be structured according to the specific social structures of this particular people, including their rites, myths (albeit purified from elements that contradict the Christian faith), traditions, and cultural heritage. Gutmann succeeded in establishing a particular Chagga church mostly in line with older Chagga traditions including neighborhood relations, kinship, and age group structures. While these orders of creation, of necessity, had to undergo a Christ-oriented purification and refreshment, the Christian faith had to find its local expression through these social-cultural patterns of a particular ethnic group.

This missiological approach would, after the Second World War, come under significant criticism due to its popularity within National Socialist ideology. Without question, the general missiological position refused to see the Aryan race as the highest race of humankind, and it certainly did not view ethnic groups and cultures as plant and animal species with specific abilities that enabled them to survive within the struggle for life. But there were points of agreement: the first resided in the rejection of "internationalism" as destroying culture, and the second in the positive notion of the orders of creation and of God working through these orders. As an illustration of the pervasiveness of this idea, §7 of the "Principles of the German Christian Faith Movement" (1932/1933) states that "German *foreign mission*, on the ground of its experience, has for a long time told the German people to 'Keep your race pure,' and has said to us that faith in Christ does not destroy race, but rather deepens and sanctifies it."[3] We will return to this issue in the analysis.

---

[3]"Richtlinien der Glaubensbewegung 'Deutsche Christen' 1932/1933," in *Kirchen- und Theologiegeschichte in Quellen*, vol. 4, *Neuzeit*, ed. Heiko Augustinus Oberman, Adolf Martin Ritter, and HansWalter Krumwiede (Neukirchen-Vluyn: Neukirchener Verlag, 1977), 117-21.

The matter is complex and confused, with a number of different and shifting reactions including those of sympathetic advocacy to outright rejection. **Hilko Wiardo Schomerus** (1879–1945) is an example of one who questioned the idea of primal ties. A Lutheran theologian, between 1902 and 1912 Schomerus served in South India with the Leipzig Mission and was concerned with the encounter between Christianity and popular Hinduism. Prevented from continuing in India by the onset of WWI, Schomerus became a minister in the city of Rendsburg in northern Germany (1914–1920). In 1926, he was appointed to the position of professor of mission studies and the history of religions at the University of Halle. A well-known Indologist and translator of texts in South Indian languages like Tamil, Schomerus was also an outspoken critic of the Nazi regime and of the theology of primordial bonds or primal ties (*urtümliche Bindungen*). This is seen in his 1935 book *Missionswissenschaft* (*Mission Studies*), where he addresses the topics of "group conversion" and "people's church."

For Schomerus, the first converts from any ethic group require a strong grounding in the faith and high levels of personal commitment because these are the people later generations would look to for direction. Conversion of the individual is, by extension, the most urgent need. When a small group of Christians forms, this community should not distance itself from the local environment but make plain that they still belong to the local people. The missionary aim is the Christianization of the whole ethnic group, for this helps lessen the tensions between the Christianized and the non-Christianized parts of a people. Foreign missionaries will never succeed in this task as they will never be able to understand the needs and feelings of the native people. Christianization occurs only by way of the testimony of Christians within this group. As a result, these local Christians are the ones to develop the theologies, songs, liturgies, and the ethics of the local church (*Volkskirche*).

Schomerus opposes the ideas of primordial bonds and the orders of creation (against Gutmann) and of a particular Christian culture (against cultural Protestantism and Troeltsch). Nevertheless, *Volk* remains the key conceptual framework for his understanding of the relationship between culture and the forming of the church.

It was possible to be both a member of the Confessing Church and to express support for Nazism.[4] But it was also true that the missionary cause needed advocates during the National Socialist period and here one would find mediating voices. This was the role played by **Siegfried Knak** (1875–1955).[5] Knak's singular standout contribution was as a mission administrator, serving for twenty-seven years as director of the influential Berlin Mission Society (1921–1948). As an influential spokesperson of German missions, he participated in the World Missionary Conferences of Jerusalem (1928) and Tambaram (1938). From 1950, he served as professor of missiology at the Kirchliche Hochschule Berlin (the Confessing Church seminary), and as lecturer at the University of Halle. During the early political ascendency of the Third Reich, Knak articulated some sympathy with Nazi ideology. He would distance himself from it in 1934 and become a member of the Confessing Church, and yet he still saw in the National Socialism a coordination with the missionary account of how God works through culture and this should be understood as a positive boon to the missionary task.

Like Gutmann, Knak affirms an authentic and pure folk culture (*Volkskultur*) in opposition to the destructive Western civilization (spread through world trade, world politics, and industrialization). The doctrine of original sin, in his estimation, prevents any attempt to hold blood or ethnic bonds as a source of religious insight. Mission is called to maintain the particular cultural character of a people, but the gospel is and remains the criterion and critical benchmark of all peoples and cultures. Even though Knak rejects the dogma of races (*Rassedogma*), he nevertheless argues against the mingling of races (*Rassenmischung*). Knak adhered to the "organological" understanding of *Volk*. This static approach understood cultures and ethnic groups to be enduring entities, unchanged for a long time and constantly referring back to an origin story. They exist in a more or less pure form. If a culture is less pure, if it has become polluted with other cultural elements, it can be purified. Reestablishing this pure culture, connecting with the orders of creation, is a goal in itself because God works

---

[4]Werner Ustorf, *Sailing on the Next Tide: Missions, Missiology, and the Third Reich* (Frankfurt am Main: Peter Lang, 2000), 22–23.
[5]For greater biographical detail, see Hans-Werner Gensichen, "Knak, Siegfried," in *Biographical Dictionary of Christian Missions*, ed. Gerald H. Anderson (Grand Rapids, MI: Eerdmans, 1998), 371.

through these ties. Knak expects such a purification through the strengthening of the German *Volkstum* (the character and traditions of the *Volk*) by the National Socialist regime. This political movement was itself, by extension, a movement for the reevangelization of Germany.

BRUNO GUTMANN

A Free Humanity on the Basis of Everlasting Ties
~1928~

GOD . . . FOUNDED THE ETERNAL KINGDOM of divine filiation within these organic ties.[6] As a man, he entered it by this portal. He decreed that his kingdom should be proclaimed as the kingdom of the Father and of the Son. And he also instructed this same only-begotten Son of his to do battle here on earth for the order of God. Yet this also means that he fought for our ongoing commitment toward those related to us by kinship ties—a commitment that surpasses all artificial relationships. . . . The word *friendship* . . . is understood differently, depending on whether it is used by a native of the soil or by someone detached from the soil. When the urbanized man—which includes everybody in Germany who no longer belongs to the rural classes—thinks of friendship, he thinks of elective community, of a brotherhood among people who are foreigners to each other, one that comes about on the basis of some or other mutual appreciation and that may be dissolved again at will. In the urbanized world, which proudly calls itself "civilization"—an unnatural phenomenon—each individual has been worn by constant friction into a rock-hard piece of soul grit. He prides himself on grinding against a fellow piece of blue grit the one day and a red piece the next, yet remaining yellow himself no matter what! And the grumbling and rumbling of the cogs and gears, powered by the water force . . . that propels him and all the other pieces of grit along relentlessly, with or without their say-so, he calls progress, development. How differently the word *friendship* sounds to the person still rooted in German agrarianism! For him, friendship does not mean associating himself with others whom he has freely elected,

---

[6]Bruno Gutmann, *Freies Menschentum aus ewigen Bindungen* (Kassel: Bärenreiter-Verlag, 1928).

but rather a God-given order, the natural association with his kinfolk. His clan—that is his definition of friendship! That friendship has kept him and his neighbors true to their roots, thereby preserving the German kind for his benefit. . . .

It is still that way in mission work. As congregations form, they are provided with elders who are elected by majority vote, in other words, according to the parliamentary model. The elders are joined by teachers who are first educated and then appointed, thus following the model of the bureaucratic state. As a result, these bodies often closely resemble the Sanhedrin, which was ruled by the Pharisees and scribes. That is difficult to avoid as long as missionaries neglect the structure foreordained in the depths of God's creation, as long as they do not bring the leaders on board whose leadership is predicated by their natural position in the organic association with those of their kind.

....

BRUNO GUTMANN

"Primordial Ties and Sin"
~1934~

THE OBJECTION PEOPLE BELIEVE to be most capable of refuting the concept of primordial ties is the claim that primordial ties can no longer exist for the simple reason that all human relationships have been corrupted by sin.[7] People honestly believe that the effects of sin have stripped the primordial ties of their divine authority and of their original essence. . . . What if it were incumbent on us to infer from the reality of sin that the primordial ties are indispensable and categorically imperative! "Everyone who sins breaks the law; in fact, sin is lawlessness" (1 Jn 3:4). Here John is simply saying that whenever people "step out of themselves," as it were, they are confronted by realities inherent to the world, and that the world demands that they comply with its basic blueprint. But in this blueprint they encounter God himself; first, and inescapably, in their parents, their spouses,

---

[7]Bruno Gutmann, "Urtümliche Bindungen und Sünde," *Neue Allgemeine Missions-Zeitschrift* (1934): 20-31.

their children, and their kinfolk. This then is also the point where the sin that clings to them manifests itself most obviously and persuasively. . . .

We keep on forgetting how biological processes are organized in our own bodies. . . . It is possible, is it not, to portray the operation of the so-called noble organs in our bodies as a relentless purification of fatigue-causing products and metabolic toxins? And the significance of this ongoing process of detoxification is emphasized as being vital like none other, is it not, when we hear that the failure of just one of these organs leads to the death of the individual?

These kinds of detoxing organs are present to an even greater extent in the body politic, in this wonderful kinship association with its spiritual organic form. We are talking about none other than the primordial ties. There is sin in them; sin was not added at some later point. . . . Sin permeates them like blood laden with impurities permeates the noble organs. . . .

It is compulsion, nothing but divine compulsion that preserves the effective original association between the basic elements of the visible world. And this compulsion is not derivable from anything else.

The foundation of humanity is also divine providence, the compulsion of blood that not only forms us as individual units, but also arranges us in kinship groups, the compulsion of the earth that renders us the service of linking us together, and the compulsion of childhood that associates us with each other.

Even if we were to form social groups with each other a hundred times over in the name of Christ, sin would cast the deciding vote. In fact, sin often does this while masquerading as a respectable figure wearing either the splendid robe of piety or the austere cloak of self-denial. There is only one thing that compels us to be completely honest in our struggle against the inborn self, and to maintain our vigilance against the primordial toxin: When we demonstrate Christ's love to those whom we have not personally elected to be our neighbors but who have been associated with us in God's foreordaining; when we wholeheartedly forgive those who show no love to us, the way all true neighbors should, or who commit offenses against us; when in this estate, into which we were thrust involuntarily, we serve as substitutes without being required to do so, playing the role accruing to us when we are called to be there for others in times of need, the role that accrued to Christ for the benefit of us all. . . .

It follows that we should exploit the primordial ties for the benefit of church development—not despite the sin with which they are encumbered, but precisely because of the struggle against sin. . . .

And if this is so, then these primordial ties may not be seen as a merely subordinate means for the expression of communal Christian life . . . ; rather, their systems should be subordinated to Christ as a divine mandate: from that point forward, they will play the primary role in determining the self-administration of the church and its ongoing self-detoxification. They are the most important organs of the filial spirit that intends to pervade the church of Christ. We cannot fashion any other organs for this spirit; rather, all those who administer Word and sacrament in the church must for the sake of these divine mysteries become proficient in ensuring that the primal filiation keep in step with the eternal filiation, and in restoring the balance between the two on an ongoing basis. The entire New Testament can be read along these lines. . . .

Modern civilization, along with all of secularized Christianity within it, is nothing but the replacement of the basic obligations of human beings with a surrogate proxy.

It is for this very reason that the primordial ties are of key importance for the kingdom of heaven, for they alone firmly anchor human beings in their human-fraternal relationships, so that, being locked into them, they can no longer evade God. And this is the only way for them to encounter themselves, that is, their fallen sinful kind, and feel the desire for atonement in the presence of God and among their kin.

Hilko Wiardo Schomerus
"Mission and Volkstum"
~1935~

WHEN CHRISTIAN MISSION is working among the national customs and traditions of the *Volkstum* [customs and traditions of a *Volk*], it needs to take two things into account, ... (1) that the diversity and characteristic feature of the *Völker* [races and peoples] is according to the will of God and so have to be respected, (2) that as empirical realities the *Völker* without exception do not fully correspond to the will of God, that is, they in some respects developed in ways other than the will of God.[8] ... From a Christian point of view, the abilities, capacities, and possibilities of development, and so on, of the different *Völker*, without doubt, can be traced back to God as Creator and to his will. However, one has to hesitate to draw the same connection concerning the particular social institutions, customs, mores, and states of heart and mind. The person, according to Christian understanding, is equipped with a free will and the capacity to use the God-given abilities and virtues according to his or her own responsibility, and so perhaps in a manner different to the will of God. ... One has frankly to admit that it is impossible to separate with any accuracy the elements of a *Volkstum* according to the headings: intended by God and against God's will. One continues to face great difficulties even with the addition of a third heading beside these two, that of *adiaphora*.

With regard to morals and above all ethics, some expressions of the *Volkstum* need to be rejected as against God's will: anthropophagy, human sacrifice, the abandonment of unwanted children and especially girls, slavery, polygamy and polyandry, child marriage, the disdain of women and especially widows, and many other things. However, some customs and mores have been unjustly rejected. It was wrong to oppose the topknot in India and the pigtail in China in the name of Christianity. On the other hand, one cannot treat everything as *adiaphoron*, even if at first glance it appears this way. One needs to account for the circumstances and the basic motives and purposes. Even things that seem good at first might be doubted on a closer inspection. ...

In recent times, some have vaunted the kinship bonds of the so-called primitive people as primal ties in accordance with God's will. These ties are to be regarded as the foundation of life in its entirety, and must be made the nuclei of the larger associations such as the congregation, the *Volk*, the

---

[8] Hilko Wiardo Schomerus, "Die Mission und das Volkstum," in *Missionswissenschaft* (Leipzig: Verlag Quelle und Meyer, 1935), 136-49.

church, and the state. By contrast, institutions like the Chinese extended family and the Indian caste have been subject to repeated criticism and opposed in a harsh manner. . . . But do we really have the right to view the kinship bonds of the Chagga in the Kilimanjaro as intended by God and the institutions of the extended family and the caste as opposed to God's will? . . . This forces a question on us: do the institutions that seem damnable to us and contrary to God's will like the extended family and caste really have their ground in themselves? Might they be judged only as excesses that are the result of human imperfection and sin? Could it not be possible that they are according to God's will? If one does not recognize this as an option one risks the danger to which some American mission circles have fallen prey: to regard a particular order like democracy as alone in accordance with God's will, or, in other words, to reduce all of humankind to a single level in the name of Christianity. . . .

What holds true for the social order, holds true also for the culture of a particular *Volk*, regardless of their type, whether primitive or highly developed. . . . Christianity stands above cultures and is able to fulfill the God-given task among all people regardless of their culture. . . . Christian mission has to oppose what stems from sin within these cultures, but only this and not more. Furthermore, mission has to do this according to the spirit of the Gospel and not out of a spirit of rigorous legalism. That means, sin has to be opposed where it resides. It resides solely and alone in the human heart. Taking a legalistic approach against the so-called harm within a *Volkstum* mission might succeed in destroying this or that custom in an existing culture and in replacing these with elements of the different European culture or with new customs and mores. But mission will then quickly discover that this has no effect over sin. Quite the opposite, this opens the doors and gates for sin.

The proclaimer of the gospel mission . . . serves God's saving will. This cannot contradict God's will as Creator, but means the possibility of restoring creation as it has been tainted by sin, and even the restoration of the *Volkstum* as it has been led astray by sin. Where this proclamation resounds, there arises the possibility that the God-given abilities and virtues of a *Volk* develop in the direction intended by God.

SIEGFRIED KNAK
"Mission and Church in the Third Reich"
~1935~

TO DATE, THE RELATIONSHIP between church and mission still has not been regulated in the Third Reich.[9] On the contrary, the governing bodies of the mission societies are still in charge of the mission work on the mission field, of the education and all the activities of the missionaries, and of the entire life of the mission here at home, just as they were prior to January 30, 1933.

1. Organizational plans. To be sure, concepts for restructuring the relationship between church and mission have already been submitted. As early as the fall of 1933, a representative assembly of all the German mission societies came to an agreement about the basic aspects of such a restructuring process. But the antagonism and the turmoil in the church prompted the church leadership to delay taking a stand on the draft submitted by the conference alluded to above, the Conference of German Protestant Mission Societies. This draft consolidates two points of view: first, the viewpoint that the *church leadership needs to take more responsibility* in overseeing the mission to the heathens and Muslims, and in managing the mission here at home, than it did before . . . , since mission is "the church's act of confession before the world"; and, second, the view that the *living conditions of Protestant mission work here in Germany need to be preserved*. These living conditions comprise four aspects: (a) it needs to be ensured that mission seek nothing more than to be the bearer of the message of salvation in Christ to the nations; (b) the ministry of mission—meaning both the mission work done abroad on the mission field, and the involvement of local church members in mission here at home—must retain a character of *volunteerism*; (c) leadership must remain in the hands of competent persons and boards; and (d) the close contact between the mission leadership and the friends of the mission who support the work financially may not be severed.

These four conditions mean that mission must continue to be carried out by independent *societies*, albeit in some kind of a relationship with the

---

[9]Siegfried Knak, "Mission und Kirche im Dritten Reich," in *Das Buch der deutschen Weltmission*, ed. Julius Richter (Gotha: Leopold Klotz Verlag, 1935), 240-44.

church leadership. That being said, careful consideration must be given to whether amalgamating the many operations and organizations working abroad and at home might not take in hand the deplorable fragmentation of the missionary strength of German Protestantism. Instead of waiting for the church to take a position, the mission bodies have taken appropriate steps themselves in order to advance matters in this direction. It is still too early to discuss these in detail. What we can report is that at the above-mentioned meeting, a break was made with the past in that every single one of the mission organizations joined to form the Conference of German Protestant Mission Societies. The executive body of this conference is the Council of German Protestant Mission Societies.

Regardless of how the organizational issues presenting themselves will be addressed, . . . what is far more important is the matter of what position the mission activity of the German Protestant church is to hold in the Third Reich—*what effect the new situation has on its task and purpose*. After all, this finding cannot but have a deciding impact on those other questions. That is why we now turn our attention to this matter.

2. Purpose and task of mission in the Third Reich. It is no accident that the issue of how best to structure the relationships between the mission societies and the church has been left for last. The activity of mission is simply too closely linked with the heartbeat of the church. The relationship between the church and the Third Reich has not yet been clearly and unequivocally established. The fact that German Protestant Christianity has mission fields, as well as the experiences it has acquired there, can help shape this relationship in any one of a number of ways.

Even within the German Protestant church, people argue about whether the church should still engage in mission to the heathens and to the Muslims today. The reawakened sense of race and the belief that we should devote all our strength to saving the German nation and its national values and traditions, often make it unpopular to promote mission work. Of course, if we were talking about the Gustav Adolf Society, then yes, by all means! After all, this society cares for our German fellow believers living outside of Germany. . . . But mission to other races and distant nations? Would that not mean diluting our strength? Not to mention the concern being raised even within the church that mission alienates other nations and races from their own unique character. We will need to return to this concern that touches on the nature of the Christian faith at a later stage!

First, we need to bear in mind the fact that German Protestant Christianity *has* mission fields as it is.... This means that our question today should not be, "Is it our task to begin doing mission work now?," but rather, "Do we have the right and obligation today to turn our back on these mission projects?" If we did so, a *threefold collapse* would ensue. On the mission fields, the *mission churches would fall to ruin*; the legacy of the labor of two centuries would be lost. The *Roman Catholic mission*, Islam, and a renascent heathenism would fill the void left by the recalled missionaries, and the only thing left would be the stunted remains of native churches. Furthermore, this would grievously undermine the *trust of other nations*, both colored and white, in the Christianness of this new church in the Third Reich, and it would call into question the claim that the Third Reich affirms Christianity. At present, every steeple in the mission field pokes a hole in the fabric of foreign lies claiming that the new Germany is a heathen entity. Every German missionary, by virtue of his mere presence and especially by his behavior, invites trust in and friendship toward Germany—he cannot help it. In contrast, a collapse of German mission would fuel the most vicious rumors about the spiritual attitude of the Germans in the Third Reich. At the same time, the trust Bible-believing Christians at home hold in the religious convictions of the ruling men and powers in their own church would be shaken to the core. For it is not only its full-time workers who consider mission to be necessary and important; the same is true for the overwhelming majority, if not every single one of the most faithful of the church's faithful.

Let us return to the question whether mission alienates other nations and races from their own unique character. The question in and of itself shows how much *cause the church has to persevere with her mission work*, and especially at the present time. For only in doing so can the church proclaim before all the world and her own nation the truth by which she lives and for which she exists, namely that Christ is the Savior of all people and of all nations, and that the only reason he is there for the Germans too is that the word *all*, by which the message of the gospel stands or falls, also includes the German people. It is precisely at the point where the church needs and wants to be more in touch with people that she needs the mission to the nations. The church needs mission to remove all doubt that the only service she can render to our nation in and of herself is to proclaim the message of Christ and to embody a community of people whose life lies in this Word. The church lives by her commission to go to all nations. If she were to default on the word *all* in her scope of duty by allowing her mission work to go to rack and ruin and by consciously dedicating herself only to her own nation, then she would in effect sever the root of, and cut the heart out of, the commission entrusted to her. *Mission* truly is the church's *confession in action*, and she can least afford to abandon it at the present time when current events in the state and nation command her, yes, urge her to give a clear answer to the question about the purpose of her existence in the Third Reich.

In her foreign mission work, the church in no way disputes the purposes and intent of the Third Reich. More than anything else, mission can on the basis of its experience reassure the church so that she can approve of the intentions of the Third Reich *joyfully* and with a clear conscience. For the Third Reich intends to embody the values and traditions of the German nation. Now, it is mission above all else—German mission, at any rate, like all other mission work sprouting from the soil of the German Reformation—that persuasively teaches us to recognize the significance of national values and traditions for humanity and history. The opinion that mission destroys the national values and traditions of other nations is based on an unfortunately widespread ignorance about all things mission. The true agencies behind this work of destruction are Western civilization; global trade; global politics; the industrialism conquering Asia and Africa and atomizing the nations in order to create willing "worker peoples" for harvesting the raw materials of the other continents; and the cultural imperialism seeking to subject all of humanity to the influence of the Western lifestyle and the Western world of ideas. Long before there was a Third Reich, German mission recognized that its task is to counteract these destructive and disintegrative forces by helping distant people groups to recognize and take ownership of their own unique national or racial attributes. For it is precisely by their becoming spiritual devotees of Western culture that they become unable fully to receive and to grasp the gospel. Mission seeks to establish national churches in accordance with the natural attributes of each particular nation in Asia, Africa, and Oceania, and it does so with all the power at its disposal. For mission has recognized that the *unique national character* of the various nations is a gift given by God, the ruler of history. And mission is well aware that it has been called not to break down and destroy the handiwork of God, but rather to fulfill and preserve it. This awareness is all the more important and convincing because mission did not have it from the outset, but first had to learn it in the school of God. So mission now returns to the Christians in Germany with a lesson that makes it easier for them to feel at home in the Third Reich. For while proclaiming the gospel abroad, mission became strongly convinced of the value of each nation's unique national character, a value the Third Reich intends to safeguard.

In the process, the church received a lesson in outlook it needs to keep our nation from an *unwarranted* overemphasis on the concept of ethnicity. This refers to the dogma of race. Too many in our nation have fallen under its thrall. To be sure, racial differences exist, and they are not abrogated even when people convert to the Christian faith. It is incumbent on mission to issue a stern warning about miscegenation. Mission does not teach uniformity; quite the contrary, just like the New Testament, mission teaches that there are differences between people—in this world, at any rate. Mission witnesses and therefore teaches that even though there is just one gospel for *all people*, among the different people groups and races the one faith *expresses itself in different forms*. But mission shows that all races and people groups belong to the one family tree of fallen humanity, and that for this reason, "blood" can never serve as the measure of religious truth or as the fountain of religious knowledge. On the contrary, each race and each people group needs the gospel in order to reach the peak of its historical purpose. Moreover, each race and each people group is indeed capable of understanding the gospel. The goal of history according to mission is not a uniform humanity, but a humanity subdivided into various people groups. The chancellor has publicly declared that we not only claim for *ourselves* the right to preserve the unique ways of our nation, but that we concede the same right to every other nation concerning its own national values and traditions. On the basis of its history and experience, mission finds itself in agreement with this view. Wherever the gospel is rightly proclaimed, the result is not the destruction of a nation's unique character; rather, when that happens, the nation is led to the only fountain and source from which each nation can imbibe its life force, to the Word of the world's reconciliation through the death and resurrection of Christ.

The church owes the following twofold truth to our nation in the Third Reich: each nation's national character comes from God; but without the gospel, every national character must perish. Mission opens the church's eyes to recognize this truth. The experiences gained in mission return to the church a spiritual profit that more than makes up for the men and means the church contributes to mission.

Our nation as a whole should learn from the example and the outcome of mission that fighting only for one's own existence is simply not enough. Our highest task is to be a thriving, vigorous nation drawing its greatest strength from the gospel in order to be of service to humanity and to the glory of God.

....

ANALYSIS

The punitive Treaty of Versailles following the conclusion of World War I reinforced in the minds of German missiologists their suspicions regarding the basic imperialism of the Anglo-American approach to mission. A stress on German particularity developed in response. For Warneck, in opposition to this imperialism, it belonged to the "special charisma" of German missions to enter into the cultures of other peoples. On the one hand, this points to a critique—sustained over subsequent decades—concerning the problem of missions confusing conversion with colonization, the gospel with a particular cultural expression of the gospel. On the other hand, the special German understanding of what a local embodiment of the gospel might look like traded on the idea of *Volk* and *Volkstum*, and its configuration of the customs, mores, and associated rituals of a people. It was because the German people could appreciate their own *Volkstum* that they were able to appreciate it and cultivate it in other peoples. Whatever the self-appreciating rhetoric, it remains true that German mission theory of the period foreshadowed many concerns basic to contemporary missiological reflection. As such and due to its later relationship with National Socialism, it also serves as a salutary lesson.

Bruno Gutmann, notorious for his complex writing style, was the most accomplished theorist of *Volk* missiology.[10] The first element of note is the strong distinction between individual and communal identity. In the first reading, he sets the discussion of "eternal" and "primal ties" in his own German context. Though he begins with a christological affirmation, the focus is on kinship ties and friendship and how these appear differently in an urban versus an agrarian environment. And, for Gutmann, the urban or "civilized" environment is a soulless place: a place of individuals he terms "grit," who live a life confirming their own identity (yellow versus blue versus red) and relate only by grinding against one another. The Christianity found in the city can only be "secularized" because, no matter the liturgical form, it has forsaken the primal ties—through which God works—for this life of disconnected association. Those living an agrarian life, by contrast, are free, not living according to relationships that they have chosen, but in a "natural association with his kinfolk." This is the German version of a clan, and faithfulness to the clan is faithfulness to the root of German identity, preserving that for the whole of the German-kind. Building on this pattern, Gutmann distrusted Western civilization because it only succeeded in dissolving the primal ties he saw as basic to human being and to the human relationships with God.

The second text examines the possibility of sin destroying these primal ties. His simple answer is no. Primal ties, for Gutmann, belong to the order of creation, the "blueprint" of reality. It is through these that humanity encounters God: "in their parents, their spouses, their children, and their kinfolk." To be sure, sin has infected these ties, but the ties themselves serve to "detox" the body. Sin, in this sense, magnifies the importance of the kinship association because this "spiritual organic form" serves the "body politic," the wider social and national identity. Negatively stated, herein lies the danger of the urban and civilized—it undoes these ties and so the possibility of purification from sin and communion with God. Positively stated, with this detoxifying function, primal ties should be "exploited" for the development of the church. They have a primary function in drawing the church together as a body and Word and sacrament serves

---

[10]For a good summary of Gutmann's position, see P. Hassing, "Bruno Gutmann of Kilimanjaro: Setting the Record Straight," *Missiology* 7 (1979): 423-33.

the development of these relationships. This, Gutmann argues, is the direction of the entire New Testament.

Though Gutmann dominated the discussion, not all agreed with his approach. Schomerus too explores the relationship between the *Volkstum* and the effects of sin. In similar manner to Gutmann, he understands local customs to be part of God's will as Creator and that these are affected by sin. He differs, however, on the question of criteria. What criteria exist for one to judge whether a local custom reflects God's will or is a departure from it, or whether it is *adiaphora*? *Adiaphora* refers here to a matter of "indifference," a cultural custom that is neither for nor against the gospel. On the one hand, Schomerus agrees that certain practices are to be repudiated as antithetical to the gospel. On the other, he sees an arbitrariness in judging ties within a tribal setting as of God and ancestral filiation in China as against God. Without maintaining an open position, the danger lies, Schomerus suggests, in flattening the world into one sociocultural pattern. The example he gives is that of America and democracy, but the undercurrent is that of Germany and *Volk* and it is noteworthy that Schomerus did not press this issue in more explicit terms. Part of the problem lies precisely in how the *Volk* establishes the idea of culture. However legitimate Schomerus's concerns and to whatever degree he rejected the reduction of the *Volk* to an ideology, this was the only language available to him. His concluding point agrees that mission seeks to restore the *Volkstum* and that this is to be developed in the direction intended by God.

Though Gutmann was the key exponent of the *Volk* approach and this de facto affirmed the nationalist position that contrasted the German approach to that of the Anglo-American, the rejection of civilization and its political order was central to his position. The available evidence suggests that he did not himself affirm National Socialism. However, his work was read by many as, not simply affirming, but contributing to the conceptual landscape of that ideology. For Siegfried Knak, who understands himself in the line of Warneck and Gutmann, a direct connection existed between *Volk* mission theory and the Nazi state. More than this, Knak makes an argument for National Socialism as an evangelistic movement: as God works through cultural ties, so Christianity would grow with the rediscovery of German culture encouraged by Hitler.

Knak's text addresses the formal regulatory discussion concerning the relationship of the state church to the Third Reich. As a mission administrator, Knak's desire lay in protecting the place of missions, especially after the devastation of the removal of German mission territories by the Treaty of Versailles. Part of the worry rested in a logic that considered mission impossible because other races were not capable of receiving the gospel. If impossible, then funding would be withdrawn and missionary activity would come to an end. Knak's defense promotes missions as a way for the Third Reich to demonstrate its Christianness to those outside Germany—and, more importantly, to those within it. Mission does not alienate peoples from their own particular character. Christianity affirms them in their nationality. Foreign missions is part of this because it confirms that God is for *all* people, and so also for Germany. Christian mission, in his understanding, serves German culture by recognizing that every culture is a particular culture and therefore has its own worth and dignity. Christian mission reminds the German people that all cultures have to be recognized as unique.

But the key defense lies in the 'how' of how God works through and confirms these national identities. While Knak does distance himself from National Socialism, he nevertheless qualifies that distance by affirming God's work in relation to that regime: mission can with joy and a clear conscience approve the intentions of the Third Reich. In another article titled "The Total Claim of the State and the Total Claim of God on the People," Knak makes the same case in a stronger fashion: "The church can and must answer Hitler's state with a fundamental and wholehearted yes."[11] Why? German missions were the first to teach the importance of national values and traditions for human being. Missions have helped counter the "disintegrative" force of Western civilization, with its cultural imperialism and reduction of the nations to raw materials for an economic system. It did this through encouraging local peoples to own and develop their "unique national or racial attributes." Insofar as the Third Reich seeks to recover and develop the unique German spirit, so it affirms the lessons of mission and helps cultivate the means by which God speaks. The re-Germanization of Germany being experienced under Hitler constitutes the recultivation of the

---

[11]Siegfried Knak, "Totalitätsanspruch des Staates und der Totalitätsanspruch Gottes an die Völker," *Neue Allgemeine Missions-Zeitschrift* 10 (1933): 407.

primal ties of blood and soil through which God works: the greater the recovery of German identity, the closer to God.

How might one evaluate this *Volk* approach and its eventual connection to National Socialism? First, there is much to affirm. One might see in the interest with locality and the encouraging of local and popular forms of the faith not beholding to Western standards a remarkably contemporary approach. It is possible to find continued support of its attention to the cultural heritage and its embodiment in social institutions and customs, along with the importance of communal structures.[12] As evidenced by Knak's concern for balance vis-à-vis the race question, this approach argued for difference in Christian embodiments in relation to different peoples. No single Christian form exists and mission seeks not to create a uniform humanity. Cultural diversity is itself a gift of God. Recognizing this included a caution against identifying the gospel with its German, English, or American expressions and so against the problem of missionary imperialism. Its basic circumspection regarding Western civilization, with its atomization of human being and the reduction of all things to raw economic material, was prescient. Relative to the Anglo-American missiology of the period, the German approach had much to commend it.

Second, one should not too quickly dismiss the link that developed with National Socialism. Yes, the Volk approach looked first to local culture, but Volk and *Volkstum* provided the very lens for defining and shaping this culture. Gutmann's romantic reference to agrarian life indicates well the concern. The country village, with its social coherence, becomes the ideal. It establishes the vision of what a "body" and maturity in the faith looks like. To encourage primal ties is to encourage this type of community. As to where one might find this community, first, the experience of missionaries found seeming validation among tribal peoples. Here was confirmation of a located German account of culture and so of the associated missionary approach. Second, it was found in the past, prior to modern life and the entrance of civilization with its acids of individualism. "Blood and soil" become important because of this relationship to land and to one another.

---

[12]Timothy Yates, *Christian Mission in the Twentieth Century* (Cambridge: Cambridge University Press, 1994), 39-56; Stephen Neill, *Colonialism and Christian Missions* (New York: McGraw-Hill, 1966), 401.

The eschatological move toward the kingdom of God consisted of a backward-oriented repristination of the orders of creation through which God's immanence flows. The understanding of culture, in other words, resulted from the German experience of its own nationhood as interpreted through the lenses of romanticism and idealism. As a result, it is obvious to find missions affirming the National Socialist ideology because they both stemmed from the same root.

Third, the entire approach received developed theological legitimation. One finds intricate biblical arguments, reference to tradition (especially Luther), and constructive theologies of mission, the nature of God, and the church. The theology and the Volk understanding of culture were bound together. With this theological structure confirmed by German experience of the Volkskirche, to criticize the underlying account of culture was to promote a disembodied church and to undo a key element of German identity. As we will see with Hans-Werner Gensichen in the next chapter, however much one might agree with the criticisms applied to the Volk approach in the postwar context, it leaves the question of how the church is established and structured. And, given that this approach to creation and identity constituted the nature of the body itself, the temptation was to rationalize the inherent difficulties away and reaffirm the original position as 'necessary' to the establishment of the church.

As a postscript to this chapter, given its compromise with National Socialism, one might be tempted to treat this missionary approach as an exceptional historical moment, one that has nothing to do with our contemporary experience. This would be a mistake. While we should not overstate the connection, there exists some ongoing relationship between this *Volk* missiology and a key approach to missions within American Evangelicalism: Donald McGavran and his theory of church growth.

Christian Keysser (1877–1961) was a contemporary of Gutmann and likewise a main theorist of the *Volk* approach. In 1899, he was sent as a missionary by the Neuendettelsau Mission to Kaiser-Wilhelmsland (the northeastern part of Papua New Guinea). He served among the Kate people until he was prevented from doing so in 1920 due to the post–World War I political situation. On his return to Germany, he taught at the mission seminary in Neuendettelsau and was a leading figure within the German mission administration. Unlike Gutmann or Knak, Keysser would become a card-carrying member of the Nazi party. He did this because he considered Nazism to be the fulfillment of his concept of mission and Hitler a confederate in his concern for the *Volk* over against individualism.[13] He maintained this position through the war and would lose his positions of leadership within German mission administration during the post–World War II period of denazification. Much of the history during this complex period remains to be written, but Keysser does not appear to have retracted his association with National Socialism from the time after the war until his death in 1961. Nor is there any secondary literature on Keysser during the war or in the postwar period. Keysser, in other words, was explicit in tying his mission theory to the ideology of National Socialism and never expressed any contrition over his position.

The tie between McGavran and Keysser lies in a 1929 text Keysser wrote titled *Eine Papuagemeinde*, which McGavran had translated in 1980 with the title *A People Reborn*.[14] This text was Keysser's main expression of his theoretical framework. In his forward, McGavran defends Keysser against a key critic of *Volk* mission theory, J. C. Hoekendijk, and affirms the main lines of Keysser's approach. McGavran agrees that the missionary should engage in a process of Christianization through the preservation of a "people consciousness," and the creation of a *Volkskirche* or "a people church."[15] He observes how Hitler brought the term *Volkskirche* into "disrepute," but nonetheless still affirms the importance of "*Volk* movements."[16] More than this, for McGavran, the *Volk* approach confirmed Waskom Pickett's study of "mass movements" in India, which informed McGavran's 1955 work *The Bridges of God*.[17] McGavran notes his own use of the term *people* within this text: "The concept of people movement embraces clans, tribes, classes, and even neighborhoods where the inhabitants think of themselves of one blood.

---

[13]Richard V. Pierard, "Völkisch Thought and Christian Missions in Early Twentieth Century Germany," in *Essays in Religious Studies for Andrew Walls*, ed. James Thrower (Aberdeen: Department of Religious Studies, University of Aberdeen, 1986), 144-45; Yates, *Christian Mission in the Twentieth Century*, 54.

[14]Christian Keysser, *A People Reborn* (Pasadena, CA: William Carey Library, 1980).

[15]Donald McGavran, foreword to Keysser, *People Reborn*, x.

[16]McGavran, foreword to Keysser, x.

[17]Donald A. McGavran, *The Bridges of God: A Study in the Strategy of Missions* (London: World Dominion Press, 1955).

'A people' is an endogamous society. It marries within itself and sees itself as 'thank God, quite different from other peoples and from the mongrel assemblages of individuals which compose so much of urban society.'"[18] The language is identical to that found within the *Volkschristianiserung* tradition stretching from Warneck, including the binary of the communal-rural and individual-urban. Despite acknowledging Hitler's use of the same language, nowhere does McGavran refer to Keysser's Nazi ties nor to any potential link between Keysser's theory as developed in *A People Reborn* and the ideology of National Socialism. Instead, McGavran finds confirmation of a position he already held, which would develop into the "Homogeneous Unit Principle," the subject of a Lausanne Occasional Paper and much debate within evangelicalism.[19] Exponents of this position remain today: reference to the Homogeneous Unit Principle appears even within the Fresh Expressions movement.[20]

McGavran remains one of the most influential voices within American evangelical mission thinking. Church growth still plays an important role within evangelical missions. While one might well question the extent to which McGavran's position entered and flows today within the evangelical bloodstream, the German experience of this position nonetheless functions as a cautionary tale. It is not difficult to find contemporary rhetoric that links the faith to the agrarian (heartland), to the importance of this group as the safeguarders of national identity, and to God's working through family (primal ties). As they hold the national character, so this people need to protect their own purity. Nor, as a consequence, it is difficult to find a rejection of urban and metropolitical centers as individualistic and liberal (civilized) and destructive of national identity. As this cosmopolitan group erodes the national character, so it is against the God who gave the people this character and this authority. To attack key identity markers of this national identity is to impinge on the church and its embodiment (religious freedom). With the national character related to the heartland, it is a small

---

[18] McGavran, foreword to Keysser, xi.
[19] *The Pasadena Consultation: Homogeneous Unit Principle* (Wheaton, IL: Lausanne Committee for World Evangelization, 1978).
[20] Archbishop's Council on Mission and Public Affairs, *Mission-Shaped Church: Church Planting and Fresh Expressions of Church in a Changing Context* (London: Church House Publishing, 2004), 108-9.

step to connect the eschatological future to the pristine past in which that character first came into being as a movement of God. This people have a particular mission, both to the nation and to the world, and it includes the transmission of this people's values even as it expects different forms (they belong to God's people, but not this people and its special charism). This allows for a conflation of religious and political identity. God's calling is above and apart from the national character even as that character is the means through which God works (constitution, democracy, freedom). Even if no direct tie exists between McGavran's position and the contemporary experience of American evangelicalism, there is sufficient commonality between these themes and the *Volk* approach that we should pay heed to the lessons of history.

3

Eschatology and Agency

Introduction

Whatever the potential cross-pollination of ideas between mission theory and the ideology of National Socialism, the institution of German missions struggled for its survival under that regime. Such struggles, in part, reflected wider challenges presented to missions during the early part of the twentieth century. The bright optimism apparent at the World Missionary Conference held in Edinburgh, 1910, soon dulled. The First World War (1914–1918) and its millions of dead undid the European claim concerning the good of its civilization. As this civilization provided a key warrant for the spread of Christianity, so the loss of this authority prompted questions concerning the right and basis of missions both within and outside the West. Oswald Spengler's 1918 book *The Doom of the Occident* expressed a dark pessimism concerning the possibility of Western culture. With the Russian Revolution of 1917, communism embraced a secular framing of life and proclaimed an antireligious message that gained success around the world. The International Missionary Council conference held in Jerusalem, 1928, revealed deep fractures within the missionary movement as it tried to reformulate the meaning of mission after the violence of imperialism. While it identified militant secularism as the main new foe of the church and its mission, it could itself describe mission in humanistic terms, a trajectory that culminated in William Hocking's infamous 1932 report, "Re-thinking Missions: A Laymen's Inquiry After One Hundred Years."[1]

---

[1] William Ernest Hocking, *Re-thinking Missions: A Laymen's Inquiry After One Hundred Years* (New York: Harper and Brothers, 1932).

Compared to John R. Mott's confidence in the ongoing "conquest" of the Christian faith at the conclusion of Edinburgh 1910,[2] Stephen Neill describes Jerusalem 1928 as "the nadir of the modern missionary movement."[3] Much had changed in eighteen years. By the time of the 1938 International Missionary Council conference held in Tambaram (India), "crisis" dominated mission's understanding of itself and its place in the world. There was an urgent need to reformulate the fundamentals of Christian mission. In Germany, Karl Hartenstein and Walter Freytag drew on the work of Oscar Cullmann (1902–1999) and his book *Christ and Time*.[4] For Cullmann, the New Testament places Jesus Christ at the "center of time." In Christ, the history of God with Israel and with the world finds its center, and salvation spreads out from this center to the world. This account of *salvation history* (*Heilsgeschichte*) meant that God's saving action should be understood neither in terms of evolutionary history (Troeltsch) nor as a history of decay (primal ties). The focus of salvation history was on the history of God and God's acting. This affirmation is basic to understanding Karl Hartenstein and Walter Freytag.

Karl Hartenstein (1894–1952) was raised in the tradition of Württembergian Pietism associated with the name Johann Christoph Blumhardt (1805–1880).[5] From 1925, Hartenstein served as director of the Basel Mission, until 1939 when he felt called back to serve the Lutheran Church in Württemberg as a representative of the "Confessing Church" during the time of National Socialism.[6] In terms of his own theory of mission, Hartenstein draws a direct link between missions and this period of salvation history, the time between the ascension and the final parousia. Mission is

---

[2] John R. Mott, "Closing Address," in *World Missionary Conference, 1910: The History and Records of the Conference, Together with Addresses Delivered at the Evening Meetings*, ed. Robert E. Speer (Edinburgh: Oliphant, Anderson and Ferrier, 1910), 347.
[3] Stephen Neill, *The Unfinished Task* (London: Edinburgh House Press, 1957), 151.
[4] Oscar Cullmann, *Christ and Time: The Primitive Christian Conception of Time and History* (Philadelphia: Westminster Press, 1950).
[5] For greater biographical detail, see Jürgen Schuster, "Karl Hartenstein: Mission with a Focus on the End," *Mission Studies* 19 (2002): 53-79; Gerold Schwarz, "Karl Hartenstein 1894-1954: Missions with a Focus on 'the End,'" in *Mission Legacies: Biographical Studies of Leaders of the Modern Missionary Movement*, ed. Gerald H. Anderson et al. (Maryknoll, NY: Orbis Books, 1994), 591-601.
[6] Much has been written on the Confessing Church, but for two brief introductions, see Jeremy Begbie, "The Confessing Church and the Nazis: A Struggle for Theological Truth," *Anvil* 2 (1985): 117-30; Matthew Hockenos, "The Church Struggle and the Confessing Church: An Introduction to Bonhoeffer's Context," *Studies in Christian-Jewish Relations* 2 (2007): 1-20.

"the obedient ministry of witnesses of a confessing church [*Bekennende Kirche*] insofar as it is directed to the world of heathens. It is done by believing in the church and awaiting the Kingdom of God."[7] Mission is witness and witnesses point not to themselves, but to the object of their witness. Christians witness to Jesus Christ as the Son of God who came into the world, was crucified and resurrected by God for the redemption of all, and who will return at the end of time to judge the living and the dead. The time in-between, the time between the "already" of Jesus Christ's presence and the "not yet" of his return, is the time of mission. Christians are called to an *obedient* ministry of witness, meaning that it properly belongs to Christian being. It is obligatory on all to witness to God's revelation of the reconciliation found in Jesus Christ even and particularly when faced with hardships and to the point of death.

The source text illustrates this position with reference to a particular hardship: the financial crisis of German missions during the 1930s. Under this pressure, mission exists due to the sacrifice of the congregation in providing its resources of time, prayer, and goods to support the mission. Faith and love cannot be demanded, only freely given. The financial crisis, by extension, was not a crisis of money; it was a crisis of faith and commitment. Against the intention of the "German Christians" (*Deutschen Christen*) to force the mission societies under the authority of a single and Führer-led German national church, missions must remain free to do their work. As a free endeavor, Christian mission abroad reminds the local German church that, if it is to be and remain a "true" church," it can never remain within the borders of a particular people. Mission, on this basis, rejects the "Aryan paragraph" of the National Socialists. (This was a collection of laws and regulations that reserved certain rights for those of the "Aryan race" and discriminated against individuals that were regarded as non-Germans, most especially Jews and those of Jewish descent.)

Mission and church exist on the ground of faith and prayer, not on the ground of money and goods. This refusal to locate the possibility within physical contingencies is part of the call for the church to free itself from improper ties with the state, society and culture. Mission is eschatologically

---

[7]Karl Hartenstein, *Die Mission als theologisches Problem: Beiträge zum grundsätzlichen Verständnis der Mission* (Berlin: Furche Verlag, 1932), 13.

grounded, oriented to the second coming of Christ, and this relativizes all earthly bonds.

Walter Freytag (1899–1959), like Hartenstein, was raised in the Pietist tradition but as a Moravian.[8] He studied theology and philosophy at the University of Tübingen before serving as a solider during World War I and later continuing his studies at the Universities of Marburg and Halle. His intention was to become a missionary to China, but this proved impossible given the political circumstances of the period. After completing his dissertation on Chinese religions at the University of Hamburg in 1925, Freytag was appointed first secretary and then director of the Deutschen Evangelische Missionshilfe, an agency for the promotion of mission, and later as mission director for the churches of Hamburg, Bremen, and Lübeck. He also lectured in mission at Hamburg and Kiel. Freytag was removed from office during the Nazi regime but was reinstalled after World War II. Freytag was without doubt a leading figure in German missiology, and in 1946 became the chair of the German Protestant Missionary Council (Deutscher Evangelischer Missionsrat) and later vice president of the International Missionary Council. His main contribution lay in giving more formal shape to the above eschatological insights.

In a 1950 essay titled "The Meaning of World Mission," Freytag distinguishes four different types of eschatological thinking and four resulting approaches to mission method.[9] First, Pietism locates mission within the urgency of final judgement and damnation. It is a subjective eschatology framed by a certain understanding of individual spirituality and ethics, with the movement of mission from individual soul to individual soul. The kingdom of God is the sum of the converted who have been saved from this world. Second, the Roman Catholic Church, more or less, identifies the kingdom of God with the institutional church. Mission, within this account, becomes the expansion of the institutional church. Third, some missions within North America followed the Social Gospel and its view of the kingdom of God as the improvement of social conditions and betterment of

---

[8] For greater biographical detail, see Hans-Werner Gensichen, "Walter Freytag 1899–1959: The Miracle of the Church Among the Nations," in Anderson, *Mission Legacies*, 435-44.
[9] Walter Freytag, "Vom Sinn der Weltmission," in *Reden und Aufsätze*, ed. J. Hermelink and Hans Jochen Margull (Munich: Chr. Kaiser Verlag, 1961), 207-17.

the society. As an immanent reality, mission is working for the social good. Fourth, some Christians understand the kingdom of God as only appearing at the end of time, for which the Christian community waits. This world is not redeemable, and the missionary responsibility lies in proclaiming the gospel and remaining pure through separation from the world. For Freytag, every approach contains positive as well as problematic aspects. Mission has to achieve a balance between individualism (Pietism) and collectivism (Roman Catholicism), between immanence (Social Gospel) and transcendence (apocalyptic). Like Hartenstein, Freytag regards mission as the meaning of history, viewing the current period as a "pause in the history of salvation" (*heilsgeschichtliche Pause*).

Though this eschatological approach represents one significant attempt to distance missions from an undue compromise with National Socialism, the ties were not so easily severed. Without question, there is advance, but there is also overlap and the desire to conserve and even validate earlier models. The article from **Hans-Werner Gensichen** (1915–1999) represents an instance of such overlap.[10] Shaped by Walter Freytag, Gensichen completed his doctoral studies in 1942 and his Habilitation in 1950 at the University of Göttingen, before teaching in theological colleges in Tranquebar and Madras (1952–1957). Upon his return to Germany in 1957, he was professor of the history of religions and mission studies at the University of Heidelberg to 1983. He also held the post of Africa-Secretary of the Theological Education Fund (1961–1964), and was from 1965 to 1990 chair of the German Society for Mission Studies (*Deutsche Gesellschaft für Missionswissenschaft*).

The selected reading is Gensichen's response to an extended critique of German missiology and the basis of its compromise with the Nazi State by Dutch missiologist Johannes Christiaan Hoekendijk. Gensichen's concern focuses on the grounding of the church as a body of believers. He acknowledges the basic thrust of Hoekendijk's critique: the goal of mission can neither be the founding of a church or not the expansion of an already

---

[10]For greater biographical detail, see Hans-Werner Gensichen, "My Pilgrimage in Mission," *International Bulletin of Missionary Research* 13 (1989): 167-69; Theo Sundermeier, "Gensichen, Hans-Werner," in *Biographical Dictionary of Christian Missions*, ed. Gerald H. Anderson (Grand Rapids, MI: Eerdmans, 1998), 238.

existing church. In both cases, the end result is confessionalism, a church merely reproducing itself in a different cultural context. Contra Gutmann, Gensichen agrees that the church is not "first creation," it does not belong to the *order of sustainment* (*Erhaltungsordnung*). Yet, contra Hoekendijk, the church is "new creation" and belongs to the *order of salvation* (*Heilsordnung*). As to how one might describe the process of gathering a community, Gensichen replaces the terms "founding" or "expansion" with a neologism: the "coming-into-being" of a church (*Kirchwerdung*). The grammar of this term is noteworthy because of its oddity: it includes no identified acting subject—a church simply emerges. This emergence Gensichen ties to the encounter of the faith with the different cultural customs of local people. This requires both respect for those customs and a care not to blur the boundaries between church and ethnic group. Indigenous theologies must evolve *in loco,* but do so in both *bondage* and *freedom.* Gensichen's question is vital: while one might critique past practices of forming communities of faith, the issue remains as to how those communities form to become part of the body of Christ.

Karl Hartenstein

"What Is Our Obligation in Light of the Mission's Financial Situation?"

~1934~

1. WHEN IT COMES TO MISSION, what matters is substance, not finances.[11] Mission stands or falls by the reality and truth of the living *Christ*, by his Word, and by his sending. If he is present—and he is present—then there will be mission, even in times of the greatest poverty and financial difficulties. Therefore, mission today is called to examine itself continually before God from all angles, and to see whether it is what it is meant to be: *Missio Dei,* the sending of God, indeed, the sending that Christ the Lord

---

[11]Karl Hartenstein, "Wozu nötigt die Finanzlage der Mission," *Evangelisches Missions-Magazin* 79 (1934): 217-29.

imparted to the apostles: "As the Father has sent me, I am sending you" (Jn 20:21)—, and the answer to the call that the apostles by their word extended to the church of all time: "Therefore go and make disciples of all nations" (Mt 28:19). The main thing, the decisive factor by which Protestant mission stands or falls is the Lord of mission and the call the living Lord issues to his church to be of service to the world. Do we give glory to the Lord of our noble ministry? Do we listen to the voice of the Lord of mission—and to no other?

The second factor is inextricably linked to the first. It is the issue of proclamation, of "authoritative" preaching. The word *authoritative* implies a double calling. First, we use it to mean that the message we proclaim is the living Word of God, of the God before whom there are no other gods. It is therefore the living Word that is valid for all time and for all nations. It is also the Word that does not return empty, in which there is power and Spirit and life. Second, we use it to mean that this authority has been "entrusted" to us, that it has been entrusted to the male and female servants of the Lord who is the Word and who places it on their lips and in their hearts as their witness in his name. The question of authority is therefore the question of the *Spirit*, of the Holy Spirit by whom the Lord intends to equip his messengers and without whom mission is nothing more than a resounding gong or a clanging cymbal.

Third, mission stands or falls by the restless, unconditional *affirmation of faith*, of believers who know themselves to be joined and obligated to Christ not only in terms of their speech, but in terms of their entire lives. That is to say that they are willing to suffer for him, and this willingness is the only way in which we today can once again credibly bear witness that this is about the one thing that is needful, which all people need—the Word of the living God. This affirmation of faith is expressed in very different ways. It consists in the willingness to serve among the nations, in the perseverance of the messengers in severe climates, in hardship, and in imprisonment, in the struggle against their own weaknesses, in their fight against the demons. But it is also expressed in the faith of the congregation that intercedes for the messengers with prayer, love, and sacrifice. It is expressed in the confession of the church that is aware that mission is a key indicator that she is alive and an expression of her God-given existence.

Finally, mission stands or falls by the church's unforced willingness to give and to make *sacrifices* to make this kind of mission possible. The confessing church knows that her gold and silver are not her own, that she is not free to dispose of her wealth as she sees fit, but that it belongs to the Lord and is to be used in service to him—that is to say, either she knows it or she has forgotten it, in which case no gifts, no "days of sacrifice," no collections, and no propaganda will achieve much at all. Mission does not live on monies given under constraint, nor on organized propaganda, nor on ecclesiastical dictates, but on the faith and love of the church *compelled* to give precisely because she believes and because she loves. But it is impossible to enforce faith and love; either they are present, and mission is therefore also present, or they are lacking, in which case all attempts to resuscitate them by whatever means may perhaps meet with success—but what good would that be to mission? At any rate, they would bear no fruit. Not to put too fine a point on it: ultimately, mission does not subsist on gifts, but on *givers* who are conscious of the task of mission and who carry it out.

To address problematic finances, we therefore need to begin and end by talking about the key *substance* of mission: about the Word of the living Christ, about the authority to proclaim, about the dedication of the witnesses and of the church, and about the true sacrifice of the church, that is, about the awareness that our means belong to the Lord and therefore need to be surrendered to the Lord so that his work may be done. The public financial difficulties currently facing continental European mission as a whole and German Protestant mission in particular compel us to begin and end by enquiring into the ultimate *mandate* to do mission, and by engaging in comprehensive introspection as to the essence of mission and the status and role it deserves.

2. German Protestant mission engaged in such introspection when it gathered in Barmen in October of 1933. The confession formulated there, a unanimous expression of German Protestant mission, represents an instance of standing or falling by the highest aspiration to which Christ alone calls us, namely a knowledge of being rooted in the king to whom the world belongs. This article must therefore be cited in this context. It states,

> As the church's act of confession before the world, mission is the bearer of the message of salvation in Christ to the nations. In this capacity, it accomplishes

the mandate the Lord gave to his church, the *una sancta* of the Christian confessions. In German Protestant mission, the German Protestant church expresses its association with the *una sancta* in a largely visible manner. The mission of German Protestant Christianity carries out its unique service to the nations by bringing to them the legacy given to it in the Reformation and the accompanying revival movements. Under the leadership of God in history, the militant forces of the believing church united to carry out this service. As a result, the church received unique and indispensable tools to accomplish her mission mandate.

But the most important consequences of this confession are found in the conclusions drawn from it. They state that a church that is aware of her task and of the content of her message must take an interest in *promoting* mission, that such a church will recognize the mission societies in her midst, and that she is called to use all the means at her disposal in support of the service these mission societies offer to the church. Furthermore, they state that in the context of such an association between church and mission, the church must grant to mission the necessary leeway to act, to call and to train its personnel, and to govern and bring to completion their service both at home and abroad. They go on to state that mission as the church's act of confession before the world must remain completely independent of the wrangles and church politics taking place within the church itself. They also state that mission fundamentally rejects the implementation of any legislation related to the Aryan paragraph in the church; being an ecumenical enterprise, mission must stand on the foundation of the New Testament church and must also resist every effort to apply church-political measures to the sphere of mission by force. Finally, they state that it is the responsibility of mission to bundle its strengths and to employ them cohesively and in consensus, in order to do justice to the global nature of the task given to the church.

In so doing, mission resolutely articulated its basis, namely the church's confession, and it unequivocally confessed the practical consequences of the Christian church acting in mission. It is only on this foundation that the issue of the financial crisis, its causes, it needs, and its prospects may be rightly viewed. . . .

With deep gratitude to God, we realize that the financial crisis has also brought with it tremendous *blessings* in all areas. It became evident that

God's Spirit is especially active in times of scarcity, and that it is particularly in those areas where human help fails that he opens new doors in his omnipotence and awakens independent responsibility and creative love in the native churches in completely unexpected ways.

More and more baptisms are being recorded in almost all mission fields, particularly in western, southern, and eastern Africa. Even Borneo, which offered such dismal prospects for so long, and which Basel took over from Barmen thirteen years ago, is now experiencing a booming revival. People are beginning to express a strong desire for literature, especially in China and India; in many areas, a real hunger for the Bible has arisen, especially as a result of the service of revivalist preachers coming from the Chinese church itself.

Furthermore, the crisis has sifted the chaff from the wheat among the teachers and catechists. Those who were in it for the money rather than for reasons of faith have left mission work, thereby making it purer. We are pleased to see the work of evangelism making good progress all over the world. This is especially true in Africa, where a strong revival is taking place everywhere—here we may name especially Cameroon (particularly the grasslands) and East Africa. Everywhere, the churches are coming to realize that the church is built not by might nor by power, not by money nor by external means, but by faith and prayer alone, by the living Word of God alone....

Thus one of the prominent signs of the financial crisis is that God particularly uses times of poverty to produce the wealth of his heavenly goods, namely faith and sacrifice, prayer and devotion. He does this in a completely different manner than would be the case in times of more abundant supply from the home base. It is safe to say that not only do the hardships and blessings of the financial crisis balance each other out, but that this time of poverty has been especially profitable for the divine history of mission, which is written in eternity and whose most profound meaning is hidden from our human eyes. In fact, God could not have brought this about in any other way....

Above and beyond this, mission has an important service to render to the organized church. The *church* is in grave danger of wasting its strength and means on organizational issues, of associating itself too closely with state and politics, and of breaking apart in the process. Mission may not tire of pointing out what a vibrant church looks like, a church based on the Word, living by the Word, and faithful to its confession. We believe that in today's church struggle, the experiences made in the mission field empower mission to say that the *living church* is still the basis for every true church of Christ, and that for mission, too, in terms of faith, sacrifice, and prayer, the *living church* is the sole basis for an authoritative proclamation of the eternal Word of God throughout the world. The future of German Protestant mission is closely tied to the emergence of a living church, which has been the case in recent months here in Germany—a miracle of God. Whenever the church believes and confesses, it also heeds the mission mandate and carries it out without much hype, propaganda, or human hustle and bustle.

Finally, the financial crisis has a profound effect on us—it compels us to complain less and to *pray* more, to make fewer cries of distress and to be more deliberate in approaching the heart of God from depths of woe, pleading with him to direct the forces of eternity in service of mission both at home and abroad. Such pleas and requests for the spiritual revival of our church and for victory over the spiritual powers of heathenism are the only weapons mission has at its disposal.

WALTER FREYTAG

"Mission in View of the End"
~1942~

AT THE LAST MAJOR mission conference, the German delegation made a declaration on the main problems facing mission work at the present time, based on the line from the Apostolic Creed that we believe Christ "will come to judge the living and the dead."[12] Our delegation drew conclusions from this statement regarding the correlation between the gospel and national traditions, the gospel and religion, and the gospel and social issues. Now of course the aspect of the eschaton has always been a core consideration in

---

[12]Walter Freytag, "Mission im Blick aufs Ende," *Evangelische Missions Zeitschrift* 3 (1942): 321-33.

German mission theology. At the same time, it is remarkable how one-sided the emphasis on eschatology has been. This emphasis can only be understood in light of the church's situation as viewed from the German delegation's perspective at the time of this most recent overview of mission. Whatever has happened since then in mission and in the church confirms the necessity and importance of this point of view. That is why we propose to consider mission here in view of the end. As we do so, we will address three issues: the rationale for mission, missionary proclamation, and the goal of mission work.

The view of the end supplies a key basis for mission. In making this statement, we are not aligning ourselves with the concept of eschatological justification held by a number of mission movements founded in the nineteenth century. What fundamentally drove Hudson Taylor to pursue his China Inland Mission and what determined his entire, very productive life was the notion that roughly one million people died in China each month without any hope of salvation from perdition because they did not know the gospel. The American, English, and Scandinavian Alliance Missions were also founded in view of the end. Led by men like Simpson, Grattan Guinness, and Franson, these missions put others to shame by raising an enormous amount of funds and by sending out many missionaries—more than four hundred thousand marks were collected in a single evening, and thousands of missionaries were deployed in just a few years. These missions were founded as a result of the idea that our Lord's return purely depends on the gospel being proclaimed throughout the world. In 1887, it was calculated that if twenty thousand missionaries were sent out immediately, the evangelization of the world would be completed by the turn of the century, meaning that the end would then take place. This is not the view of the end we mean. . . .

Our basic premise is that the church of Jesus exists in the interim period between the resurrection and the return of Jesus, between the reconciliation of the world and the consummation of the world. We are once again coming to realize the profound significance of this premise. The church lives in the "not yet." She inhabits the period in which the Lord is delaying the visible consummation of salvation. If the reconciliation of the world and the consummation of the world had taken place simultaneously, then there would be no church as we know it on the basis of the New Testament. The church is "saved—

in hope." She is the body of Christ. She shares in what God has already accomplished in Christ; she is justified. But she also shares in the hiddenness of Christ. She is in the world, enduring the sufferings of this present time caused by a defeated enemy's final rebellion against God, and waiting for the glory to be revealed. That is her existence in the interim period, the tremendous tension in which she lives. In this tension, she is called to persevere, to keep watch, to remain faithful, to confess, to be ready, to wait, and to conquer.

But the interim period is more than just a timeframe the church inhabits. The meaning and purpose of this period is for the church to be gathered. The only reason Scripture provides for the delay between the inception and the consummation of the new creation is that the church of Jesus must be gathered from all nations.... Because the gathering together of the church is the purpose and meaning of history, she operates with two watchwords in view of the end. Her first watchword is to persevere, to confess, and to be ready. And her second watchword is the proclamation of the gospel, that is, mission.

We may summarize the relevant New Testament passages and their implications in the following three points:

A. We should always bear in mind that in the New Testament, missionary instructions and missionary proclamation are subordinated and constrained to fixed time limits. "First" the gospel must be proclaimed, "then" the end will come. In the interim period between the two points in time, the Word of God proceeds from one nation to the next as a present moment in time moving from place to place. "Who is now being preached to you beforehand," Peter says in Acts 3:20.[13] "But now [God] commands all people everywhere to repent," Paul preaches in Athens (Acts 17:30). Daybreak does not occur everywhere in our world at the same time; rather, sunrise takes place successively, hour after hour. In the same way, the time of salvation dawns on one nation after another, separating what used to be from what begins "now" and will be consummated "then." By delivering their message, Christ's ambassadors usher in the dawn of the time of salvation and of the end times from one nation to the next. Bearing in mind the "first" and the "then" and the eschatological "now" in which mission takes place attaches

---

[13]This is an English translation from the 1912 edition of the Luther Bible.

Eschatology and Agency

an incomparable importance to mission. The whole meaning and purpose of history and the trajectory of salvation in history are accomplished in and by means of mission. From the perspective of the New Testament, all of human history takes place under the aegis of the maturation of the demonic in this world. But here in mission, God is accomplishing his purpose in the midst of and under and in spite of the demonic, namely, to gather together the church. As a result, mission remains inwardly unaffected by considerations of timeliness; as a matter of fact, Jesus locates mission in the midst of "wars and rumors of wars" (Mt 24:6). To Jesus, mission is the real event on which everything else depends.

B. Mission is one part of God's eschatological action. It is striking that the sentences recorded in Mark 13:10, "The gospel must first be preached to all nations," and Matthew 24:14, "This gospel of the kingdom will be preached . . . , and then the end will come," stand apart from their immediate context in terms of their form. In both cases, the context is that of a speech, much of which is addressed to the hearers in the second person plural. Besides admonitions like "watch out" and "you will be handed over" we find here the simple statement: the gospel will be preached. Mark emphasizes it by adding the word δει—it is necessary—which alludes to the whole weightiness and immutability of the divine will and determination. This has nothing to do with human beings—God is at work here. Mission is the signal of the eschaton which he has established. Its dignity does not depend on the goodwill of human beings; even less do human actions constitute an adequate basis for bringing about the coming end. But wherever mission occurs, God shows that his hour is drawing nearer. . . (Rom 13:11-12). Since mission is one part of God's eschatological action, it contains within itself the assurance of God. Mission is the inevitable signal of the eschaton. The gospel will be preached; it is happening and it will happen. Even if a thousand witnesses were to be muzzled and entire Christianities to be silenced, it is happening and it will happen. In fact, such distress and outrage at the Word is the most conclusive sign that the Lord is on his way.

C. At the same time, mission is oriented toward Jesus' eschatological commission to his disciples. In Acts 1, they ask the resurrected Lord whether he is about to restore the kingdom, and he answers by promising them the Spirit and by commissioning them to be his witnesses to the ends of the earth. The Great Commission (which is undeniably linked to Dan 7:13-14) is also more closely associated with a view of the end than we often realize. The composition of the Daniel passage reflects the underlying three-stage structure of an oriental enthronement ceremony, namely elevation, proclamation, and conferment of authority. In the same way, Matthew 28:18-20 features in immediate succession the bestowal of authority, the proclamation of the lordship of Christ among the nations, and the promise of eschatological consummation. Mission is the eschatologically oriented lordship of Christ. Mission is the church's central commission. The church does not remain stationary. To use a military analogy, she is not condemned simply to sit and wait until the machine gun fire dies down. She may, yes, she must move forward. In terms of the proclamation of the gospel, the passages referring to the end never speak only of preaching, although many seem to prefer this restrictive misconstruction; no, they speak of the progressive proclamation of the gospel. This sending is the only answer Jesus gives to the "when" question, which gets people so riled up these days. It is the act of hope that keeps the view of the end grounded. It subsists on the hidden glory of Jesus in all its fullness. This sending is not just about the salvation of souls; it looks to the coming world of God. Neither does it occur simply as a dutiful response, as we have repeatedly emphasized over the last decade vis-à-vis other mission motives; rather, it reaches forward to the promise. It is the action of the church that testifies like none other that

> at the name of Jesus every knee should bow,
>> in heaven and on earth and under the earth,
> and every tongue acknowledge that Jesus Christ is Lord,
>> to the glory of God the Father. (Phil 2:10-11)

From no other perspective does mission emerge more clearly as an essential feature of the existence of the church of Jesus Christ, than it does in view of the end.

The message of the end is an essential aspect of missionary proclamation. At first glance, this seems self-explanatory. This is how it is in the missionary proclamation of the New Testament—we might think of the Acts passages cited above, of 1 Thessalonians 1:9-10; 4:15ff; 1 Corinthians 15:51ff; 2 Corinthians 5:10; and whatever passages we may relate in this regard.

But how are things today? Overall, whereas missionary proclamation—and here we are speaking of what is initially preached during the first encounter with heathenism—certainly mentions the resurrection of Jesus, it has much less to say about his return, the resurrection of the dead, the final judgment, and the time of the end. . . .

[There is] no genuinely missionary preaching. . . without a fundamentally eschatological perspective. The following five points will serve to demonstrate that as soon as churches are founded, missionary preaching manifests such an eschatological perspective, and that the church accepts this preaching.

1. The eschatological "now" vis-à-vis the religions. . . . Just like in the New Testament, statements made about heathenism in missionary proclamation have in mind a form of heathenism "now" considering the offer of salvation. And now this heathenism can no longer remain what it was. It must either surrender itself or turn into anti-Christianity. . . .

2. God's demand is unconditional: when a Papuan tribe's first Christian convert selects for herself the name Benuana, meaning "before the face of God," then it is quite obvious that what the missionaries proclaimed before the church was founded vividly evoked the concept of judgment. At Mount Hagen in the interior of New Guinea, which was discovered as recently as 1929 and where mission work commenced in 1935, a major turnaround occurred as a result of a sermon about the resurrection of Jesus, his return, and the judgment. Tens of thousands were moved to renounce heathenism. It is significant that it was the fact of being accountable to God that overcame these heathens with its novelty and intensity and led to the momentous conversion. It is only by preaching judgment that God's unconditional demand is enunciated and that understanding begins to dawn about what sin is. Having to appear before the judgment seat of Christ breaks down the separation between religion and morality prevalent in all heathen cultures. The proclamation therefore rapidly proceeds to the announcement of the judgment, because this is the only point where the proclamation of the law and the promise of the gospel properly intersect. Talking about the judgment intensifies the demands of the law to the point where every form of self-praise becomes impossible and where even those who keep the law are

shown to be sinners. It imbues the promise of the gospel with such gravity that the hearers simply have to make a decision, to respond with the answer of faith. "Work out your salvation with fear and trembling, for it is God. . ." (Phil 2:12-13). This excludes any possibility of viewing the Christian proclamation either purely as a lesson in morals or purely as a religious form of comfort. When people's attention is directed to the end, they readily adopt a mindset of willingness. Hartenstein would sometimes tell the story of his encounter with a young Indian merchant in Colombo. Recognizing that Hartenstein was a German, the merchant immediately directed the conversation to the subject of the last things. At the end of the conversation, he confessed, "Every day when I hold my morning devotion on the roof of my house, I conclude with the petition that the Lord would find me ready if he should come today."

3. The message about suffering: it is often said that in the initial stages of the proclamation, the heathens would ask: "Tell us, Mr. Missionary—is it true that if we listen to you, we will not die anymore?" All forms of heathenism subscribe to the notion that happiness and salvation are identical, or that success is proof of being saved. On this point, the missionary message is fundamentally different. The message has to penetrate the constriction of purely temporal thought. It can only do so by clearly talking about the "not yet–ness" of our life in this world, by shifting the emphasis from this life to the true goal, by showing that God leads our souls to this goal by the path of suffering. It is truly miraculous when people come to understand this. We often read in our mission reports how, say, recently converted Christians testify about their hope in the face of the death of their children. And we hardly pay any attention to it at all, simply because we do not understand how miraculous it is for people to comprehend that happiness and salvation are not the same thing. Junod mentioned something in a report from South Africa I found particularly memorable: A woman with two children converted to Christianity and then had two more children. These children, who were born as Christians, then died. Naturally, their heathen grandmother immediately responded by saying to the woman, "The ancestors are punishing you for departing from their ways." The woman simply answered, "Have you forgotten our customs? The punishment for stealing from our

fields is death. But when a friend walks past our fields and is hungry, then he is permitted to take from the fields. He only has to leave visible tracks so that we can know it was our friend. Before I knew God, he did not take away my children. Now that I know him, I say this: He is my friend; he is permitted to take." That is African logic, and yet it speaks of a powerful new insight; the woman understood that the purpose of God's dealings is not happiness, but something else.

4. The message about death: I do not need to elaborate on this point, because it is well known that this is where the young church most clearly shows that it has grasped what is to come. Missionary Fischer reported that a negro from Togo was once asked without prior notice, "What is the best part about the gospel?" He answered, "What awaits us after death." We receive testimonies from all the various mission fields about people dying with joy. These reports are astonishing because they clearly prove that the most important thing to these people is not some notion of perpetuating this life, but the idea of going to be with Christ with whom they were buried through baptism into death in order that they too might live a new life. Last year, we read the most recent report about the death of a Christian lady from East Africa. Her final words were, "I am now going to be with the one I saw when I was baptized." This is the same new insight that made such an impression in New Guinea that the heathens soon started to talk about the "new death" to be found among the Christians. It is especially interesting that former Muslims tend to take the entire Islamic eschatology about the end that comes to all people, and to narrow it down after their conversion to this focus on Christ. For instance, one such former Muslim said, "Every day I pray that the Lord would at some point allow me to enter into eternal life; that is all I want right now."

5. The message of the hiddenness of God's children and their future glory. . . .

The eschatological perspective is a definitive characteristic of the objectives of mission work. Oddly, the German declaration we mentioned at the beginning also bases its comments about the problem of national customs and traditions on the reminder that Jesus will return. That is no accident. After all, three key things follow from the eschatological perspective with regard to the objectives of our mission work:

A. We are called to observe the basic structures of human society for the very reason that we still live in the world of the "not yet," in which these structures still apply. Ignoring them would mean preempting what we have received only in hope. For this reason, mission insists that the church should be autochthonous, since it has been called to establish the obedience of faith in this world. In this way, the view of the end safeguards the objectives of our work from fanaticism.

B. On the other hand, the view of the end grants us complete freedom from all issues related to ethnic composition and ecclesiastical structures. The church of Christ never becomes fully identical with such things. They characterize her, but they do not own her. The church that lives by faith that Christ is alive and will return will not be bound to any of the probabilities and prospects awaiting these things in the final judgment. The young church in New Guinea is a textbook case of an autochthonous church. Nowhere else were a village community and a church community as synonymous as there. . . . Or we might consider their counterpart. Given their ethnic mixture, it seems impossible to establish autochthonous churches in Asian metropolises. From the outset, it seems impossible to create autochthonous structures in places like Singapore, or Shonan-to, as it is now known, where sixty-eight languages are regularly spoken, and where churches must hold worship services in eleven different languages. But that does not mean that church is impossible.

C. When it comes to mission work, the view of the end provides us with what we may call illusion-free certainty. We are under no illusion when it comes to the future—we expect to encounter temptations and many failures among our mission churches. We know that our mission work will give rise to churches, but there are no guarantees that they might not ultimately wither and become all crusted over like the old Syrian church in India or like many churches in the Middle East, all of which once came into being through great missionary sacrifices. In the face of the difficult circumstances about to affect large parts of our mission fields, we must be absolutely clear that such things may well happen. Even so, in view of the end, we are certain that the Christ will preserve all who wait on him and keep them safe throughout these times of distress, until the day arrives Scripture describes not as "the day of victory of the demons," but as "the day of harvest."

Hans-Werner Gensichen
"Basic Issues Concerning How the Church Comes into Being in mission: A Discussion with J. C. Hoekendijk"
~1951~

CRITICISM ALWAYS HURTS.[14] The only question is whether criticism causes hurt for the sake of hurt, or whether criticism causes hurt in order to stir up powers of healing and aid. Without a doubt, German mission finds painful the sweeping criticism it has incurred because of J. C. Hoekendijk. ... All of these references take nothing away from the impression that with his topic of "church and nation," Hoekendijk has distilled, as it were, all the pertinent models promoting a critical reconsideration of mission thinking, and has drawn attention to their core aspects.... It seems especially necessary to pick up on Hoekendijk's promptings and to push them forward in those areas where they will have the strongest impact: In thinking about the church, in thinking about how church comes into being and is formed as a result of mission work, and in thinking about church as the *purpose* of mission.

1. Defining the problem in this way already sets us on a course that will take us to the heart of the matter, to the fundamental issues related to establishing church in mission. Hoekendijk himself has recently and emphatically warned of even associating the objective of mission work with the expansion of the church. In his view, it is unacceptable to define mission as a "path leading from the church to church." True, we side with a respectable tradition if we endorse this definition, but it does not become any less questionable just because many stubbornly insist on espousing it today. Now of course, from St. Thomas and the medieval Roman world mission all the way to the Roman mission theorists of today, *plantatio ecclesiae*—in the sense of the purposeful expansion of the Roman church—has been the leitmotif of Catholic mission and has become even more so....

Without a doubt, this *plantatio ecclesiae* concept has also had a strong impact on the Protestant mission.... It is well known that it often led to

---

[14]Hans-Werner Gensichen, "Grundfragen der Kirchwerdung in der Mission: Zur Gespräch mit J. C. Hoekendijk," *Evangelische Missions Zeitschrift* 8 (1951): 33-46.

disastrous consequences in the mission field, and especially in terms of the severe developmental issues facing those young churches that were and continue to be founded as a result of the denominational problem. The danger to the mission churches at home is just as great, that is, to those mission churches that insist on defining their missionary task solely as denominational self-affirmation and as the formation of Christians and churches according to their own image.

That being said, if we recognize these obvious dangers and if we abandon the awkward language of "building the church" or "expanding the church," is it then really necessary to do away entirely with the concept of *establishing* church when we define the purpose of mission? From the perspective of mission history, at any rate, it would seem rather oversimplified to equate all Protestant efforts to establish churches in mission with the Roman *plantatio ecclesiae* model, or to see it purely as a relapse into the medieval *Corpus Christianum* ideology. . . .

2. In mission praxis, basing the establishing of church simply on the power of the life-giving gospel has always posed problems. Of course, the whole point was that church came into being and began to exist in very particular circumstances. This raised the question as to the extent to which the circumstances and customs of the natural world should impact the establishing of church, or should at least be considered in the process. The more recent mission history has shown that especially in those cases where people took Word and sacrament very seriously, this issue was sometimes decided to a large extent by the application of supplementary norms which were secondary to the gospel. There were two possible sources from which such norms could be drawn: they could either come from the sociological structures the missionaries encountered on the mission field, or the missionaries could import them from their home context. In the case of German mission, the latter possibility, the danger of transferring Western sociological norms to the mission field, never really became acute in the sense of the mission degenerating into mere cultural propaganda. Even Herder warned about it, and just as the colonial era was providing a fresh impetus to mission, and Martin Kähler was emphatic in his repetition of this warning.

Admittedly, Herder was also the one who came up with those romantic concepts that have dogged German mission ever since, a kind of legacy that was handed down from the fathers but is by no means harmless: that Christianity should not alter but rather ennoble the character and the type of fruits yielded by the national entities sprouting like trees from the root of German Christianity. At a later stage, it is possible to adapt in large part and on this basis the home-grown forms of community used by the natives. This adaptation in turn makes it possible to transplant the concept of the national church familiar to the missionaries from their home context to the mission field. This gives rise to a curious mix between the two kinds of foreign influence on the process of establishing church—a type of middle course seeking to factor in the national customs and traditions of the heathen while remaining faithful to Western ideals as well, although priority is given to the former. This is the path of establishing church Hoekendijk traced all the way through its various stages and bifurcations.

Hoekendijk even detects ominous undertones in the writings of the Lutheran mission thinkers of the nineteenth century already: when it comes to establishing church, they assign important roles not only to Word and sacrament, but also to people's natural desire for community. Of course they assert the primacy of the church above all naturally occurring forms of community. But from this point on, two factors have been in play, and as a result, more and more emphasis has been placed on the aspect of ethnicity. One of these factors is the mission's practical experience of conversions of tribes and ethnic groups, which appear to confirm that it is legitimate to define the purpose of mission work as the establishment of a national church. The other factor is theological in nature. It consists in the discovery of the intrinsic theological value of the orders of creation, which are seen in a positive light when it comes to the establishing of church in that they help "prepare the soil to receive the gospel" (Gutmann). In addition, the romantic awe of that which developed in the course of history plays a role in German mission when it comes to implementing the notion of national church, as does a type of sociology unilaterally proceeding on the basis of the concept of "nation." All of these factors played a part in the "national-organic" definition of mission coming to prominence in the time following the First World War. People came dangerously close to conflating the concepts of "forming a church" and "forming a nation," and the main accent of mission work shifted from the Third to the First Article.[15] The fact that individual representatives of German mission have been purposely working at breaking this spell ever since about 1930 should not leave us in any doubt as to the extent of its impact.

To be sure, this distortion of the process in which church comes into being is found outside of German mission as well. . . .

In essence, the Bantu sects have the same position, except that they approach the racial aspect from the reverse angle. They are living proof of the ultimate result of this kind of overemphasis on natural phenomena: not the gospel, but myth, not churches, but sects. Incidentally, we join Hoekendijk in viewing the key characteristic of sects not as a unilateral focus on one or the other aspect of the message of the gospel, but as the displacement of the gospel from its central position (it is thus very well *possible* for a "national church" to become a sect in this sense!).

We must come to the preliminary conclusion that where the forming of church is no longer based only on the life-giving power of the gospel, and where the corporality [*Leibhaftigkeit*] of the church is modeled after natural phenomena, what comes into being is not truly church, and that the body of Christ must necessarily begin to compete with secular forms of community which constantly threaten to engulf it. The church's corporality comes at the price of the church necessarily surrendering its intrinsic hiddenness and its character as the church of the Third Article. While she then is a body indeed, she is no longer truly the body of Christ.

3. What would happen if we were to avoid the problems related to the establishing of church by defining the objectives of mission in such a way as to make no allowances for the orders and customs of the world, nor for the visible, constituted church with all its weaknesses? Times of great eschatological tension have always led the church to wonder whether it is actually still worth building ecclesiastical emergency bridges for the heathens, seeing as the imminent end would soon usher in the lordship of the coming Lord over all the nations en bloc. Bengel predicted that the parousia would take place in 1836. When it failed to materialize, many awakened Christians like Basel mission inspector Wilhelm Hoffmann believed that 1848, the year of

---

[15]Editor's note: this language refers to the articles of the Apostle's Creed. The first article refers to God the Father and to creation, the second to the Son, and the third to the Holy Spirit and the church.

the revolution, would usher in the end times. Should the church really expend its energy on converting people even at that late hour? Since the mission societies were perhaps about to complete their task, was it not perhaps time to adopt a radically expanded focus and "to subject entire tribes and ethnic groups to Christian treatment," so as to introduce them into the coming kingdom immediately, in other words, by skipping the intermediate level of the visible church?

Hoffmann only alludes to these concepts. In terms of actual mission history, we find them gaining traction in England and America. Hudson Taylor, the founder of the China Inland Mission, calculated on the basis of maps and the Bible that it would take one thousand evangelists one thousand days to present the gospel to every single Chinese person. Grattan Guinness deployed droves of itinerant preachers to Africa in an effort to attend to the final delays to the imminent parousia at the eleventh hour. With his rousing slogans, John Mott stirred up thousands of students to help carry out the "evangelization of the world in this generation." Elsewhere it was said that only twenty thousand more missionaries were needed to reach the great goal before the end of the so-called missionary century, and then—according to Matthew 24:14—the lordship of Christ could manifest itself in all its fullness before the whole world.

The eschatological pathos which drove these mission endeavors could not prevent them from being carried along by the rising tide of Anglo-American world domination and thereby degenerating significantly to mere propaganda. We will not add to the criticism already leveled at the often impulsive and hasty methods of this work, seeing as Anglo-American missions have for the most part long been aware of the questionable nature of these methods.

Elsewhere, the eschatological pathos was focused inward. It outpaced the mission's goal of establishing church in that missionaries began directing their efforts toward visibly establishing the pure church of the end times. Looking into the more recent mission history, branches of the American mission, operating with the principles of Methodism, reflected this intensification of the goal of mission in a particularly characteristic manner. After the initial so-called Haystack Prayer Meeting of 1806 and the subsequent founding of the American Board of Commissioners for Foreign Missions (1810), many consciously decided to work for *revival* and not for the founding of churches. The revival movement spread like wildfire, and it appeared to be able to realize the true communion of saints on earth at last. This communion needs no ecclesiastical support; after all, the idea is that this communion itself consummates the coming kingdom of the Lord here on earth. Today's Alliance Missions continue to endorse this notion as their operative objective: the idea is that the true church will surpass the various particular churches—whose divisions are cause for great concern—in the here and now, and that the promises of the Bible can only pertain to this true church. However, as Heinrich Frick put it, the end result of this idea is that "the true concept of church has been destroyed"—nothing more, nothing less.

We need to consider that in contrast to the former, more extensive impact of the eschatological pathos, the founding of churches still remains firmly in place. People cannot and will not forgo the corporality of the church. The only difference is that it is not based on Word and sacrament any longer, but on the faith and sanctification of the members. This comes down to an underlying wariness to equate the true church with the visible institution of salvation, a wariness which is at first only too justified. But then it goes too far. Granted, these people stop short of spiritualism, which should have been the logical conclusion, and which would have disappeared the church and turned it into a *civitas Platonica*. Nevertheless, they want to isolate the true Christians from the world and from the institutionally established church and have them join to form the pure church of the perfect. After all, they say, the end is near, and so the "pure wheat" must now be separated from the weeds. Luther once said, *Latent sancti*. This is the exact opposite: it is only and exclusively on the basis of the faith and sanctity of its members that the true church takes on form.

Once again, South African sects demonstrate what the outcome of such an objective *can be*, specifically the "Zionist" sects, many of which grew out of the work of American missionaries. Their emphasis is on being totally "spiritual." The members select biblical names, they resort to the Bible directly for guidance in forming and ordering the church, but—and this says it all—not to the New Testament so much as to the Old. "While proclaiming freedom by the Spirit, they allow themselves to be oppressed more and more by the letter of the Law." Spiritual freedom is shoved aside by the constraints of theocracy; the gospel is shoved aside by the law. Small wonder, then, that behind the biblical façade, these sects welcome back the old ethnic legacy with open arms. The Bantu believe themselves to be the rightful heirs of the Old Testament people of God, and it is this very thing which throws open the doors to the Gospel being swallowed up by myth.

Now of course the Bantu sects are little more than a caricature of what the mission initially wanted to achieve. Even so, the actual results must necessarily give us food for thought. At the very point where people try to preempt the consummate church, where they try to establish church on the basis of a purely otherworldly *theologia gloriae*, they are at risk of relapsing into the *theologia naturalis*. It is precisely this radically "eschatological" understanding of church development that can become so hopelessly entangled in ethnological ties. The main reason for this is doubtless that here too, the church is no longer an article of faith, that people can no longer endure its intrinsic hiddenness. Instead, in looking for that which makes church to be the church of Christ, they search for it in places other than the gospel—in this particular instance, not in sociological phenomena so much as in the fanatical prolepsis of the heavenly communion of the perfected.

4. Mission locates the establishing of church not in the *theologia naturalis* nor in the *theologia gloriae*, but only in the *theologia gratiae*. Only the gospel of saving grace, the Word of the cross, has the power to found church. It is only by virtue of the preached Word and the response of faith that church keeps on becoming an event. To be sure, this event occurs not only in isolated cases and like flashes of lightning, but wherever the church is gathered. No matter how weak and lowly it may be, the church knows itself by faith to be the true body of Christ on earth. The church is corporeal and visible, but remains hidden in the world nevertheless. She lives by faith, not by sight. She is in the world, but not of the world. Formally speaking, on the basis of this eschatological character of hers, her relationship to secular research on community is defined in two ways: as withdrawal and return, and as detachment and devotion.

a. Whenever the objective of mission work is defined as establishing church, no independent or even supplementary value may be attached to the laws governing the objective of mission work. Without a doubt, one of Hoekendijk's greatest achievements is that he formulated this basic principle with the necessary incisiveness. Church is not the church of the original creation, but of the new creation by the Word of the gospel. She is based not on the First Article, but on the Second and Third. She belongs to the order of salvation, not to the order of preservation. When these distinctions become blurred, a danger arises Gutmann already recognized: the gospel no longer rules over the orders of creation, but becomes their slave. . . .

b. Most of what may be said about this *orientation* and about the church's proper and positive assessment of the orders of creation goes beyond the domain of the *objective* of mission and falls under the heading of the *method* of mission. From the perspective of establishing church, we need mention only the following point, which incorporates two aspects: wherever church as the body of Christ, as the church of the gospel becomes reality, it is not under the compulsion of the law, but under the *freedom* of the gospel. This applies in the same twofold sense in which Luther described the life of the individual Christian—not only in the sense of freedom *from* the world, but also freedom *for* the world. The same freedom applies to the church and her mission as well. It can only be a freedom to serve. . . . Mission is about establishing church as a result of the gospel, and therefore about church coming into being in the world and for the world, and specifically for the respective local context.

Undoubtedly, this local context of the nascent church may never be the determining factor in the church's process of truly becoming church. At the same time, it certainly constitutes the space to which the church is assigned in its freedom to serve. In the recent past, other mission theologians before Hoekendijk (like J. Merle Davis and Hendrik Kraemer) already contemplated the significance of this "space of proclamation" [*Verkündigungsraum*]. In essence, it can only refer to the proper understanding and the appropriate application of what the New Testament says about the obedience of faith. Christians are strangers on earth; even so, they are called to render obedient service within the constraints of the orders of creation. What holds true for the individual Christian also holds true for the church: "The event of the new creation is not endless; rather, it is fulfilled *here and now*." Hoekendijk is again the one who stands out by drawing attention to the inseparable link between *kerygma* (the proclamation of messianic salvation), *koinonia* (the community of those participating in salvation), and *diakonia* (the freedom to serve within the community) today. In this way, he essentially averts both the danger of prematurely bestowing religious sanction on the orders of creation, and the danger of theocratic fanaticism.

Luther's much misinterpreted doctrine of the two realms is really nothing but an attempt to discern and describe the positive relationship between the church and the orders of creation in an appropriate manner by steering clear of these two dangers. The intent of this doctrine is everything but to isolate the church in some fictitious sphere of interiority; on the contrary, the intent is to locate the church in the world, since she is obligated to proclaim the Word and to render the service of love to the world.

Finally, this background also supplies the right setting for the efforts made by the German mission from the very beginning to ensure that the church of the heathen Christians be properly grounded in her native context. We should not deny that the "nationally organic" ["*volksorganisch*"] concept popular among mission theorists after the First World War was commandeered and made to espouse a dubious theology of the orders of creation. At the same time, we may not forget that in its praxis and in terms of church development on the basis of the gospel, German mission took seriously the "space of proclamation" and with it, its own responsibility for the environment as well. Hoekendijk's recapitulation of such efforts in the form of his demand for a new "ecology" is not simply an antithesis to the work of German mission to date; in fact, he is able to build on approaches taken by others in German mission long before him. After all, Nommensen, J. Warneck, Johanssen, even Keysser and Gutmann, as well as many others besides made a point of carefully studying this very *oikos*, that is, the "space of proclamation" presenting itself to them, and they allowed it to come into its own. Of course, everything will depend whether the missiologists of the present can come up with an ecology geared toward the fragmented mass society of today, instead of frantically seeking to revive the ecological results of previous eras. At any rate, mission is still obligated to bring the gospel to the uprooted masses of today. Even though national and tribal orders of creation are disintegrating in the mission field, it is still both necessary and possible to establish the *koinonia* in which people already live out their salvation here and now. Mission will only be helpful in this regard if it continually disengages from the world so as to be free to serve the world; in other words, if it doggedly clings to the one fixed goal of building up the body of Christ (cf. Eph 4:12), even though its environment constantly changes.

Analysis

The eschatological position developed by Hartenstein and Freytag is consequent on the significant political and social challenges of the period. After the ravages of World War I, the claims of the West to be a rational and ethical civilization were no longer credible for those outside the West. Christianity and European modernity diverged in the perception of the intellectual elite. The cultural Protestant interpretation of European history, culture, and civilization faded from view. The 1917 Russian Revolution manifested a militant form of antireligious sentiment that Europe and North America feared as the end toward which generic forms of secularization lead. The colonial territories experienced a revival in traditional religions and discovered that technical development could occur apart from a Christian culture and faith. In stark contrast to the concluding optimism expressed at Edinburgh, 1910, Hartenstein could in 1928 observe that "we have learned in these last years to think differently about the superiority of European culture. Every heathen throws our own words back into our faces."[16] This general loss of authority was, for German missions, accompanied by the confiscation of their missions in the Treaty of Versailles and by the withdrawing of funding during the period of National Socialism. In this context of increasing challenge and the diminishing missions, Hartenstein and Freytag respond by grounding mission within an eschatological horizon of the end.

If for no other reason, Hartenstein's article is of interest because this is the first use of the *missio Dei* formula in its contemporary missiological sense. Though it does not include any trinitarian formulation, it links mission to John 20:21 and to the notion that the church is itself constituted within this being sent. Its strength lies in detaching missionary activity from human capacity and present opportunity. God is the Lord also of mission, and this mission is located within the person of Jesus Christ and his being in the world.

Though Freytag does not himself use this language, the key argument for both lies in identifying history as the place where God conducts this mission. In reference to 2 Thessalonians 2:6-7, mission gives meaning to history, and history constitutes the time and space for witness. Mission is the purpose of

---

[16] Karl Hartenstein, "Was hat die Theologie Karl Barths der Mission zu Sagen?," *Zwischen den Zeiten* 6 (1928): 66.

the time between "already" of the present kingdom and the "not yet" of waiting for its final revelation. It matters not whether one views history as leading creation to development or to atrophy. In both cases mission becomes contingent on warrants found in historical accident. The only proper lens with which to view history is that of the reality of the eschatological end, of the return of Jesus Christ and the judgement of all things in him.

This starting point helps purify mission. Mission is not a duty somehow external or secondary to the Christian life. Mission is not made possible by adequate funding, or new opportunities (the discovery of other lands), or by a lack within the church (falling numbers). Mission strives not for the ennoblement of cultures (Troeltsch), nor the expansion of Christendom, nor the establishment of a people's church (Warneck), nor is directed by primordial divine orders (Gutmann), nor is it grounded in a human desire to be saved (*Heilssehnsucht*). Mission occurs in expectation of the coming kingdom of God. The mandate or rationale for mission lies in the promises of God—or, in the judgement of God. This is a message true to the ends of time and to the ends of the earth.

In terms of mission method, the primacy of mission societies remains. Yet, though neither Hartenstein nor Freytag use the later language of a "missionary church," the eschatological perspective moves mission from simply an external activity to something which belongs to the church's own self-definition. Hartenstein draws attention to faith and the compulsion that comes from faith and love, and to the need for a living church as the basis for the "authoritative proclamation of the eternal Word of God throughout the world." Where the eschatological fervor of the Anglo-American position concentrated on the urgent need to save souls and so minimized the church, for Freytag and Hartenstein, the "time between the times" points to the embodiment of the church. This translates into the gathering of a community that witnesses to the truth of the kingdom even as it withstands the evils around it. Freytag characterizes the period as one of tumult, of the maturity of the demonic. Against this, the church assumes a stance of perseverance and preparedness, and also of proclamation. Both Hartenstein and Freytag highlight the authority of the church and the need for sacrifice.

One major benefit of this position lies in how it understands the provisionality of all church forms. Within this eschatological horizon, the church cannot be identified with any politics, any culture, or any ethnicity. It can only be identified with the coming kingdom of God, "for here we do not have an enduring city" (Heb 13:14). This not only creates space for, but mandates the establishment of "autochthonous" churches. But this affirmation is itself based in the ongoing idea that the orders of creation govern life in the "not yet," and it is in these structures that the local churches will find their ground.

The eschatological position is an attempt to extract German missions from the evident problematic ties between its theology and National Socialism, even while attempting to maintain reference to the orders of creation. The statement by the German delegation at the International Missionary Council conference held in Tambaram (India) 1938 and referred to by Freytag illustrates well the type of concern.[17] Against the perceived dominance of an American position that equated the kingdom of God with historical progress, it begins with a simple statement of the basic eschatological position: already Christ has conquered sin and overcome the word, but this reality is hidden with Christ and evil rules this current world until the Christ's return. Three conclusions follow. First, in this "period of transition" there remain "distinct orders which God has established and ordained from the beginning of history," that is, the "orders of sex and family, nation and races."[18] Second, in relation to religious heritage, the "judgement of Christ" means "a radical breaking with the bonds of one's religious past," and not a process of "evolutionary fulfilment." Third, the church is the "interim body" that witnesses to the "coming Lord and His Judgement" through its life and its sacrificial service. But the church is not called to bring about a "renewed world order," or a "Christian state." Thinking of mission within "the horizon of the end," in other words, succeeds in withdrawing the church from the state, a problem within Germany but equally applicable to the Anglo-Americans. It establishes the church as the main organ of God's acting in the world and provides a clear basis for conversion: due to the coming judgement of God and not the good of Western civilization. This radical clearing nonetheless requires some account of the human space, of the embodiment of this church

---

[17] For this statement, see "A Statement by Some Members of the Meeting: Presented by the Chairman of the German Delegation," in *The Authority of the Faith*, ed. John Merle Davis and Kenneth G. Grubb (London: Oxford University Press, 1939), 183-85.
[18] "A Statement by Some Members of the Meeting," 184.

between the times, and this is found within the orders of creation which are now subject to adaptation and not revolution.[19] While the church began to be conceived within these missionary terms, the overriding method remained the same as with previous generations of German missiologists.

Nor did this line of thinking simply fall away after the Second World War. In 1948, J. C. Hoekendijk wrote an extended critique of German mission theology and the associated method. It proved especially forceful given the links he drew between the origins of this mission theory within German Romanticism and Idealism and the compromise of missions during the period of National Socialism. Gensichen, writing six years after the conclusion of World War II, sees Hoekendijk's main critique as addressing a definition of mission that understands its key task as planting the church and so an activity that consists in the church validating its own self-image.

Gensichen acknowledges this difficulty when speaking of "building" or "expanding" the church, but he questions whether one can abandon "establishing" the church. Whatever critique might follow, Gensichen's question is vital, and though the form it takes through the twentieth century varies, it frames much contemporary mission theology. If the church's form should not derive from the "sending" churches in the West, and if the faith critiques also the (every) local context creating instead a new thing, how does the church "come into being"? Out of what does the "corporality" of the church grow? This leads Gensichen to the "coming-into-being" of the church, a passive and emergent idea without any acting subject.

His answer lies in differentiating between two dangers. The first looks to natural phenomena, understood either as the transference of Western norms to the mission fields, or as the reduction of the church to local "natural phenomena." As to the importation of Western structures, Gensichen understands that German missions protected against this. It failed, however, to protect against the importing the notion of a "national church." This set the discussion fully within the doctrine of creation to the neglect of Christology and pneumatology, to the neglect of its eschatological hiddenness. The corporality of the church became an instance of *theologia naturalis* (theology of nature), a mere reproduction of ethnic structures.

---

[19]Karl Hartenstein, "Adaptation or Revolution," *The Student World* 28 (1935): 308-27.

The second danger lies in ignoring local orders and customs and, by extension, the visible church. This non sequitur should already alert us to the key problem: the orders of creation constitute the only ground of the church's embodiment. To eliminate them is to eliminate the church as a body. Nevertheless, Gensichen ascribes this neglect of the orders of creation to the eschatological urgency and resulting "impulsive and hasty methods" basic to the Anglo-American position, to a *theologia gloriae* (theology of glory). Without attention to the church's establishment, "propaganda"—defined within German missiology as the process of reproducing carbon copies of oneself—is the necessary result.

Gensichen's solution lies in a *theologia gratiae* (theology of grace), the dynamic of the preaching of the Word and the response that leads to a gathered body. The eschatological theme repeats in understanding the church as both visible and hidden, meaning that the church is possible only in a coincidental closeness to and distance from other forms of community. Yet, in expanding on this point Gensichen returns to Gutmann and to the issue of mission method. The gospel is not spoken into a vacuum but within a "space of proclamation," a local context. While the above problems must be avoided, including the drift into notions of the organic national church, it is nevertheless the case that local churches are to be grounded in the native context. This legitimates, in Gensichen's estimation, German missiology from Warneck to Gutmann.

The evident critique of Gensichen lies in his deafness. Though he accepts Hoekendijk's critique at a certain national point, Gensichen understands Hoekendijk as in final agreement with German missiology. When Gensichen gives examples of the problems of theologies of nature or of glory, he looks to the African (Bantu, South African Zionists) and the Anglo-American churches. There is no notion that the German church might itself have drifted into an improper naturalism. The opposite is true: Gensichen promotes the special German character of grounding the church in the native context. This form of contextualization is the only one that will result in the visible church. Gensichen reinforces this by reference to the theology of Luther and to the relationship of law to gospel. Reference to the eschatological, in this instance, failed to encourage sustained self-criticism.

The eschatological ground of mission remains an underdone point of concentration within the mission studies more generally. Hartenstein and Freytag's contribution is an important one, but theirs is a dark eschatology, reflecting their time and local Western experience. Its positive aspect lies in creating a breach between mission and the range of human motivations and historical circumstances which shaped the mission enterprise during the colonial period. The church cannot be identified with any particular nation, politics, or cultural form. They did not think of God as the agent of mission per se. Rather, it was the ferment of the eschaton that unsettled the church into twofold action of persevering and proclamation. The bigger problem, as Werner Ustorf suggests, is that "after Freytag and Hartenstein had removed the liberal or neo-protestant [sic] tradition from the equation, it became difficult to relate the eschatological approach to the cultural and philosophical experience of the 20th century."[20] Their approach condemned contemporary history to an addendum beside the process of all becoming Christian. Even as it undid liberal accounts of human existence, it failed to provide any other ground for human history. Without this ground out of which to build, they returned to the established forms. Little changed in terms of actual missionary structures, and the theory developed following the old guidelines: the rationale or mandate for mission, the content or substance of mission, the structures or method of mission, and the goal of mission. The mission society maintains its priority in contexts where the church does not yet exist, and the orders of creation remain the main mechanism for grounding a local church. Matters would soon change, however, with the first slow recognition within Western missions of an independent non-Western Christianity.

---

[20]Werner Ustorf, "'Survival of the Fittest': German Protestant Missions, Nazism and Neocolonialism, 1933–1945," *Journal of Religion in Africa* 28 (1998): 258.

4

The Widening of Horizons

INTRODUCTION

The period immediately following the Second World War proved to be somewhat thin in the area of constructive German missiology. Prior dominant theories bound to the orders of creation could no longer be forwarded in the same manner and the eschatological emphasis, while it helped create some distance between mission theory and its appropriation during the Nazi period, seems itself to have been limited to that period. As to why, one might speculate that the movements of political independency marking the end of the colonial period and the associated (slow) discovery of theologies outside the West altered the type of missiological questions being asked within the West.

The various movements to political independency sparked two major developments within the missionary enterprise. First, the legitimacy of missions and the assumed right that they be conducted were being questioned by political authorities, by local churches and by the so-called sending churches of the West. The mass expulsion of Christian missionaries from China and the resulting "China crisis" within Western missions marks the end of colonial-era missions and necessitated a revision in the definition and theology of mission. *Missio Dei* theology (1952) developed as a response and located the missionary endeavor not in human capacity, but within the being of God—God is a missionary God. However, while a positive theological advance, it did little to change the forms and methods of mission. Key difficulties remained, leading to Freytag's observation at the 1957–1958 International Missionary Council (Accra, Ghana), that, while previously missions had problems, now they had themselves become a problem. The issue, he argued, lay with the historic and basic theological rationales for mission and the associated methods within this postcolonial political context.¹ Mission, in his definition, "means taking part in the action of God, in fulfilling His plan for the coming of His Kingdom by bringing about obedience of the faith in Jesus Christ our Lord among the nations."² While this definition maintains reference to mission organizations, the accent shifts: the "main missionary service" is now "Christian decision, Christian living and Christian action."³ Mission no longer followed Warneck's geographical definition: the sending of especially called and trained people from Western nations into the rest of the world. It was starting to be located within the body of the congregation.

The Division for World Mission and Evangelism conference of Mexico City (1963) took place under the motto "Mission in six continents." The West was itself part of God's missionary activity. This essentialization of mission and of the term *sending* shifted the focus to social and political movements. At the Fourth General Assembly of the World Council of Churches held in Uppsala, Sweden (1968), a cosmic and messianic account of missions dominated. Social and civil developments were regarded as God's working amid different cultures. Development and progress provided greater space for freedom and individual self-determination. The stated goal of mission was the *new human being*.

Second, the independence that led to the establishment of nation states created the necessary space for the local or "younger" churches (to use the WCC nomenclature of the period) to also gain their independence and to develop local leadership. For these churches, the relationship to their cultural and religious heritage became a matter of intense activity. At a formal ecumenical level, the WCC and the Roman Catholic Church engaged in interreligious conferences on dialogue. But it is the great number of dialogue initiatives undertaken by the churches in Asia and Africa that captures missiological attention. First, these local Christian communities had and have to prove that their faith is not simply an imported religion and that they are not simply a traitorous people who owe their allegiance to foreign

---

¹Walter Freytag, "Changes in the Patterns of Western Missions," in *The Ghana Assembly of the International Missionary Council, 28th December, 1957 to 8th January, 1958: Selected Papers, with an Essay on the Role of the I.M.C*, ed. Ronald Kenneth Orchard (London: Edinburgh House Press, 1958), 138-47.
²Freytag, *The Ghana Assembly*, 146.
³Freytag, *The Ghana Assembly*, 147.

powers. Second, these communities had and have to demonstrate that they contribute socially and politically to the well-being of the wider society in which they are born. Third, these communities had and have to reformulate the universal theological claims that accompanied Western colonial expansion in terms of living in contexts of religious plurality; they have to engage in vital interreligious cooperation. The overriding theological assertion is that Christianity is everywhere a local religion and that the religious experiences and forms of gathering of these communities are authentic in relation to their cultural and religious heritage. How this affirmation works its way out in terms of structures, liturgies, symbols, rites, hierarchies, institutions, and theologies shapes missiology to today.

Johannes Christiaan Hoekendijk (1912–1975) was among the first (and certainly the most notorious) to apply the critique of missions to established Western accounts of the church.[4] The son of Dutch missionaries serving in Indonesia on the island of Java, Hoekendijk expected to follow in his parents' footsteps until he was prevented from doing so by the Second World War. After the war, he completed his doctoral thesis titled "The Church and Volk in German Missiology," which appeared in Dutch in 1948 and in German translation in 1966. A key ecumenical figure and exponent of the "Dutch theology of the apostolate," Hoekendijk served between 1949 and 1953 as the chair of the Department of Evangelism of the World Council of Churches, before moving in 1953 to become professor of "practical theology, apostolate, and biblical theology" at the University of Utrecht, and then in 1965 to his death in 1975 as professor for world Christianity at Union Theological Seminary in New York. He made a significant contribution to the International Missionary Council conference held at Willingen (Germany, 1952) and to the WCC study program on "The Missionary Structure of the Congregation" (1962–1967).[5]

The selected text comes from a special appendix written for the 1967 German translation of his dissertation. Titled "On the Question of a Missionary Existence," it provides a mature summary of his thinking as it had developed

---

[4]For greater biographical detail, see L. A. Hoedemaker, "The Legacy of J. C. Hoekendijk," *International Bulletin of Missionary Research* 19 (1995): 166-70. For more on his theology, see John G. Flett, *Apostolicity: The Ecumenical Question in World Christian Perspective* (Downers Grove, IL: IVP Academic, 2016), 187-240.
[5]This was published as *The Church for Others, and the Church for the World: A Quest for Structures for Missionary Congregations* (Geneva: World Council of Churches, 1967).

through the 1950s and '60s. Taking clues from Hartenstein and Freytag, Hoekendijk advances an eschatological approach to mission. He differs from them by relocating the eschatological driver from a vision of the end to the messianic. The church takes part in God's own sending, God's acting within history. From this comes Hoekendijk's sustained critique of "church-centred" or "ecclesiocentric" mission thinking that he saw as basic to traditional missiology. The church is neither the main actor nor the main goal of mission. The primary goal is the kingdom of God, witnessed to through proclamation (*kerygma*), fellowship (*koinonia*), and diaconia (*diakonia*) with the aim of spreading shalom.

Because God's own mission is to the world (Jn 3:16), God's sending activity does not follow the sequence of God-church-world, but rather God-world-church. This attributes a different theological status to the world. It ceases to be the church's "front lawn" or "not-yet-church," becoming instead an independent and mature entity. The church exists for the world's sake, not vice versa. Mission as the messianic involvement in history means that the church is free to change its structures in service to the world. Hoekendijk criticizes what he calls a "morphological fundamentalism." Taking its clues from "biblical fundamentalism," the basis of the church is understood as lying in its structures (*morphe*), most notably that of the parish system. These structures, however, are all "come-structures" and reflect a missiology that places the church at its center. The contemporary context requires "go-structures," as the church needs to make its way toward its neighbors. Exodus and the promises of God provide the basic theological clue: to be in mission is to be under way.

Though the question of other religious expressions and spiritualities informed German missiology from its inception, **Hans Jochen Margull** (1925–1982) is among the first to develop a mission theology through the lens of interreligious dialogue. From 1961 to 1967 and his appointment as professor of missiology at the University of Hamburg, Margull served as the secretary of the WCC Department for Evangelism. During this period, he was instrumental both in the study on "The Missionary Structure of the Congregation," and in the preparation for the WCC General Assembly held in Uppsala (1968). His major work, *The Theology of Missionary Preaching: Evangelization as an Ecumenical Problem*, reflected his interest in reshaping Western church institutions, in becoming the "church-for-others."[6] In 1975, he

---

[6]Hans J. Margull, *Theologie der missionarischen Verkündigung: Evangelisation als ökumenisches Problem*

became chair of the WCC Department for Interreligious dialogue and this reflected a widening in his own understanding of mission.

Whereas Freytag's mission theology held the greatest influence over Margull's thinking during the 1950s, in the 1960s his attention shifted to the liberation theology then developing in Latin America. Including this experience and embodiment of Christianity beyond Europe into his own perspective lead to his invention of the term *Tertiaterranität*. A cumbersome term, it sought to counter the dominance of the *Mediterranität* (Mediterranean) in theological discourse. Margull lamented how the telling of Christian history concentrated on the story of Christian churches around the Mediterranean Sea (Middle East, Europa, North Africa). This, in his view, produced a distorted view of contemporary Christianity. A fuller account needed to recognize and respect the developing forms of the faith. *Tertiaterranität* points to the different forms of expression Christianity assumes in the *Third World* (*terti-aterranity*) context. This includes different modes of acting and different ways of thinking. In the 1970s, Margull urges Western theology to take these new developments seriously for they create what is popularly termed today a "third space." Within this third space lies the possibility for liberation. According to Margull,

> The interpretation of the Third World in terms of social history . . . has to be preferred over against a geographic interpretation. On this basis, one recognizes a tertiaterranity of Christianity wherever Christ Jesus is authentically believed to stand on the side of the down trodden (and so especially in Christianity overseas) and where Christian faith is authentically understood as an act of comprehensive historical liberation.[7]

Where Hoekendijk saw the society as point of reference of the *missio Dei*, Margull expanded the horizon to include the sphere of international relations, focusing especially on the dependency of the South with respect to the North.

In this, Margull used liberation theology's "theory of dependency." According to this theory, the majority of social, economic, and political problems experienced within Third World result from their dependence on

---

(Stuttgart: Evangelisches Verlagswerk, 1959). A shortened version was published in English as Hans J. Margull, *Hope in Action: The Church's Task in the World*, trans. Eugene Peters (Philadelphia: Muhlenberg Press, 1962).

[7]Hans J. Margull, *Zeugnis und Dialog: Ausgewählte Schriften* (Ammersbek bei Hamburg: Verlag an der Lottbek, 1992), 211-12.

the industrialized Northern nations. Dependence theory gives an alternative explanation for international relations than the one forwarded by the theory of development. Whereas development theory expects the social improvement of Southern countries to take place via aid and an economic "trickle-down effect," the theory of dependence focuses on power and structures of domination and the need to struggle for liberation from these powers and structures. Jesus Christ is the liberator and so the relation of mission to culture itself becomes a political movement.

The selected Margull text deals with the idea of vulnerability (*Verwundbarkeit*), a theme that issues from his experiences in interreligious dialogue. Dialogue initiatives spread very quickly after the 1960s as a new phenomenon in the history of religions. Dialogue concerns itself not only with past wounds (historical incidents between religious traditions such as wars justified by religion), but also with wounds in the present (the rejection by one party of an invitation to dialogue). But one further wound experienced by Christianity lies in recognizing that the era of Western missions had come to an end. Vulnerability becomes basic to the definition of mission because it is the way of God, who becomes vulnerable in the life and crucifixion of Jesus Christ.

Swiss theologian **Walter Hollenweger** (1927–2016) served as executive secretary of the WCC from 1965 to 1971 and then taught missiology and intercultural theology from 1971 to 1989 at the University of Birmingham. Hollenweger was himself raised in a Pentecostal Christian tradition. Not only did this have a lasting impact on his theological thinking, it alerted him to a dominant voice within world Christianity largely ignored by theorists to this point.

Like Hoekendijk and Margull, Hollenweger took an active part in the discussions on the missionary structure of the congregation. His emphasis differed, however, in that he concentrated on the corporeality (*Leiblichkeit*) of Christian life and practices. This becomes clear in his interpretation of a theologoumenon developed by Dietrich Bonhoeffer: the church-for-others. Even today, this idea informs theologies concerned with the capacity of the church to change its structures in service to its mission; Hollenweger's approach differs in that he sets this idea of the church-for-others in relation to pneumatology and a theory of symbols. This establishes a basis by which to critique Western missiological attempts at dealing with the challenges of secularity. How should the church embody and express the gospel vis-à-vis secularized people and culture? Must the faith undergo a process of demythologization? Hollenweger's answer is a simple no.

Hollenweger focuses on how language functions and the uses people make of language worldwide. Language is far more than just words; it is clothed in symbols and expressed in performances. Language requires myth. A myth Hollenweger defines as something people believe in, either individually or collectively, and is itself a "medium of communication." The missiological question of mission and culture leads Hollenweger to the consequent question of how an indigenous or local theology comes to expression. Theology "happens" or "takes place" through the use of media like rituals, symbols, dances, and bodily forms (*Formen von Leiblichkeit*). Any mission theology must take these forms into account: the message is communicated through these forms (language) and is itself given shape and meaning in being spoken through these forms.

This, Hollenweger argues, is pneumatologically important. The Holy Spirit manifests itself in different forms. The Western approach, which reduces the Holy Spirit to the "religious, ecclesiocentric and individualistic," misconstrues the Spirit because Christians in other parts of the world experience the Spirit in a very different way. Hollenweger describes the Third World not from the perspective of social history or that of liberation theology, like Margull. His interest lies in its medial character: What is it that bestows power on the forces of liberation? Or, to use theological language: What media does the Holy Spirit work through?

JOHANNES CHRISTIAAN HOEKENDIJK

"On the Question of a Missionary Existence"
~1967~

THERE IS A CALL FOR MORE THEOLOGY, and also for a different kind of theology; not a theology formulated in the ivory tower of some monastery or academy, but one which is at home in the market square and on the street, the way it used to be.[8]

---

[8] J. C. Hoekendijk, "Zur Frage einer missionarischen Existenz," in *Kirche und Volk in der deutschen Missionswissenschaft* (Munich: Chr. Kaiser Verlag, 1967), 297-354.

1. Let us return to the perspective of *God—world—church* (not God—church—world). That is the truly (theo-)logical approach. As soon as we speak of God, we take it for granted that the world is the theater of his operations. And the church is the first to know and respect that. In confessing God, she has already implicitly admitted her own ex-centric position. She hopes she will one day be instrumental in ensuring that the world receives its due in terms of its intrinsic value and its intrinsic purpose. Consequently, this ex-centric church will not be able to insist on maintaining its own structures. She has no sociology of her own; instead, adopting a purely functional approach, she uses the existing structures of the world to the extent that it is feasible. This is of course neither new nor surprising. It is the way it has always been: House churches formed because the existing social unit of the *oikos* seemed to be useful. The dioceses, parishes, associations, and societies were formed in a similar manner.... People failed... to notice that.

2. The *world*, which is our concern here, is *constantly changing*. That is no coincidence, nor is it some accidental side-effect. When God focused his plans on the world, he allowed it to enter the stream of history. After all, he is no Baal who settles down somewhere and commands that a *fanum* be established for him; rather, he forges ahead and leaves each *fanum* behind when he has dealings in the *profanum*. In this way, the world as the living horizon of God's action is also set in motion. It is open to the future, that is, it is historicized: deprived of the secure existence of an ontocracy (van Leeuwen) eternally at rest in itself, divested of the well-established harmony of a cosmos, and liberated from the tyranny of sacral order.

For this reason, the "secular structures" that the church adopts and accepts in its historicity must be recognized and distinguished. They have no "ontological status," nor any fixed ordinological value. They are snapshots in the ongoing process of destructuring and restructuring, nothing more; they are always contingent arrangements and therefore ad hoc in nature, dependent on the context. From the perspective of salvation history, the entire complex of sacral *morphai* with its inherent tendency to "morphological fundamentalism" (along with the apology it sometimes offers) has long been superseded and stands offside.

3. We could use the term *missio Dei* as shorthand for this history-making action of God. To use this term is to praise him as the one who initiates,

performs, and concludes this comprehensive economy of mission, in which he lends expression to his will to be among the people. Understood correctly, *missio* is an attribute of God, and it is therefore no accident that the term was used in the doctrines of the Trinity, Christology, pneumatology, and ecclesiology. After all, God organizes the "entire cascade of the *missiones*" (Congar) of which the biblical testimony continually speaks. We only know the truth about this God in the form of a message. The *missiones* are the promise that the truth will achieve its goal in the form of a message. Provision has been made for this: *missio Dei*. And the world as history is his "mission field." The church can only authenticate herself as the church of this "apostolic" God by allowing herself to be used in this *missio Dei*. She must demonstrate her apostolicity (both in terms of doctrine and in terms of her constitution) by way of the apostolate. *Missio Dei* is the concise summary of the good news that there is a God who has revealed himself with the intent to be God-for-others. The church that corresponds to this God is found wherever she becomes church-for-others.

The "secular" and "historicized" structures the church adopts will therefore only prove their "usefulness" if they serve as structures-for-others. Paul dared to consider the ignorant and the unbelievers to be the criterion for what rightfully belongs in the worship service. This, in my view, constitutes a canon for the entire destructuring and restructuring of the life of the church. Only those structures may be considered authentic that make it possible for the uninformed and the unbelievers to discover their human existence and to conclude that the *missio Dei* has reached them as well (1 Cor 14:24ff.).

4. Naturally, the *content of the missio Dei* can be described in various ways. In reaction to all of our Christianization programs of yesterday, people have placed a great deal of emphasis on the keyword *humanization*. The idea is that God wants human beings to be fully human once more, instead of mere *homines religiosi*, who have never been anything more than chained convicts. This humanization got off to a start with cross and resurrection, and it serves as a fermenting agent in culture. We may conclude that whenever people are liberated to embrace their true humanity, the *missio Dei*—once again!—achieves its goal.

Personally, however, I prefer a different description, and I am happy to see that others are also experimenting with it. In all apostrophic brevity: I believe that *missio Dei* is about what I would like to call the *shalomatization* of all of life, which will make it possible for people to be people again (without *personas*, i.e. masks; "God is no respecter of *personas*") and for things to be things again (and not idols or material). In the horizon of creation, shalom is the promise of life; in the horizon of history, there are indications that justice will be recreated (in the full spectrum indicated in Ps 85:8-13); and wherever that happens, a messianic horizon opens up all around us and provides us with an untrammeled view of the kingdom of God. Thus to shalomatize means to be so involved with life, so engaged with it, to have our hands so dirtied by it (though not by joining the false prophets in crying "peace, peace") that these three horizons of hope (life, justice, kingdom of God) manifest around us. I would like to refer to this as the "messianic lifestyle," which is characterized by a unique blend of impatience ("how much longer until he returns") and patience ("but he will come"). If we are looking for a model, we will need to listen to Deutero-Isaiah's suffering servant and to Philippians 2:5-11. Years ago, this model of life (and model of mission as well!) was summarized in five keywords: being predestined (to)—serve—witness—self-identify—suffer. And all of that stands in the hopeful perspective of shalom.

In this view, the content of the *missio Dei* may be described as everything God does to share this messianic lifestyle with people so that in the perspective of shalom, the horizons of hope open up for all.

A church that shares in this *missio Dei* (which is another tautology, since she would not be church if she did not share in it) has no option but to structure her life around the focal points of society where this shalomatization is specifically offered or already in progress. Globally, it is impossible to stipulate where exactly that will be. It is also impossible to stipulate ahead of time whether the center of attention will be the *praesentia realis* in Word and sacrament of him who is shalom, or the equally real presence of Christ in and among the despised and those deprived of their rights (Mt 25:31). It is also totally uncertain whether this will take place in the quest for a "personalism of salvation" (even if our liturgical heritage gives this impression). "Shalom" is more comprehensive than *salus*, and if we must distinguish between salvation and well-being (which is unlikely in light of the word *shalom*), it is no foregone conclusion that the church must always choose salvation.

This might be the appropriate place to say something about the so-called *heretical structures*.... For one thing, I believe that we should stop applying this concept of heresy purely to intrachurch situations. For another, we would then need to realize that heretical structures come into being as soon as the church withdraws from the history she shares with the world (does she know of any other kind of history?), proceeds to write her own story, and aims at self-affirmation by meticulously studying (it certainly cannot be labeled "doing theology," in my opinion) her own private totem pole on which she has carved the faces of her "own" fathers.

5. The "offices" in the church should be oriented toward the *laity*. Most people believe that it has become necessary to distinguish between the ministries. This process of distinction directly refers to the laity, as does the prospect of a comprehensive restructuring of the missionary church. The laypeople are, after all, the visible representatives of God's missionary people (*laos tou theou*)....

When the laity once again truly serve as the reference group (i.e., no longer simply consuming what the office bearers have to offer), then there will once again be room for a new style of theology as well. Being a true *apologia*, this theology will be able to account for itself before the world. In the market square and on the street, it will gain the reputation of a *theologia publica*, the way it used to be, or—and this would be my preference—of a political theology (i.e., a theology "for the *polis*").

6. Up until now, we have spoken of the "world" only in the singular. It was necessary to simplify things this way for the purposes of our argument, even if doing so introduced some problems and was not entirely realistic. Admittedly, no church deals only with a single world. As soon as she is somehow present in the world in the sense of being present in history, she encounters an unlimited number of "worlds" ("a world is that which concerns us"). Then we can also no longer speak of the church assuming the form of a *single* "predominant social entity" and seeking to serve others as such. The church is not tied to any one normative model, nor is it obligated to social deformation by some sacral ordinology. As an "organization" and on a purely functional basis, the church is able to use anything which seems usable. A society like ours is characterized by three fundamental processes: that of *differentiation*, which leads to pluralism; that of *being concentrated* into

greater ecological unity than before; and that of *mobility*, which is turning our cities into "mass movements" (Harvey Cox). In such a society, the church will therefore also be present in a pluriformity of structures without being homesick for the relatively uniform model of the past.

....

HANS JOCHEN MARGULL

"Vulnerability: Remarks on Dialogue"
∼1974∼

IT MIGHT SEEM EXCESSIVELY arbitrary to select vulnerability as a keyword in the discussion of dialogue and the problems of dialogue.[9] ... What is indeed arbitrary is that as I prepared to write this article, I struggled to get past the ever more frequent and ever more intense criticisms of the dialogue program of the World Council of Churches I am currently engaged in ..., and that ... I caught a glimpse of the harm apparently caused in the dialogue process. The person being criticized is not the only one harmed; the person who criticizes does so because of the way "dialogue" harmed "mission." But it is far more important to bear in mind the instances where, say, Hindus, Buddhists, or Muslims turned down invitations to dialogue because they believed it would be pointless to dialogue with Christians, and especially because they claimed that dialogue would only reopen old wounds caused to them or to their communities by Christian mission, or even make them worse. ... Vulnerability should therefore be understood in the dialectical sense, as it were: everybody and everything is vulnerable, but everything comes down to whether and to what extent people can endure being vulnerable, thereby imbuing vulnerability with meaning and purpose. But the key aspect of vulnerability on which we are focusing here is that when I again tried to zero in on the Christian view of dialogue ..., what caught my attention was the novel indication of the centrality of the vulnerability of God. We will need to devote more attention to this issue; for now, we will content ourselves with the assurance that our keyword is not arbitrary after all.

---

[9]Hans J. Margull, "Verwundbarkeit," *Evangelische Theologie* 34 (1974): 410-20.

Naturally, vulnerability does not denote the obvious aspects of dialogue, nor (at least, not yet) its historical significance. Rather, what is striking is the *speed* with which dialogue began to take place along the winding boundaries between religions, cultures, and ideologies (let us use this terminology for now), the *global scope* dialogue was able to achieve, and the *novelty* with which it was perceived. . . . In 1964, in the encyclical *Ecclesiam suam*, Pope Paul VI declared that the Roman Catholic Church was willing to engage in dialogue. In 1965, the declaration of the Second Vatican Council on the relationship between the church and non-Christian religions was promulgated and the Vatican Secretariats "for Non-Christians" and "for Non-Believers" were established. In 1967, the World Council of Churches . . . issued its first statement on dialogue . . . , in 1970, the first game-changing multilateral dialogue took place between Hindus, Buddhists, Christians, and Muslims in Ajaltoun, Beirut; and in 1971, the program for "dialogue with people of living faiths and ideologies" was established.

In summary, it took twenty years at most; practically speaking, it was much less—symbolically, let us say seven years. This was rapid and astonishing change in the history of humanity and of religion. . . . It was and still is . . . a torrential transformation. It took place in the torrents of the present-day history of humanity.

Vulnerability? But it was where these torrents occurred that the wounds of this history were inflicted. To name only the most obvious: the genocide of European Jewry; antisemitism in Christianity; a mindset of extermination prevailing between communism and Christianity; Western imperialism; Christians disdaining, if not despising non-Christian traditions; threats to global peace; and sin and judgment, at least as far as Christians were concerned. Dialogues began to take place at the sites of these wounds, along with these wounds, for the purpose of binding up the wounds, and for the purpose of preventing additional wounds.

"Binding up the wounds" is an ambiguous phrase. Naturally, it refers first of all to the treatment of wounds and the elimination of their causes. . . .

In the process of treating mutually inflicted wounds, a significant measure of unanimity was achieved; however, many a dialogue never went beyond that to a point of basic respect and to ongoing consultations. Even so, most dialogues managed to transcend the immediately presenting problem of sensitization by speaking to the issue of the very deep wounds that had already been sustained at the points of profound religious disagreement and social difference in the history of humanity. This issue essentially concerns Judaism, Christianity, and Islam; it is just as prominent and relevant to this day in the relationship between Hinduism and Buddhism; and it is clearly manifest also in the association between Christianity and Marxism. Naturally, some parts of the dialogue spoke to the joint impact of Marxism and Christianity on history, as well as to the integrity of the history of religion, the purpose of its findings, and its virtual portrayal. . . . Initially, a religious history that has not yet been concluded will inflict wounds on existing religious systems, corporations, and communities. The cultural circulation in the present-day history of humanity that Richard Friedli took as the subject of his theology of religions is already demonstrating the following: (1) increasing encounters with and coexistence between people of different cultures and religious traditions, along with the rapidly increasing exchange of information across all the old boundaries, have demolished traditional religious safeguards; and (2) in the quest for new meaning and for sanctuary, people are arriving at new religious self-conceptions and creating new religious forms. It is likely that . . . a new mindset will assert itself in the process; when people interact, the question will no longer be "what truths have been handed down and preserved in the various systems," but rather "is the other person's faith or sense of meaning and purpose true here and now, and if so, to what extent." Above and beyond that, we can already begin to discern the wounds being inflicted by the historicization and anthropologization of modern thought—some more pronounced, others less so. Religions are always vulnerable. One of the vulnerabilities of Christianity became evident when the end of Western Christian mission occurred. It was a torrential development for Christianity. Few have understood it to date, and today especially, more and more Christians refuse to accept it. But this is a verdict Christian historicity will have to accept. The verdict includes a judgment against the propagation of the absoluteness of Christianity supported by politics and culture. Our dialogue soon made it clear that the verdict does not include any incrimination of the absoluteness inherent to people's subjectivity, that is, not only the absoluteness intrinsic to the choice of the Christian faith. . . .

Since the Protestant faith community is once again asserting the legitimacy of Western-Christian mission, we can speak of its (admittedly historically effective) end only in principle. At the same time, we need to make a point of considering the distinction between Christian mission and the specific form of mission unique to nineteenth-century Western Christianity, even though doing so is tedious and unsettling. After all, over the two thousand years of its history, Christian mission has proven itself to be extremely diverse, and it is now searching for a new form of expression. It is simply not true that Christian mission always automatically means Western Christian mission. Western Christian mission is not the norm for mission in general. The end of Western Christian mission (not of mission per se!) took place in one form as a result of what happened in China, in another as a result of the sense of independence, presence, and witness of the churches to which it gave rise abroad, and, finally, in a third form as a result of its highly controversial stance vis-à-vis the history of religion. In short, we may say that contrary to all Western expectations, its bold, but nevertheless expansionist attempt to overpower the non-Christian religions and by means of Christian mission to bring the history of religion to an end failed. . . . At any rate, we now face not the conclusion of the history of religion, but rather its intensification. One example of this is the phenomenon of the renaissance of some non-Christian religions—a renaissance that cannot be explained without considering the distress imposed on them by Western Christian mission. As a result, especially those Christians living in the mission fields have had to face the religions as a reality with profound and extensive social networks. In doing so, they demonstrated their ability to endure vulnerability in a meaningful way, thereby substantiating the ongoing nature of the history of religion. Also, as adherents of the Christian religion, and not knowing what the future would bring, they wanted to preserve the open-endedness of this history of religion by engaging in dialogue. In this respect, the present-day dialogue is their present-day Christian mission. The gospel is not a quotation, let alone one single long quotation.

What form can this mission take? Kenneth Cragg, whose reference to the "vulnerability of God" was mentioned above, came up with this spiritual term in an attempt to introduce the theology of the cross into the dialogue with Muslims in terms of its significance in the history of religion, or rather in the history of faith. Proceeding from the center of the Christian faith, he tried to connect with the center of Islamic faith, that is, with its doctrine of God, by proceeding via the point of divergence between Islam and Christianity constituted by the cross of Jesus. Now of course he was familiar with the many apologetic reasons that Islamic theologians (let us agree to use this term) have furnished to explain the problematic discrepancy between God's authoritative claim to all people—as demonstrated by Islam's ultimate authority—and the fact that most people reject this claim. Even so, he believed he was able to bring this problem up to date, that he was able to reclaim the question about God from the formulaic manner in which it was traditionally answered, by approaching it via a sense of the tragedy with which events were imbued at the time. In the process, he formulated a truly daring question, namely, Might the greatness of God (Allah) not also perhaps entail an aspect of vulnerability, and hence the crucifixion of his prophet Jesus? We are less concerned here with such a dialogue's chances of success, and more with the blueprint for dialogically exploring the key concepts of another tradition. What is even more important is the reference to the attempt to engage in dialogue with others by purposely talking their difficult or potentially painful problems over with them. During the Yom Kippur War of 1973 between the Arabic states and Israel, Kenneth Cragg reflected on the uninterrupted, unquestioned, definitive, and paradoxically parallel claim each side would probably once again lay to the rightfulness of its respective history, that is, of Jewish and Islamic history. He wondered whether there are Islamic reasons in Islam that, if highlighted or at least rediscovered, might shed light on the problem this poses to Islam and to all of humanity in an ongoing history which might not proceed as expected. Might it be possible to find points or strata where a faith defined as expectation and ossified in its claim to God might still give a sense of faith and thus of being liberated from every kind of inevitability, including a self-imposed one? Cragg risks offering counsel in this regard. He begins by referring to a modern Muslim interpretation of *shirk* (attributing a partner to God, polytheism), according to which *shirk* may also mean absolutizing a nation, class, or system. He then refers to Surah 49:13, which speaks of the arrival of some desert Arabs who said, "We have believed [*amanna*]," to which Muhammad is directed to reply, "You have not believed. You should say, 'We have submitted' [*aslamma*]. For faith has not yet entered your hearts." "This significant distinction plainly involves the fact that *Islam* politically could and did happen without *Islam* religiously, and that the disparity (or contradiction) should be detected and repaired." Thus far an example. We may succinctly summarize the ethos of dialogue as follows: one partner strives to understand the other the way he understands himself. This ethos is also the point at which dialogue is vulnerable. To begin with, in an attempt so much as to identify one or the other point that might make it possible to accomplish the task, dialogue partners postulated certain commonalities in the midst of almost impassable hermeneutical terrain. For instance, people talk of the history of revelation common to Judaism, Christianity, and Islam. If nothing else, in a multilateral dialogue where nontheistic Hindus, Buddhists, or perhaps Marxists are present, this commonality, which is of course highly fragile, becomes temporarily real by virtue of the fact that Jews, Christians, and Muslims can speak about God among themselves and collectively vis-à-vis the other dialogue partners. Those sharing the views of Cuttat, along with Cuttat himself, have proposed what I would like to call a shared history of spirituality, one that has met with the approval of Hindus. It identifies common ground between the "hemispheres" of the Indian religions and the Eastern religiosity of Asia, on the one hand, and the monotheistic religions, or Christianity, as the case may be, on the other. . . . As part of this type of quest for convergence, when it comes to Christianity and Marxism, we might join Milan Machovec, for instance, in speaking of a shared future history and a shared history of change. A recent dialogue between Christians and adherents of "primal," especially African religiosity stipulated that one point of commonality lies in the quest for the wholeness of life. It is a reflection of real-life dialogue, at least the way I know it, when I summarily terminate the discussion of these efforts at this point. In the same way, a dialogue conference usually breaks off just at the moment when it finds itself facing the evidence of such commonalities in the brutality of everyday reality and their respective contemporary constellations. Praxis waits for no man. Since interreligious dialogue has to do with religion, it must confront not only doctrines, cultures, and history, but also spiritual actions or acts of worship, albeit to a lesser extent; in such a dialogue, the crisis presents itself not only when the bold attempt is made to engage in a joint exercise, but as soon as the dialogue partners make an effort to discuss "spirituality" together. . . .

Now as our understanding of dialogue becomes more profound—which is possible not only in mysticism, and initially seems desirable in, say, present-day Indian dialogues—we may discover that the meaning and purpose of dialogue may be found in remaining silent together, as opposed to speaking separately. But even then, we may in no way preclude the other vulnerability of dialogue, which consists in monologue. It is tendentially present both in shared silence and in speaking together, and for this reason, in this context too, commonality may only be presumed. . . . But do dialogical traditions actually exist?

The Christian tradition is certainly not a dialogical one. The dialogues of the ancient church were in fact monologues. While the weightiness of monologue was overcome for once in Nicholas of Cusa's *De pace fidei*, even the present-day statements on dialogue of the Second Vatican Council and of the World Council of Churches begin with words like *church* or *lordship of Christ*. When we take recourse to the biblical tradition, . . . we initially find only indirect references in Isaiah 53:5 and Philippians 2:7: wounds, the form of a servant. In some theological conceptions or ancillary arguments by representatives of especially the Orthodox, Catholic, or Anglican mentality, the doctrine of the incarnation is fundamentally abstracted as a dialogue between God and human beings . . . on the basis of Philippians 2. But in addition to this abstraction, we will also need to consider all of the implications of believing in a God who makes himself known not in a general sense, but "dialogically" in the form of a servant; that is to say, by taking on the form of a servant, he became (still is/wanted to be?) vulnerable. . . . As yet, not every knee has bowed before him and not every tongue has confessed him; he continues to have different names, and the decision to remain nameless seems to be becoming more prevalent than the decision to call on his name. Christianity is tremendously vulnerable. The cross remains real, as do the wounds. Everything beyond that appears to Hindus, Buddhists, Jews, Muslims, Marxists, and so on, to be nothing more than a quotation, often just one single long quotation. The cross can also be misunderstood— absolutely in our own case, relativistically in the case of others. Jesus can be an avatar, a Bodhisattva, a (cross-less) prophet, a lord, a physician, a human being, a brother. He was and is vulnerable. He shows what is and what will be.... Could invulnerability, could an invulnerable person turn out to be an idol in the end?

WALTER J. HOLLENWEGER
"The Church for Others—a Myth"
~1977~

IN AUGUST 1944 IN HIS PRISON CELL in Tegel Dietrich Bonhoeffer drafted his conclusion for a planned book on the church: "The church is the church only when it exists for others. To make a start, it should give away all its property to those in need."[10] The church that this position brought into view can be summarized as follows:

1. The church must be there for others because there are others. Bonhoeffer understands these others to be religionless and mature.

2. The church can be the church for others because Jesus is "the man for others."

3. The church is for others if she does not drive through the world like a "sealed up train in a foreign land" but keeps her doors open to the world, which can be a dangerous journey but corresponds to the nature of the church.[11]

4. The church is for others if she lets these others remain others and does not try to make them her own.

5. The church can be radically for others because these others already belong to Jesus Christ.

6. The church for others is not merely a reinterpretation of ecclesiology but inspires a change in her budget and investment policy, in her building programs, in her liturgies, and in her theological education.

---

[10]Walter J. Hollenweger, "Die Kirche für andere—ein Mythos," *Evangelische Theologie* 37 (1977): 425-43. Quotation is from Dietrich Bonhoeffer, *Letters and Papers from Prison* (Minneapolis: Fortress Press, 2010), 503.
[11]Dietrich Bonhoeffer, *Discipleship* (Minneapolis: Fortress Press, 2003), 260.

The opposite to the church for others is best documented by the *Oxford Dictionary of the Christian Church* (1974). While one finds such esoteric entries as *eclecticism* and *ecphonesis*, vital topics for the Church in Great Britain such as *economics* are missing....

Thirty years after Bonhoeffer's martyrdom, the *Oxford Dictionary of the Christian Church* conveys the picture of an irrelevant church, a church turned in on herself, a church with a pathological relationship to the world, a church which suffers from being "totally estranged from today's world."[12] This may be an *Oxford* dictionary, but it is certainly *not* a dictionary of the *Christian church*.

The structure of a missionary congregation. In contrast to the *Oxford Dictionary*, Bonhoeffer's concept was taken up by the ecumenical study of "the structure of a missionary congregation."...

The ecumenical study *The Church for Others* starts "very far outside," that is, with the question of the changing world.

> Perhaps it may be said that the method of correlation, as applied by Paul Tillich in the sphere of theological thoughts, is applied here to Church action: the changed world confronts the congregation as a question. The answer, which the congregation alone has to supply on the basis of the Gospel, has not yet been formulated. The answer will not come in a vacuum, but within the horizon of the question presented to the congregation by the world.[13]

Krusche describes the main tenor of the study in these shorthand phrases:

- not the mission of the churches, but the mission of God
- the church is not central, but the world
- the churches do not stand over against the world, but before it, not in opposition to it, but in solidarity with it
- the church does not stand remote from the changes of history, but is responsibly involved in the changes of history

---

[12]M. Linz in an analysis of sermons on key texts on mission from 1900 to 1962: Manfred Linz, *Anwalt der Welt: Zur Theologie der Mission* (Stuttgart: Kreuz-Verlag, 1964).

[13]Werner Krusche, "Parish Structure—A Hindrance to Mission? A Survey and Evaluation of the Ecumenical Discussion on the Structures of the Missionary Congregation," in *Sources for Change: Searching for Flexible Church Structures*, ed. Herbert T. Neve (Geneva: World Council of Churches, 1968), 53-54.

- not the expansion of the church, but the raising up of shalom
- not the integration of the others into the existing church, but the expectation of a new church
- not normative once-for-all-time-structures, but flexible, differentiated, and coherent structures

The study became one of the main sources for section 2 of the Full Assembly of the World Council of Churches at Uppsala (1968). The draft of that section report was hotly contested in Germany and Scandinavia and also in the Anglo-Saxon world. Some Norwegian delegates went so far as to threaten the resignation of the Norwegian Church if this draft were not withdrawn. . . . The critics understood the document. In particular, they understood that the style of the document's nonrhetorical *questions* called into *question* their own church reality [*Kirchlichkeit*]. . . .

In the realm of Western theology, a vast number of ecclesiological, liturgical, and missiological studies have taken up, modified, and adapted the impulses of the ecumenical study. . . . This processing of the history of ideas [*Ideengeschichte*] should not be undervalued, but what interests me more is the history of the reality [*Realgeschichte*]. The study of structure began with the express goal of helping the churches come to a changed understanding of the world and so to help their own reality, to inspire a churchly reality in which the churches no longer stood in their own way, contradicting their declared goals and intentions by the very way in which they operated. Has the study achieved this goal?

It is true that almost all churches have appointed committees on structural reform. Yet, in most cases, the churches did not follow the ecumenical study by starting their enquiry far outside, in the *missio Dei* in the world. On the contrary, they began with a *theologia perennis* [an eternal theology], an already-known task, and perceived as effectively the only one. And, if "there really is a fixed task, then all structural changes are only to be understood as marginalia, as cosmetic operations which correct but do not really change anything."[14] Structural change would be degraded to socially tactical tricks, keeping the hypostatized task of the church within the borders that belong to it. . . .

---

[14]Wolfgang Marhold, *Fragende Kirche: Über Methode und Funktion kirchlicher Meinungsumfragen* (Munich: Chr. Kaiser Verlag, 1971), 90.

From the history of ideas to the history of realities. I want to compare this with the real history of a "church in the power of the Holy Spirit." Do we see the beginnings of this? One can think of some specific indigenous Pentecostal churches in the Third World and some minority groups within the charismatic movement that are hardly known in the West. To describe the whole charismatic and Pentecostal movement as a "church in the power of the Holy Spirit" would mean to confuse the history of ideas with the history of the reality. But one can observe such a history of reality in some lands, like Ireland and South Africa, where charismatic, Pentecostal, and independent movements and churches operate at the intersection point of political and racial struggles. Should this history of reality be written, the fascinating experience of these groups would be poured into the ideology of a religious, ecclesiocentric, and individualistic understanding of the Holy Spirit. . . .

The difference between language and experience, between ideas and reality is paradigmatic for other differences. Language can not only semantically hide and camouflage real differences, it can also obscure real consensus. That does not mean that all ecclesiological differences can be attributed to such obscuring language; it means that in other social and cultural conditions the same must be said differently so that the same might be grasped. From this comes the transcultural dignity and ecclesiological function of transconceptual language. . . . I want to clarify this with the example of myth.

"The church for others"—a true myth. There are observable facts that show that an entirely demythologized theology, a church without myth, a belief without myth, cannot be understood by the majority of Christians (including their pastors), to say nothing of the non-Christian. What are these observable facts? Almost a third of world population lives in societies dominated by Marxist ideas. Marxism claims to be a scientific materialism and denies non-Marxist sociologies, natural sciences, philosophies and theologies their scientific standing . . . but a closer look reveals that Marxism is a "metaphysical worldview." Its vigor stems from this! Interestingly, all the major themes of the Christian myths have returned: creation and fall, the chosen people, the eschatological prophet, his death and resurrection, the interim period (which lasts longer than expected), an institution that keeps its beliefs alive and interprets them, a present and future *Heilsgeschichte* that expects a new earth—all this appears in Marxism anew, and not as "metaphorical language," but as myth, a myth that is believed in and is adopted as the basis of individual and communal life. . . .

That a nonmythic language in the Third World is a nonlanguage should be clear to every halfway informed observer of Third World cultures. This is even more important for Christian theologians, should those specialists who state that the numerical and theological heavyweight is shifting from the North Atlantic to Africa and Latin America prove correct.

This nonetheless leaves the question as to whether the nonmythic language has a function in Europe and North America. If this could be assured we, at least, could demand an "indigenous theology" in nonmythic categories for the natives of North America and Europe. But even this is not the case. Our universities . . . our media and our public politics work basically with myth as their medium.

A quick look at any popular TV channel shows us myths out of the world of sports and the entertainment industry. These ritualized myths serve as a mechanism to identify with the stars out of the heaven of the sports and pop worlds. Who is able to identify with the winner, the hero, the savior is given the same dignity and status.

The world of politics is another fertile ground for the research on myths. A politician who does not read his mass on a daily basis and does not recite his breviary regularly cannot survive. As a final example, a small reference to the hospital might be allowed. So far, no one has been able to prove that an unqualified increase of medical technology advances the health of a society. Nevertheless, a tremendous amount of money is spent in support of an unproven myth, a myth that is protected by a complicated mythology: named medical science, a priesthood of named doctors (not to forget the *clerus minor*, named nurse), a liturgy complete with white gown, choir boys, and Latin formula, named medical rounds.

This is not meant as a critique but as a description, a description of an issue already observed by Tillich: "There is no actual un-mythic state of mind (*Geisteslage*). . . . And it can't be otherwise." . . .

Myth is thus a medium of communication. . . . "By chance," those people who communicate using myths are the majority of humankind who live on our planet, including the majority of Christians! Based on this empirical observation rests my assumption that an ecclesiology that clings to the history of reality [*Realgeschichte*] cannot renounce myth.

But not every arbitrary myth can assume this function. According to the example of the apostle Paul (for instance in his treatment of the Christ myth in Col 1:15-20) a myth becomes a "true myth" [*wahrer Mythos*],

1. if it stands in relation to present history [*gegenwärtige Geschichte*]: Paul relates mission and church as public entities [*gesellschaftliche Größe*] to the myth,

2. if it stands in relation to the unique event Jesus of Nazareth: Paul corrects the inherited myth in the direction of the cross as a historic event, and

3. if it expresses a surplus of promise over against history, a surplus that is not easy to read from the history of reality that we have experienced.

How might the concept "church-for-others" be understood in terms of myth? With reference to the works of Secundo and Mühlen concerning communion, I understand this to be a liturgy of a mythologized "church-for-others" ecclesiology. If, according to this myth, we should celebrate the transformation of a piece of bread into a piece of flesh, then it is not a "true myth." But if, according to this myth, it is about the solidarity and brotherhood of all Christians and vicariously about all human beings, then, to be sure, it is a myth, a myth that is not less "miraculous" and not more provable than the transformation of bread into flesh. But it is a myth that celebrates the "functionality of the church toward the kingdom of God" and forces the church "constantly toward risk itself" [*Selbstpreisgabe*].[15] The myth dismantles the barriers of our natural given sympathy or antipathy, of our political judgements and prejudices. Only a church as a church-for-others can risk its own existence again and again with such a myth of friendship. The myth contradicts our daily life experience and everything that we know about the social behavior of institutions.

Measured according to the three criteria of a "true myth," the myth of "the church-for-others" as it is currently celebrated in the eucharist meets only the third point. It expresses a "surplus of promise." It *speaks* about something that happens. But it does not happen here and now. Contrary to certain

---

[15]R. Leuenberger, "Zum Problem der Volkskirche," *Reformatio* 26 (1977): 18.

ecclesiological myths of the Third World, the promises of the eucharist myth as it appears in the West cannot be verified. What the myth says (the promise of the myth) and how it is said (its current incarnation in European history) appear as stark contradiction. No effort of theological astuteness, no rebuke from the eschatological tension, from the dialectic of communion and the *theologia crucis*, can heal this situation. The situation can only be healed, if the eucharist becomes a eucharist again, meaning a eucharist that makes the impossible—the church-for-others—visible, palpable, tangible; that means, a eucharist that does not stand in its own way by the manner of its celebration.

I have taken part in such transsocietal, transcultural, and universal eucharists. Some of them happen, for example, in Ireland, when Catholics and Protestants meet each other in a charismatic eucharist celebration and together plead for forgiveness despite the fact that they have lost some of their fathers, brothers, spouses in the civil war and will do so in the future, and despite the fact that they . . . might be ambushed on their way home. . . .

One might rightly object that all of the mentioned examples . . . are more or less located in borderline situations. . . . That is understandable. The eucharistic myth reveals its truth not in the context of normality. It is a myth that transcends borders. It *per definitionem* cannot be celebrated in a closed circle, as the stabilization of *a* class, *a* culture, *a* nation, *a* church. In the situation of so-called normality it looses its splendor and its truth. No liturgical buff can help. It transcends the boundaries between the present world and the world to come. It is a "true myth" (in my terminology) by way of its relationship between text and context, a "revolutionary myth" (Roland Barthes), an "ecumenical utopia" (Ernst Lange).

The "true myth," the Christian myth cannot be "made." It emerges if Christians start to realize their borderline situation—in the current situation this should not be too difficult any more—and if they articulate it in the myth of a "church-for-others." If only the text of the myth is valid, but not its context, then Christian myth becomes either sentimental or blasphemous, no different from the revolutionary speeches of lounge revolutionaries [*Salonrevolutionäre*].

The myth of the "church-for-others" does not transform a church that lives only for itself into a church for others. But it is an adequate medium for the self-representation of ecclesiology there where the church truly is ecclesia.

ANALYSIS

In his 1930 dictionary definition of *mission*, Julius Richter (1862–1940), the most prominent German historian of mission of his time, stated that "the spread of mission occurs everywhere today parallel with the expansion of the white race, partly in the form of colonial subjugation, partly by economic exploitation and the spread of Western culture. Mission is indissolubly connected with both."[16] In 1934, he would further observe that "Christian missions all come from the world's master races [*Herrenvölker*]. Even though the prestige of the white man has suffered tremendously ever since and as a result of the World War, he still is the schoolmaster of humanity [*Lehrmeister der Menschheit*]."[17] The evaluation of Christian missions during the colonial period is more complex and heartening than some commentaries often make out. Nevertheless, the racism, violence, and arrogance captured in the above quotes often dominated missions during the colonial era. In Freytag's estimation, the main mission methods, no matter their differences, shared one thing in common: "they all strayed into the torrent of the propagation of western civilization."[18] The mission enterprise itself came to recognize the problem and, to cite Max Warren, an "orgy of self-criticism" resulted.[19] Mission method mirrored the colonial enterprise and the end of colonialism enforced also the end of the coordinated mission strategies.

One solution lay in the *missio Dei*, the idea that God in God's own very being as Father, Son, and Spirit is missionary. God is a missionary God and it belongs to God's people to be missionary. The church is a missionary church. Far from simply validating the church, this formulation included a critical edge regarding established (Western) church structures. As an example, the 1951 Rolle Statement on the "Calling of the Church to Mission and to Unity" issued by the Central Committee of the WCC rejected the tendency to blame the colonial problem on missions as a way to safeguard

---

[16]Julius Richter, "Mission: Evangelische Mission," in *Die Religion in Geschichte und Gegenwart: Handwörterbuch im gemeinverständlicher Darstellung*, ed. Hermann Gunkel and Leopold Zscharnack (Tübingen: J. C. B. Mohr, 1930), 43.
[17]Julius Richter, *In der Krisis der Weltmission* (Gütersloh: Bertelsmann, 1934), 9.
[18]Walter Freytag, "The Meaning and Purpose of the Christian Mission," *International Review of Missions* 39 (1950): 156.
[19]Max A. Warren, "The Christian Mission and the Cross," in *Missions Under the Cross*, ed. Norman Goodall (London: Edinburgh House Press, 1953), 27.

the church and its institutions from critique. The key problem lay in the creation of church and mission as two distinct institutions and, with this, the confusion of the gospel with "the particular cultural, economic and institutional forms of the older Churches." The problems of colonial missions resulted from the "defects of the Churches from which the mission went forth."[20] The resulting question that occupied the WCC from 1961 to 1968 concerned "the missionary structure of the congregation." What changes in structure were needed for the church to become missionary and so, among other things, to protect itself against undue cultural liaisons? This question and its proposed solution in the idea of the "church-for-others" engaged Hoekendijk, Margull, and Hollenweger.

The Hoekendjik text summarizes well the main lines of his thought. Though he too grounds mission within an eschatological setting, his approach differs from that of Hartenstein and Freytag in that mission is motivated by the messianic and not the final judgment. "Mission in view of the end," for Hoekendijk, stood guilty of "ecclesiocentrism," of directing the whole eschatological horizon to the church. Nothing exists beyond the church. Grounding mission in the messianic, by contrast, sets the church within history as the realm of God's own acting. The point is an important one. Mission is not first defined in terms of geography, as the sending of the church from one location to another. Such a position succeeds only in sanctifying place and turning God into an idol grounded in a particular culture. Mission is, instead, God working in history. This undoes any claim to link the faith with a particular cultural form, as occurred during the colonial period.

As to the form of the church's embodiment, Hoekendijk directs the church to the realm of God's acting: the world. The world has its own reality and it is to the world that God in Jesus Christ comes: "For God so loved the world." For the church, this constitutes a warning against finding its identity within fixed forms. These, in Hoekendijk's estimation become "heretical structures" because they fail to serve the living God. The church, instead, is free to witness to the coming kingdom by assuming whatever form best serves that purpose.

---

[20] "The Calling of the Church to Mission and Unity," *The Ecumenical Review* 4 (1951): 70.

Without doubt, Hoekendijk owes much to the radical politics of the 1960s, but there is also more there than he is often given credit for. The basic link he forged between mission and history found confirmation in the work of Andrew Walls, Kwame Bediako, and Lamin Sanneh. He is also more biblically attentive than many missiologists. When compared to approaches that ground mission within a command, or that use the "Gentiles" to ratify forms of mission now associated with the colonial era, Hoekendijk identifies key theological themes within both the Old and New Testaments and forms his mission theology out of these.

While he informed a good deal of ecumenical mission theology during the 1960s, the charge often laid against him was that he forgot the church, that the institution of the church fell away. His radical faith in the capacity of the church to change, to reject any ontological status for church structures and the associated fundamentalism that safeguards them, drills deeply into cherished notions of the church's embodiment. Many read this as a simple rejection of the church. One can contest this point, but the larger concern reflects well the ongoing questions regarding the church's establishment, the nature of entry into this community, and, by extension, missionary forms and goals.

For all Hoekendijk's creativity, he is often read as one who deconstructed more than he constructed. As to the positive ground for the reconstruction, Tambaram 1938 already noted how Western Christianity reflected the Hellenic and Latin cultures and how "today African, Chinese, Indian, Japanese and other indigenous expressions of the Christian religion are taking shape."[21] At this point in time, this was more observation than something of material significance also for the churches in the West. By the 1960s and 1970s recognition of these local forms stimulated normative theological statements. German missiology began to discover questions, theologies, and embodiments of the faith outside of the Western experience as positive and critical realities.

This led to the widening of the conceptual field available to missiology. Margull illustrates well both this incorporation of wider experiences and using a wider spectrum of theological ideas. His beginning point is the

---

[21] *The Growing Church* (London: International Missionary Council, 1938), 295.

notion of harm: harm done to mission through dialogue and harm done by mission to the religious other. Following Kenneth Cragg, vulnerability is the name he gives to this potential to be harmed. The damage caused also by the Christian faith during the colonial era was evident, even if not accepted by all, and it indicated a vulnerability (in the sense of weakness) within Christianity itself: its capacity to consider itself in absolute terms and so to draw on the power of politics and culture. Whereas the liaison of political power and faith is often understood as something forced on the church, Margull here suggests that the faith was itself active in seeking this relationship and that this liaison continued in the attempt to reassert the legitimacy of Western missions. However, far from being normative and so necessary, Western missions constitute but one example of the diverse forms mission has taken throughout the two thousand year history of Christianity.

Margull's rethinking the form of mission takes vulnerability as its starting point, the vulnerability of God. God shapes mission in terms of both form and content. Margull's repeated comment that the religions understand Christianity to be "just one single long quotation" refers to the detachment of its words from its actions. Margull names the words *church* and *lordship* in terms of a critique that will become significant during the postcolonial period: the chosen theological lexicon married well with the colonial project—Christ as lord became a simple cypher for the colonizer as lord. Against the theological abstraction that creates space for errant forms of embodiment, the vulnerability of God is a dialogical reality. God takes on the form of a servant and, in so doing, becomes vulnerable. This is also the content of the faith. Service that proceeds from strength is arrogant. Service based in vulnerability is service with the possibility of misunderstanding, of forgetting, of failure. But this, for Margull, is the place where the possibility of "what will be" resides.

Where Gensichen could in the 1950s continue to reference the special German charism with regard to the indigenization of the gospel, Margull inhabits a very different beginning point. He feels no need to defend mission against the charges leveled against it. Quite the opposite: Margull warns that the Western church is now being confronted by its own weaknesses and feels the pain of such. To defend an approach to mission located in power, politics, and culture is to continue the way of harm. His resulting definition of mission speaks not of establishing the church, of the heathen, of conversion, of salvation, or even of the kingdom of God. Nor does he reference eschatological judgment or triumph. It is not that he rejects these theological positions. It is that without a local embodiment, one developed in the process of a living vulnerability, these ideas take form within a foreign context and serve foreign powers. They embodied Western arrogance. This leads to a definition of mission located in dialogue. The goal of dialogue is to understand the other as they understand themselves. This means silence and listening, and not a monologue that amounts to control. Margull links this approach to the nature of the incarnation. Much in the incarnation is open to misinterpretation and denial, especially if it reduces to a range of claims contradicted by the conduct of those making them. But it is in the vulnerability of the incarnation where its truth is found.

The Hollenweger article likewise extends the theological lexicon available to mission studies. Beginning with the idea of the "church-for-others," he observes the disconnect between this study on the missionary structures of the congregation and how it was received among church bodies. These bodies did not oppose the notion of structural change—as long as the change in question was only cosmetic, a modernizing of the façade while leaving the center unaffected. This approach for Hollenweger signals an intractability, a confidence in established cultural forms of the church, that inhibits the missionary witness of the church for the other. Hollenweger counters this static ecclesiocentric approach via two related points.

First, he points to the ecclesial pluriformity encountered in the grassroots evangelical, charismatic, and Pentecostal churches growing within Africa and Asia, and to the forms of unity that result. The reality of such difference intrudes on settled (ecumenical) accounts of the church. By extension, there exists no pure form of the church unavailable for structural change in service to its mission. This approach to the church he already finds within the biblical text: "The New Testament pluriformity and the conceptual 'imprecision' of the concept of the church is not a deficiency that must be corrected through a 'conceptual understanding,' but a theological fact that must be understood, reckoned with, and assumed *as such*."[22] Hollenweger raises the

---

[22] Hollenweger, "Die Kirche für andere—ein Mythos," 438n47.

further question of how this pluriformity might be treated in relation to unity. Any answer, he continues, would need to address the theological function of myth, vision, and ritual and cannot be limited to the resources available within Western "Mediterranean" culture." This directs Hollenweger to the Spirit and to the possibility that an ecclesiology of the "church for others" begins with pneumatology and not Christology.[23]

Second, this ecclesial pluriformity that nonetheless maintains its distinctive Christian identity points to a "transconceptual" language. By this he means a form of doing theology that takes on different language functions than those prescribed by a conceptual or terminological approach (one that supposes precision in definition). This transconceptual approach is not a popularizing of the theological process, but corresponds to the "transcultural" reality of the Christian world.

Hollenweger illustrates his point using the term *myth*. First, he denies the possibility of a language without myth. Even within Europe and North America, myth is part of the mundane human experience. Second, myth is a constitutive factor in any ecclesiology. This is theologically directed and concerns the story becoming actual in history. Myth draws us beyond a flat recounting of the story and toward the reality to which the myth points. That is, the myth "contradicts" daily experience and allows us to risk security for the promise of fellowship beyond every natural border. The myth proves to be true in borderline situations. This pertains both to social conditions and to events such as the eucharist. This itself suggests a borderline situation. It does not secure a particular group. It draws that group into the promise of the eucharist itself and so beyond its own borders. Apart from that movement, the eucharist is not a true myth no matter the liturgical framework. Myth as part of the "transconceptual" theological process concerns the making real or the embodiment of the faith. The myth element for Hollenweger permits both an ambiguity sufficient for cultural difference and a reality that must be lived. No single cultural instance controls this myth. Indeed, the myth calls each closed narrative toward the other precisely due to the promise to which the myth points.

In sum, all three authors indicate a significant shift within German missiology. Earlier accounts of how God works within primal ties, and the

---

[23]Hollenweger, "Die Kirche für andere—ein Mythos," 437.

related mission method that sought to protect and cultivate these ties, have given way to an approach that places the initiative for embodying the faith within the local culture itself. There is a realization that the missionary interest in local culture was an interest shaped by Western values and so a particular determination of what culture looked like and where it was to be found within particular contexts. As part of this realization, the colonial critique rebounds on the supposed normativity of established Western church forms and theologies. No single definition of the church exists, and, by extension, local culture also determines the church's shape. This directs especially Margull and Hollenweger to the capacity of theology to listen, to how language is used, and to how its formulations become real apart from their abuse within improper claims to power. This insight leads to the next generation's interest in hermeneutics.

5

Hermeneutics, Communication, and Translation

INTRODUCTION

A significant split marked the missionary movement during the 1970s and '80s. Whatever the differences in theological rationale and associated missionary method during the colonial era, the basic form of missionary activity was clear: the sending of Western missionaries to an imagined still non-Christian world. With the end of the colonial era missions required a more robust theological framework. *Missio Dei*, for all its difficulties, supplied this. But, unlike earlier theological foundations, the theology did not promote an evident and immediate missionary strategy. The key question became one of missionary structures: What form does Christian mission take?

As an institutional indicator of this theological debate, the former International Missionary Council became part of the World Council of Churches at the Third General Assembly of the WCC held in New Delhi, 1961. It was a contested endeavor. The evangelical voice of *Max Warren* (1904–1977) argued against the union based on the need to protect missions as a distinct activity, and the need to maintain mission societies as "points of concentration" for mission.[1] *Lesslie Newbigin* (1909–1998) countered that mission properly belongs to the being of the church and "integration would bring the missionary and evangelistic concern into the heart of the WCC so that all its activities would in future be infused by that concern."[2] Though the

---

[1] Max A. Warren, "Why Missionary Societies and Not Missionary Churches?," *Student World* 53 (1960): 155.
[2] J. E. Lesslie Newbigin, "Integration—Some Personal Reflections 1981," *International Review of Mission* 70 (1981): 248.

integration of the two bodies occurred, the fundamental evangelical concern remained. A divide grew.

During the mid-1960s a good deal of dissatisfaction developed in relation to the WCC study on the "missionary structure of the congregation." It was felt the traditional missionary concern for evangelization, the proclamation of the gospel and the call to conversion, had been forsaken for politics and social activity. In 1968, *Donald McGavran* (1897–1990) wrote an open letter to the WCC titled, "Will Uppsala Betray the Two Billion?," in which he lamented how the missionary movement had abandoned the eternal remedy of the gospel for a temporary palliative of giving bread.[3] Evangelicals felt that their concerns now played little to no role in WCC deliberations concerning mission. To meet this concern, other evangelical institutions began to develop. The 1966 Wheaton and 1970 Frankfurt Declarations opposed the humanitarian definition of mission then dominant within the WCC and stressed the need for evangelization and individual conversion. The Wheaton statement even reaffirmed the nineteenth-century axiom—the "evangelization of the world in this generation"—as the ground and goal of its missionary vision.

The 1973 Bangkok (Thailand) meeting of the Commission for World Mission and Evangelism confirmed the worst evangelical fears. The first conference with the majority of delegates to come from Africa, Asia, and Latin America, Bangkok resisted an identified Western theological imperialism and reinforced the call issued by *John Gatu* (1925–2017) for a moratorium on Western missionaries and money. Salvation was understood in terms of a "comprehensive wholeness," applying to every aspect of human life. It asserted the right of every church to formulate its own structure, theology, liturgy, and praxis as rooted in its own culture. It marked, to quote Emil Castro, "the end of the westernization of the Church" and the beginning of discovering the "multiplicity of different identities" that belong to the church universal.[4]

The negative evangelical response to Bangkok followed the established lines of argument. Now a sizable bloc, four thousand representatives from

---

[3]Donald A. McGavran, "Will Uppsala Betray the Two Billion?," in *The Conciliar-Evangelical Debate: The Crucial Documents, 1964–1976*, ed. Donald A. McGavran (Pasadena, CA: William Carey Library, 1977), 233-41.
[4]Emilio Castro, "Bangkok, the New Opportunity," *International Review of Mission* 62 (1973): 142.

around the world attended the 1974 Congress on World Evangelization held in Lausanne (Switzerland). With this, the worldwide evangelical movement found a platform to express their concerns. The resulting Lausanne Covenant—inspired by *John Stott* (1921–2011)—stressed the priority of the gospel as a transculturally valid and eternal message that needed to be proclaimed and personally accepted. Among other things, this safeguarded patterns of missionary sending associated with the colonial era.

Though one might point to *Peter Beyerhaus* (b. 1929), then professor of mission and ecumenics at the University of Tübingen (1966–1997), as a key evangelical voice, the dominant majority of German missiologists followed the direction taken by the ecumenical movement. The era of Western missions was at an end and the understanding and forms of mission had to change. But it was also the case that the answers to these new issues lay outside of the Western theological guild. Whatever contribution Western missiologists might make, it had to be in relation to this other.

The idea of the church-for-others dominated missiological debates for decades, and while it was subject to various criticisms, it was **Theo Sundermeier** (b. 1935) who developed a constructive alternative. The most influential German missiologist of recent time, and teacher of most of the current generation of German professors, Sundermeier first served as theological lecturer from 1964 to 1975 in Namibia and South Africa. In 1975, he returned to Germany to become the professor of the theology and history of religion at Bochum University, before becoming professor for the history of religion and mission studies at the University of Heidelberg (1983 to 2000).[5] Sundermeier viewed the church-for-others as paternalistic:

> The attitude of "existing for others" presupposes a distance from the other. Whoever wants to be there for others, wants to help the other person. [One] lives in an attitude of superiority. Help is the accumulation of power. It creates the feeling in the giver of being superior and, conversely, of being inferior in the receiver. Reciprocity is out of the question; solidarity is prevented rather than facilitated.[6]

---

[5]For further on Sundermeier, see Theo Sundermeier, "My Pilgrimage in Mission," *International Bulletin of Missionary Research* 31 (2007): 200-202.
[6]Theo Sundermeier, "Convivence: The Concept and Origin," *Scriptura* 10 (1992): 70.

In this way, the church-for-others approach extended the problems identified by colonial missions. Mission needed to begin from a different ground than that of power and self-confirmation. Sundermeier finds this within a hermeneutical approach, specifically, in a "hermeneutics of the stranger" (*Hermeneutik des Fremden*).

Sundermeier observes how much of the Occidental history of thought interpreted "understanding" as "understanding myself" (*Mich-Verstehen*). The foreign/the foreigner served as the lost half of myself, the mirror in which I am able to see myself. This tradition of thought, he argues, is found in Plato and has continued through the Western tradition, informing the hermeneutics of Schleiermacher in the nineteenth century and those of Gadamer in the twentieth. Sundermeier counters this tradition with a hermeneutics that perceives the foreign/the foreigner as something or someone that cannot be fully understood. The "other" assists self-understanding because my relation to the other is part of my self-constitution, but in this the foreign/the foreigner nevertheless remains different and strange.

This reading of the Western hermeneutical tradition leads to Sundermeier's constructive account of mission as "convivency" (*convivência, Konvivenz*), to "live-with."[7] Instead of proceeding from a position of power and superiority (helping the other), Sundermeier grounds mission in mutual help, reciprocal learning, and joint celebration. Convivency refers to a communion of life, a communion of learning, and a communion of feast (*Lebens-, Lern- und Festgemeinschaft*). The church has to live with others, on an equal footing; the church needs to be sensitive to what matters to others.

The authors through the first chapters of this book described non-Christian religious commitments using the language of *heathen*, *pagan*, and *idolatrous*. Part of the problem with this approach lies in the clean binary opposition it inserts between the otherwise complex relationship of religious beliefs, cultural customs, social institutions, and local languages. But it equally assumed the gospel to be an unchangeable object that might be wrapped in any number of cultural clothing. It became apparent, however, that one cannot find value in local cultural forms while coincidently condemning the

---

[7]Theo Sundermeier, "Konvivenz als Grundstruktur ökumenischer Existenz heute," in *Ökumenische Existenz heute*, ed. W. Huber, D. Ritschl, and Theo Sundermeier (München: Chr. Kaiser Verlag, 1986), 49-100. For an introduction to the concept, see Sundermeier, "Convivence," 68-80.

religious heritage. Nor was it possible for the gospel to be spoken in this local language without this effecting the message itself. To affirm that the gospel might be incarnated in local form, is to affirm that the local custom and religion somehow contributes to the gospel. God works through other religions insofar as religious belief shapes language and the concepts to which language points.

This complex continuation of the hermeneutical question was picked up by the Swiss missiologist and science of religion scholar **Richard Friedli** (b. 1937). A member of the Dominican order, Friedli served from 1965 to 1971 in the Democratic Republic of Congo and Rwanda, and from 1971 to 1992 was professor in the faculty of theology at the University of Fribourg in Switzerland. In 1993, he switched to the faculty of philosophy and since then has taught comparative religion with a special focus on issues of peace and reconciliation. Friedli's interest in an interdisciplinary approach was already apparent in his 1974 doctoral dissertation, "Foreignness as Home." Here he argued that all cultures and religions in our time were influenced by "sociocultural circulation": cultures encounter, influence, alter, and enrich each other.[8] This reality requires a new approach to mission, one different from dialectical theology and a theology of fulfillment. Friedli turns to the place of the foreigner as it appears in the biblical text. Foreignness constitutes the core criterion for the existence of believers no matter to which religion or culture they belong. Coexistence and mission are only possible with a fundamental sense of hope, with an attitude of tolerance, and a sense for the preliminary nature of all things. He concludes that encountering the foreigner is the very space where God can be found.

The reading from Friedli gives a concrete illustration of this point. He considers the challenges of intercultural translation using the formula found in Exodus 3:14: "I AM WHO I AM." Friedli interprets this formula first with regard to the original text, written in ancient Hebrew language, and the shift in meaning that occurs when this is translated into Greek and later Latin. The difficulties encountered here become extended when it is read within the Japanese language, for it needs to take into account Buddhist anthropology as providing the horizon of understanding.

---

[8]Richard Friedli, *Fremdheit als Heimat: Auf der Suche nach einem theologischen Kriterium für den Dialogue zwischen den Religionen* (Zurich: Theologischer Verlag, 1974).

The text from **Christine Lienemann-Perrin** (b. 1946) draws together Sundermeier and Friedli's insights. One no longer encounters the diversities of religion, culture, and thought through long travel to exotic places. In every modern society, that diversity is now our neighbor and every religious community has to address the relationship of their faith to this difference in their midst. The need for a hermeneutic of the stranger is a local need and gives shape to contemporary mission theory and practice.

Lienemann-Perrin is a Swiss missiologist in the Reformed tradition. After studying theology in Switzerland and France, she received her doctorate in 1976 from Heidelberg University though an examination of the Theological Education Fund's contribution to theological education in Asia, Africa, and Latin America and the beginnings of contextual theology.[9] After teaching at the Faculté de Théologie Kimbanguiste in Kinshasa, Democratic Republic of Congo, she became a member of the Protestant Institute for Interdisciplinary Research in Heidelberg (1977–1985). Her Habilitation addressed the political responsibility of the churches in South Korea and South Africa (1990), and between 1992 and 2010 she served as professor for ecumenism, mission, and contemporary intercultural questions at the University of Basel. Her research focuses on the intersection of ecumenism, mission, political ethics, and public theology in the area of world Christianity. Because it is interdisciplinary and concerned with North-South relationships, her methodological approach initiates and participates within research teams. This permits a wider range of voices and provides space for those voices to come into conversation.[10]

Lienemann-Perrin's concern corresponds to a key shift within mission studies: mission is no longer something to be associated with geopolitical power dynamics that permit an arrogance in relation to foreign peoples, cultures, and religions. While the work of both Sundermeier and Friedli might seem abstract and distant from historic missionary approaches, Lienemann-Perrin sets these

---

[9]Christine Lienemann-Perrin, *Training for a Relevant Ministry: A Study of the Contribution of the Theological Education Fund* (Geneva: World Council of Churches, 1981).
[10]See, for example, Christine Lienemann-Perrin and James R. Cochrane, eds., *The Church and the Public Sphere in Societies in Transition* (Pietermaritzburg: Cluster, 2013); Christine Lienemann-Perrin, Atola Longkumer, and Afrie S. Joye, eds., *Putting Names with Faces: Women's Impact in Mission History* (Nashville: Abingdon Press, 2012); Christine Lienemann-Perrin and Wolfgang Lienemann, eds., *Religiöse Grenzüberschreitungen: Studien zu Bekehrung, Konfessions- und Religionswechsel* (Wiesbaden: Harrassowitz, 2012).

same concerns within the discussions occurring within world Christianity itself. Defining mission in terms of the hermeneutic of the stranger lies now central to the missionary task. If mission is the self-explication of faith it can only occur in relation to the forms of difference which that faith encounters. Mission will take alternate forms in other places and times. Yet mission continues to be the task of embodying and speaking the faith and so being opened to all manner of social, culture, and religious difference.

THEO SUNDERMEIER

"Considerations for a Hermeneutic of Intercultural Understanding"
~1991~

THE DISCIPLINE OF MISSION STUDIES never paid much attention to "hermeneutics."[11] . . . Mission theology simply concentrated on the topic of "communication." It seems there was no doubt at all about what was to be proclaimed. Everyone knew the content. The only question was how to proclaim the *depositum fidei* to non-Christians in the most meaningful and effective way. . . . The Lausanne Congress (1974) and the follow-up conference to it continue to espouse this notion—indeed, they elaborate on it in a systematical fashion. Their only concern is communicating the Christian faith: How should people share it, what strategies should they use? What happens in the process of communication, and what could distort the message between the sender and the receiver? How does the communication channel itself affect the message? . . . "Inculturation," "indigenization," and "contextualization" are some of the concepts that were put forward to integrate mission methods and mission theology. However, their *specific differences* were lost in the process! . . .

But there is yet another reason why "mission as communication" needs to prioritize hermeneutics. Newer research in the area of communication

---

[11]Theo Sundermeier, "Erwägungen zu einer Hermeneutik interkulturellen Verstehens," in *Begegnung mit dem Anderen: Plädoyers für eine interkulturelle Hermeneutik* (Gütersloher Verlag: Gütersloh, 1991), 13-18.

studies shows that the models currently used in mission studies have become obsolete. Communication is not simply a unilateral event between a sender and a receiver; instead, the message is modified when receiver one transmits it to receiver two, when the cultural context changes, or by the means of transmission itself, the "channel," since the sender is also simultaneously a receiver. The receiver who hears the message is neither the object of the sender nor simply the object of the message, but a subject and therefore a sender as well. In the process of communication itself, the sender is also affected; in other words, when communication succeeds, it is not just the receiver who is changed. . . .

Ultimately, we are of course all well aware of this, even on the basis of our own missionary experience. But no one has drawn the consequences to date. And yet, they are highly relevant theologically. The speaker is also a receiver, and she herself is changed by the hearer in the process of speaking. To use the language of developmental psychology, "The self receives and transmits. The self uses the other person in order to be able to transmit and receive." When it comes to the hermeneutical problem of intercultural understanding that is at issue here, this observation is very significant, especially since it accords with the theological insight that witnessing does not mean simply delivering a message like a mailman dropping off a priority mail package. Rather, it means becoming involved with and lovingly relating to the person who is to receive the testimony. This presupposes that understanding takes place—that not only the text is understood, but the hearer as well, since in receiving the message she becomes part of it. She is addressed in her capacity as a subject. Understanding thus precedes communication in two ways and forms part of it. For this reason, hermeneutics must precede communication as well as accompany, if not displace, it.

II. When it comes to theological hermeneutics, it has been universally held ever since Schleiermacher that essentially, theological hermeneutics is no different to the general principles of understanding as such, that these may be applied to all areas using the same methodology. It is only recently that some theorists have dared cautiously to differ by placing more emphasis on praxis, as is the case, for example, in liberation theology. Praxis precedes understanding, a new understanding becomes possible on the basis of praxis as constellations are repeatedly torn down and reconstituted. Now of course this does not necessarily differ from the traditional humanities approach. . . . Gadamer picked up on an impulse from Pietism according to which praxis is the goal: It is only in doing that understanding finds rest and reaches its goal. . . . Theologically speaking, the obedience of faith precedes the understanding of faith. Discipleship enables understanding.

But what is to be understood exactly? It is remarkable that in the West, and especially in the existentialist view, hermeneutics always has to do with understanding myself. It is not about understanding the other person or a text that is foreign to me, but about a new way to understand myself occasioned by my encounter with the text. Even Hegel saw the Other, that which is Foreign, as a detour on the path to self-discovery, and Schleiermacher noted that it is only possible to understand the other person because "each bears within himself a minimum quota of everyone else." Ultimately, conversation toward understanding is thus a soliloquy. . . .

Now in terms of intercultural understanding, this typical Western approach is not really helpful. The point of encountering people belonging to another culture is that they are different, that I am compelled to expose myself to their Otherness, and that I cannot start out by manipulating their Otherness from the outset for my own benefit and finagling it so as to accomplish a "fusion of horizons" (the charming, but ultimately idealistic goal Gadamer set for such encounters). Understanding must take place in a framework in which the Other and that which is Foreign are allowed to stand, or else it will not take place at all. When a foreign culture is presented, it is simply false and unconstructive for the hearers to supply ready comparisons and to initiate the leveling process by uttering the phrase, "Sure, we know that from our own context . . ."

So what can we do to escape from the solipsistic circle of understanding by way of self-knowledge that has been infused into us ever since Plato? The Old Testament concept of knowing does not include a reference back to self-knowledge; rather, it is oriented only toward the other person, holding that this orientation is necessary for its own sake. Knowledge can exist only because the other person exists. The other person facilitates knowledge and therefore ultimately constitutes myself as well. At any rate, this is how Paul sees it—in keeping with the tradition of the Old Testament—when he accords absolute priority to my being known by the other person, in other words, to my being recognized. He sees it as the basis enabling knowledge in the first place: then I shall know fully, even as I am fully known! As far as I know, the philosopher Emmanuel Lévinas, who is committed to the Jewish tradition, is the only one to take a position on this topic of Otherness that is constructive as far as the hermeneutics of intercultural theology is concerned. Lévinas never sees the Other (he always spells the word with a capital letter) as the lost half of my own ego, the way Plato does, as if to say that the quest for knowledge is defined by my desire to restore the missing piece of myself. For Lévinas sees the Other very differently: by emerging from his own interiority and meeting me face to face, the Other constitutes my own ego without ceasing to be himself. . . . The reason why Lévinas seem so appealing to us is that he so clearly and distinctly regards the Other, and then draws the necessary consequences for us. In addition, his affiliation with Jewish thought makes him theologically relevant for us in that this particular relatedness to the Other reflects the basic structure of the biblical theology of the Reformation, namely justification, even though this is not Lévinas's intent. After all, in the Jewish context (and unlike the Roman context), justification does not mean that justice is done to me before the forum of the court, but rather that I am granted space to live and therefore the right to life, and that I am received into the community. It follows from Lévinas's thinking that a justified existence becomes possible for me by virtue of the Other constituting my ego's right to exist. However, this is not an individual ego existing by itself; rather, the act of adjudication constitutes community. By making it possible for me to exist, a new form of behavior also becomes possible for me: to act ethically on the basis of the life adjudicated to me. Lévinas is correct therefore when he calls the Other my "teacher." . . . The concept of the Other conveys various shades of meaning. It includes transcendentality, even if it does not always express it explicitly. It is no accident that Lévinas speaks of the face of the Other shining brightly, that he speaks of the traces and trails crisscrossing our time and making it possible for us to experience time in a new form. I maintain the polysemy of these concepts and take the liberty to go one step further. To begin with, it is important to note that the Other is not conceived of as an individualistic Thou. Third World experiences teach us always to take seriously the individual's embeddedness in a community. This embeddedness precedes the individual and constitutes her in her existence. The basic African model of how the Other is experienced states, "I am because we are." Convivency makes the life of the individual possible. It is freedom given for the purpose of learning, teaching, celebrating, in short: for the purpose of living fraternally and in peace. This living, this volition toward the Other, the striving for understanding and knowledge derives from an affirmation of life, from the knowledge of an owed life, from the experience of being affirmed and accepted. In theological terms: from faith in the Creator of all life and of the world.

Let us affirm: the necessity for a hermeneutics of intercultural understanding does not derive from the quest for more knowledge or for exotica, or from the awareness that we cannot overcome the world's problems at present purely on the strength of our knowledge. In other words, hermeneutics is not based on experiences of deficiency, but on the experience of life together. . . . By understanding the other person, my life is torn away from its egocentrism and its solipsism. In the process of understanding, it is not that the other person is assimilated toward me. I cannot assimilate a face; I can only assent to it and accept it. As a result, understanding becomes a fundamental task which precedes all action. . . .

III. Classical hermeneutics has applied itself to words; theological hermeneutics is always fixated on words. Both are convinced that in language, being itself comes into existence, that linguisticality is the ontological basis for hermeneutics in general. No hermeneutics is able to deviate from this stream of tradition. Hermeneutics is patterned toward words. Understanding cannot get by without linguisticality. Even so, we must attempt to overcome this unilaterality. Our tradition of an overly unilateral focus on words and texts is based on the iconoclasm of the Old Testament religion, which continued and persevered in ancient Christianity, to begin with, then in Islam, and finally in the Christianity of the Reformation. In our cultural arena today, hermeneutics also has to do with this tradition; art only managed to "slip in unnoticed," as it were, even though it gained in importance thanks to the Orthodox Church, the Roman Catholic Church, and the encounter with classic Greece and Rome in the time of the Renaissance and in humanism, an importance that phenomenological hermeneutics could not ignore. . . .

In contrast even to Hegel, art is not seen as the expression of an alienated spirit. . . . This is the reason why we, by comparison, attach special importance to art, simply because in the process of intercultural encounters we are confronted with cultures that do not share our appreciation of words but attach great and often equal importance to images and to nonverbal expressions, which in fact often give priority of place to these things. This is true to a certain extent for people groups with unwritten cultures where the cult is based on the notion that words and ritual performances hold equal status. It is most certainly true for the traditions of the mystic religions. Zen Buddhism in particular comes to mind. . . . Words that find their consummate expression in calligraphy are assigned a higher status than are the corresponding verbalized words.

Zen Buddhism in particular calls attention to another aspect opened up by modern research into symbols: words are more than words. They are integrated into the world of symbols and participate in it. Symbols precede thinking. They do not obscure, as even Freud still contended, but "give us food for thought" (Paul Ricoeur) instead. Thinking cannot do without words; interpretation compiles in the fullness of words what is present in symbols. But even words are a re-enactment, a compilation of something prior. Symbols impart, but not in ways that renders the recipient passive. Symbols call for an interpreter, they activate the interpreter. They demand participation. The significance of symbols is fixed as much or as little as the meaning of the oracle. Their significance changes within the receiver without giving rise to arbitrariness. Each interpretation must orient itself toward the symbols themselves and remain appropriate. In the process, symbols refuse to be downgraded into signs or to ossify in the form of allegory. Symbols are alive; like the oracle and like dreams, they are "God's forgotten language."

Does this also apply to art? Certainly not in a primary sense or by way of direct inference. . . . Since . . . reality may ultimately be expressed only by way of symbols, art also participates in this attribute. This is especially true for religious art. . . . Each work of art is a statement with multiple layers of meaning. It provides the observer with a message, and it does so by adapting itself to her ability to receive and to her willingness to do so. Because art is a human creation, its referential character may recede considerably without, however, disappearing entirely. At the same time, it offers a condensed statement far exceeding the linguistic events of everyday life. . . . Appreciating art means to expose oneself to the world of the culture in question and to its religious superelevation. And intercultural hermeneutics cannot do without this approach.

There is yet another reason why we must essentially integrate the interpretation of art into the concept of an intercultural theological hermeneutics. Having been characterized by the respective cultures in which the churches of the Third World are located, and in accordance with the considerable importance they attach to symbols, rituals, and community, theology cannot articulate itself in the first instance as veracious theology, as "armchair theology." It must identify other forms of expression, and it has done so. Songs, celebrations, short poetic texts, new symbols, and performing arts are some examples of ways in which theology may articulate and express itself. I propose that in the Third World, just as in the West, art precedes the theological insight that is expressed in words. Art creatively anticipates theological insight. . . . The truth of art antedates the insights of theology. By visually anticipating them, it renders them acceptable at the same time.

Hermeneuts of indigenous religious (Christian) art do theology in an immediate sense in that they translate into words what already exists in the encrypted format disclosed by art. We may paraphrase the statement in the first letter of John to say that art makes visible what theology will be (1 Jn 3:2).

IV. We need to provide separate reasoning for why medicine was selected as the key pillar of an intercultural hermeneutics. In doing so, we venture down untrodden, but necessary paths. . . . I needed to listen and to observe for a long time and to do a lot of research before I was able to discover that African medicine is indeed comprehensible, that it is logically coherent in and of itself, even if it is based on laws different to ours. Its logic is subject to the law of analogy, its metaphorical center is the human body. . . . The phenomenology of the body becomes a metaphor for the world, and with its help it becomes possible to decipher the world. Those who do not know this key feel lost in the world and are helpless before it. But those who have the key can feel at home in the world and face it. . . . The medicine man knows this. Usually, his knowledge is more intuitive than it is conscious. The same goes for the patient. She understands the heavily symbolic action of the healer, and this is the reason why healing takes place. Without understanding there is no healing.

Medicine also has to do with hermeneutics; conversely, hermeneuts need the phenomenological assessment of the illness arrived at by way of the medicine in order to be able to access the world of the other culture and in order to understand and translate its mode of expression, which is foreign to them. . . .

The intensive form of body symbolism is found especially among tribal cultures, for instance, whereas cosmological symbolism prevails among the Asian so-called advanced cultures. In other words, this is not about the cosmos being drawn into the world of human beings and then being interpreted on that basis, but rather about human beings transcending the world in order to enter the cosmos. . . .

V. The interpretation of religious and theological texts is usually discussed at the beginning. We turn our attention to it at the end. What these texts have in common with art and with the symbolism of a sick body is that their meaning is "open": they call for ongoing and ever more profound appreciation and appraisal. The underlying issue they intend to communicate is not fixed, as if it were like a buried brick needing only to be extricated from its cladding and its dirty casing. On the contrary, it is always open to new interpretations, and it changes as the circumstances change (e.g., as it is translated into another language and culture) and as the interpreters change, depending on their ability to observe and to interpret.

We find the problem in the New Testament already. Up until now, interpreters have traditionally resolved it by presenting an unequivocal, "objective" explanation. That is to say, the hermeneuts did not put the subjectivity and limitations of their own *summa* up for discussion—in fact, they did not even recognize them. Recently, the situation has changed. People try to solve the problem differently, arguing for multiple shades of meaning and for open-mindedness as far as the "issue" is concerned. This—according to Gadamer—is the whole purpose of the text itself. . . .

The view of text and meaning I espouse here corresponds to a notion advocated in the theory of art: that art is an open concept.

We need to elaborate on this a little, lest we be accused of arbitrariness. An artwork is open in those respects in which it does not predetermine its own meaning in an exclusive sense but presents itself to the interpreter as "a work to be completed." The basis on which a variety of interpretations is possible is the "field of interrelations" which each artwork opens up. . . . It is neither fixed nor static, but mobile. It moves the hearers/observers and interpreters. It creates associations and opens up new horizons. Being an artwork, it is subject to a kind of order, and for this reason the interpretation cannot be arbitrary, but must move within the realm of appropriateness. . . .

Therefore, the truth of the text can only be ascertained by way of the interaction of different interpretations. I do not mean this in the sense of complementarity, but rather of truth in convivency. . . .

VI. These deliberations clearly show that the aim of a hermeneutics of intercultural encounter is not to achieve harmony. It is about encountering that which is foreign. It is vital to adhere to this line consistently. In the process of understanding, it is false for the interpreter to seek prematurely to interpret that which is Foreign toward herself, to incorporate it into her own self-understanding, thereby refashioning her counterpart into a part of herself, as was the custom in hermeneutics in various forms in the past. Intercultural encounters are a form of affliction (Lévinas). Granted, the other person accords to me the right to exist, but she also afflicts me, she calls me into question. . . . Due to the proximity and suddenness with which this phenomenon encounters me, I experience it as an inescapable intrusion. . . . My outer shell does not remain intact, at least not the way it used to be. I have to face the intrusion and reply to it. The affliction always has an ethical dimension to it. . . . It is only when we appreciate the profundity of this phenomenon that we understand why it is so disconcerting when Jesus identifies himself with that which is Foreign, why, as we regard the concept and the face of the Other, we resist perceiving the referential character, the individual Other. When we do so, the only way for us to endure the challenge is by accepting it.

This means to suffer it. . . . Encountering the other person or that which is Foreign produces an experience of helplessness, of insignificance and nothingness. I do not understand that which is Other, this thing I find both attractive and repellent, which I seek to comprehend but cannot grasp. Experiencing my own limitations, even my own nothingness, makes me become aggressive. This experience is caused by the traces and trails the other person leaves in me. But I can only learn by becoming willing to acknowledge and appreciate the Otherness of the other person, not just the image I have made of her, as well as my own expectation with which I encounter her.... The Foreignness must be amplified, I must strengthen that which is Other (Gadamer). In doing so, I experience how I myself am strengthened by the other person. It is only then that we can begin to approach one another, to listen to one another, to understand. This understanding reaches its goal in action and application, since "my ego is infinitely accountable in the presence of the Other." There are various ways of translating this accountability into practice; facing up to the issue of hermeneutics is the most urgent of them all.

....

RICHARD FRIEDLI

"Culture and Cultural Plurality: Remarks on the Intercultural Translation of Exodus 3:14"

~1991~

I DO NOT PROPOSE TO formulate the issues of intercultural theology, of the transcultural meaning of the gospel, and of contextual inculturation in a definitive and universal fashion at this point.[12] A key biblical text, Exodus 3:14, states, "God said to Moses, 'I am the "I-am-there" [*eheyeh asher eheyeh*].' And he said: This is what you are to say to the Israelites: 'The "I-am-there" has sent me to you'" [author's translation]. On the basis of the translation problems posed by this text, I intend to portray the shift in values a message may undergo in diverse cultural contexts: the Semitic-Hebrew milieu, the Indo-European–Greek world, and the Buddhist-Japanese tradition.

A preliminary observation regarding methodology. In order to illustrate such difficulties in rendering the meaning, I will apply the following methodological procedures:

1. The cultural anthropological approach. According to the cultural anthropological view of the functionalist school, culture is seen as an organically coordinated and integrated holistic entirety consisting of societal factors

---

[12]Richard Friedli, "Kultur und kulturelle Vielfalt: Bemerkungen zur interkulturellen Übersetzung von Ex 3,14," in *Die Begnung mit dem Anderen: Plädozers für eine interkulturelle Hermeneutik*, ed. Theo Sundermeier (Gütersloh: Gütersloher Verlagshaus Gerd Mohn, 1991), 29-38.

(concepts, ethical demands, rituals, institution, values, etc.). These factors make it possible for a given society to safeguard life and ensure survival on the material plane (economically), on the interpersonal plane (politically), and on the level of meaning (ideologically).

2. *The communication studies approach.* The extremely complex process of translating and rendering a biblical text is reduced to three elements/factors: sender, messenger, and receiver.

Figure 1. The communication studies approach

It goes without saying that this linear portrayal of the process of communication is an oversimplification. After all, in everyday encounters the circumstances (climate, race groups, men/women, etc.) cause the feedback from the receiver to the sender to play a role in the process of communication as well.

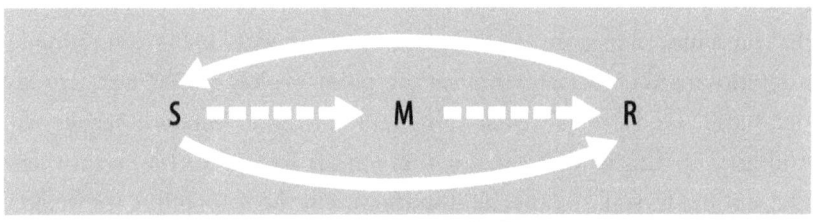

Figure 2. The communication studies approach adding feedback

Communication does not take place after the model of a stone, with its being kicked forward, but more like a dog being beaten and biting back in response.

3. *The interdisciplinary approach.* Interdisciplinary cooperation is an indispensable prerequisite for every type of intercultural work. . . . The following account would not have been possible without years of cooperation between Old Testament exegetes and experts on Japan (who helped assess ten Bible translations in this regard).

*1. **Manifest and latent culture: Enculturation.*** In order to decipher (decode) a cultural phenomenon the way it has been internalized in a given society (enculturation), it is absolutely imperative to describe the content of this cultural element. Here the empirical social sciences speak of denotation. This refers to the domain of manifest culture. When interpreting a text, denotation has to do with, say, the etymology of a term, its historico-lexicographical stage of development, or its grammatical position. With regard to our text from the Hebrew Bible, the discussion surrounding the etymology of *eheyeh asher eheyeh* is still ongoing. . . . Admittedly, the meaning of the phrase *eheyeh asher eheyeh* is uncertain and continues to be disputed. . . . From this angle, our phrase may be viewed as a preparatory, quasicommentarial explanation of the mysterious tetragrammaton YHWH in Exodus 3:15. In addition to the various possible translations . . . , some were of the opinion that God's answer is actually a form of rebuff one might translate as, "My name has nothing to do with it," or perhaps along the lines of a reference to the namelessness and incomprehensibility of Yahweh. There are various suggestions in the newer research to the effect that the statement expresses Yahweh's faithfulness to himself in the practical-religious sense, or rather that it assures the people of God's presence. Others again take it to be a reference to his ability to act. . . . The wide range of views and the discrepancy between the interpretations initially leaves an unsatisfactory impression of multiple layers of meaning.

These multiple layers of meaning are not the only point. The three-word analyses refer to three different ways to understand God and the holy. So we are not just dealing with linguistic problems here, but also and especially with different religious preconceptions and self-understandings. The label cultural anthropology uses for this setting (*plausibility structures*), which has to do with life stories, sensitivities, and value systems attaching specific "weight" to a term, is connotation. These invisible elements make up the latent culture. The hermeneutics of our text elicits three reactions to the proclamation of the name of God (M) from those who "listen to the word" (R).

1. The *salvation history* interpretation: "I am who I am." This Hebraism (main proposition with a relative clause) is intended to communicate a firm commitment to God's permanence. God is intricately involved and present in the fate of his people. This is the reason behind my preferred translation, as indicated above: "I will be among you as the one who will be with you."

2. A statement of *determination*: The polysemy resulting from the variable meaning of *hayah/hawah*, which we explained above produces a certain ambivalence in this statement. The name "I will be who I will be" leaves the receiver of the message in a state of limbo as far as its meaning is concerned.

3. In the context of *magic*: The colorful, somewhat ambiguous answer "I am who I am" is related to the archaic function of a name. A name supplies identity, competence, and authority. According to the "logic of magic," which views analogy and the mere juxtaposition between objects, persons, gestures, or sounds as a relationship of causal dependence, knowing a person's name also imparts power over that person. God, however, is not within people's area of reach (in this case, that of the Israelites). God's answer of "I am who I am" is thus tantamount to a refusal to give his name and thereby to hand himself over to the Israelites.

This brief decryption of *eheyeh asher eheyeh* illustrates the complexity of the process of translating a key text pertaining to the biblical (Hebrew) view of God. It was therefore inevitable for certain value shifts to occur in the acculturative encounter between this Semitic tradition and the Hellenistic world, since the Greek translators had to select one option from among this ambivalence and polyvalence. In this way, what was originally undetermined now became determined in the Greek culture of the Septuagint (LXX).

2. Cultural change: Acculturation. As stated above, we are delimiting ourselves to the problems of communicating and translating text into various different cultural contexts. This is not the place, therefore, to analyze the historic phases and various modalities of contact between the biblical-Jewish-Hebrew milieu and the Hellenistic culture and its linguistic potential. [Rather, our aim is simply]—on the basis of Exodus 3:14—to illustrate the phenomena of acculturation in the process of translation from the Semitic culture to the Hellenistic one. Schematically, this would look as follows:

The participial form of the Greek verb "to be" makes it possible to accommodate certain aspects of the Hebrew connotation, and especially the ongoing presence. The Greek verb "to be" also allows for the development of other dynamics. After all, the Aristotelian philosophy of being comprises the aspect of potentiality (*dynamis* and *energeia*).

When an Exodus text is translated from its original Hebrew enculturation into the Greek of the Septuagint, the cultural context changes. The translation

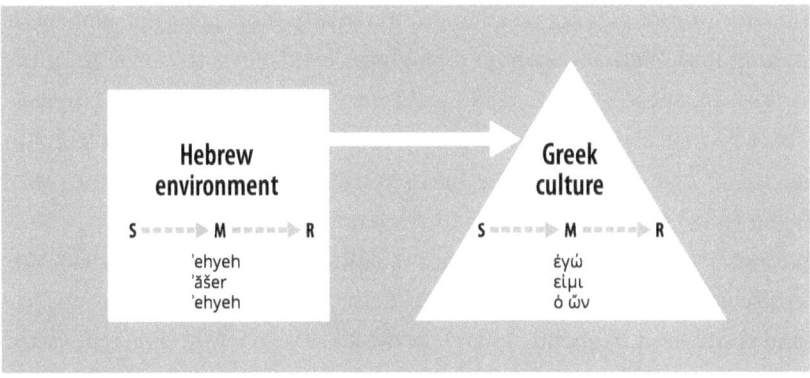

Figure 3. Translating from Hebrew environment to Greek culture

signifies not only a transition from the family of Semitic peoples and languages to the Indo-European language group, but also a shift or rather a restriction and narrowing down of the original semantic field of meaning. This means that the acculturation of translation calls for a change of values and religious perspectives. While the LXX's Ἐγώ εἰμι ὁ ὤν still includes the aseitic component of the Semitic root *hayah*, it practically excludes the aspect of God's unpredictable, yet faithful demonstration of power over and in history.

For its part, the Latin translation of the Vulgate, *Ego sum qui sum* and *qui est misit me ad vos*, lays even more unequivocally the groundwork for interpreting God's presence not so much in the historical sense, but rather in the philosophical, abstract, ontological, substance-oriented sense. . . . At this point, we will content ourselves with calling attention to the even greater problems arising from interreligious acculturation and missiological inculturation as we turn our attention to the mutual reception of Christian and Buddhist values.

3. Intercultural dialogue: Inculturation. It seems that the Japanese translators operated on the basis of the Greek version in their work. They translate Exodus 3:14 as "I am the being one": *watashi wa atte aru mono*. This translation is compiled from the following characters:

watashi	I (subject)
atte	being (participial form of *aru*)
aru	is
mono	thing, person

Here too our focus is not on attempts to translate Indo-European alphabetic writing into Chinese-Japanese pictograms or ideograms, nor is it on the various Japanese ways of reading (literary language, everyday language, polite forms). I also do not take into account the translator's difficulty in having to choose between the metaphysical affirmation of a principle of being (*aru*), being in general, and a reference to a specific person who is present (*iru*). Instead, in this context of cultural anthropology, I prefer only to discuss the sign *yu*, which was used in the 1947 translation of Exodus 3:14 (and is still used frequently today). In the Chinese context, this sign is used to represent the Sanskrit concept *bhava* (the tenth link of the twelve-link chain of dependent origination, *pratītyasamutpāda*: "being," "becoming"). According to the Buddhist understanding of existence (and not just that of Theravada), being (that which exists, that which is becoming) shares three transcendental characteristics (*ti-lakkhana*) that are common to every kind of secular existence:

anicca (p)	transience, impermanence
anitya (s)	
dukkha	proneness to suffering
anatta (p)	beinglessness
anatman (s)	

Thus the precise denotation and connotation of the selected signs shows that not only does the (older) Japanese translation not replicate the polyvalence of the Hebrew *eheyeh asher eheyeh*, but it also reverses the polarity of the fundamental rhythm of the message—an interpenetration between a salvation history dimension with a number of implications for the future, an answer of tantalizing indefiniteness, and magical refusal—so as to express its exact opposite. Using the sign Buddhism employs for *bhava*, the message of Exodus 3:14 would read as follows: "I am an impermanent, suffering-prone, and beingless ego."

4. *Final remarks on intercultural theology.* I would like to conclude these brief cultural anthropological and semantic deliberations with three fundamental considerations: . . .

1. A christological invitation. Based on the attitude to life and the value system reflected by the Hellenistic translation of Exodus 3:14 as Ἐγώ εἰμι ὁ ὤν, the theological tradition of the West has employed terms like *physis* (nature), *hypostasis* (person), and *ousia* (substance) in an attempt to convey a sense of the inexpressible mystery that Jesus of Nazareth as the Christ is located at the point of intersection between God's salvific presence and the historically, racially, culturally situated concrete human form. Buddhist culture, by contrast, does not insist on having a personal being as its substrate, but beinglessness instead; it does not insist on historical permanence, but on impermanence; not on the promise of salvation, but on proneness to suffering. The philosophers of the Buddhist Kyoto school (especially Keiji Nishitani) therefore do not read the message about Jesus the Christ based on personalistic and aseitic presuppositions as European Christians do. Instead, in keeping with the Buddhist interpretation of human existence, they favor the Philippians passage (Phil 2:5-7 ESV) that has been neglected in the West in terms of its Christology: "Have this mind among yourselves, which is yours in Christ Jesus, who, though he was in the form of God, did not count equality with God a thing to be grasped, but emptied himself, by taking the form of a servant, being born in the likeness of men."

Such a kenotic reading of the existence of Jesus the Christ is an intense and promising invitation not to miss out on the prospects offered by intercultural theology: the cultural anthropological three-step approach outlined here offers gains and losses in each case. We may schematically represent the polycultural constellation we now have as follows [in fig. 4]:

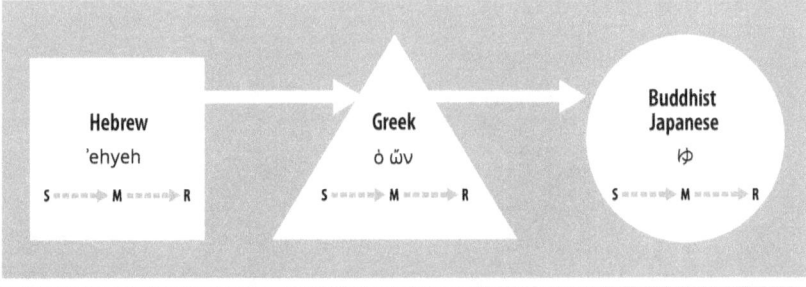

Figure 4. The cultural anthropological three-step approach

The entirety of the intercultural theological process, which we were able only to adumbrate above, leads not to a quantitative enhancement of the history of Christianity, but to a horizon I would like to characterize as qualitative ecumenism/Catholicism. The Christology stemming from a

Buddhological context highlights dimensions in Christ that have been neglected in the European perception and portrayal of Jesus the Christ.

2. *The criterion for inculturation.* A purely formal, literal translation of a text (or ritual) does not suffice to effect a successful inculturation in keeping with the gospel. It is necessary to pay close attention to the denotations and connotations in both the sending and receiving culture. So the aim is not to arrive at a literal (or perhaps gestural) translation, but dynamically to transpose the entire manifest and latent culture involved in religious texts and rituals. According to this understanding, the criterion for valid inculturation is the answer to the question whether the translation elicits the same ethical reaction of hope as the original did in the Semitic-Hebrew communication community.

3. *Asking questions of intercultural theology.* It seems to me that the most difficult question in the context of intercultural theology is whether it is normative to progress through the Western-Greek-Latin reception of the Old and New Testament message, or whether Western Christianity may be considered to be a venerable, but ultimately optional gateway for non-European Christians. In the latter case, non-Western theologians can draw directly from the Hebrew-Semitic milieu; after all, this is the culture Jesus of Nazareth also shared. By bypassing Western church history and the history of Western theology, they transpose the message of Jesus the Christ into their own respective Asian, African, Latin American "plausibility structures." Again, schematically represented, this would mean the following [fig. 5]:

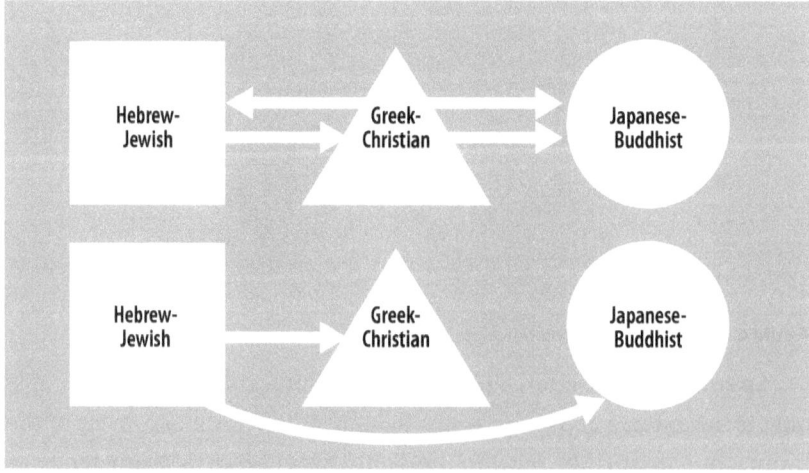

Figure 5. Western vs. non-Western gateway to the Christian message

If I gauge the prospects of "intercultural theology" correctly, then it is all about dealing with such issues that relate to the history of Christianity, culture, and salvation.

....

Christine Lienemann-Perrin

"Mission in the Turn of Eras"
~2002~

In January 2000 I took part in the tenth conference of the International Association of Mission Studies (IAMS) in South Africa.[13] Over a number of days, about two hundred specialists from five continents shared observations concerning the present state of the practice and theory of Christian mission. Taking place during the first month of the third millennium, this was an opportunity for the participants to have a look at the balance sheet and to reflect on the actual condition of Christian mission. This, however, turned out to be a difficult if not impossible undertaking. It became clear once again that nothing is as permanent in mission as the turning of eras. There is always a region in the world where mission is facing a crisis or has even come to a temporary end. In a different region, mission is in a state of transition, and in yet another, there is a new beginning leading to a missionary peak.

Europe expresses some doubt concerning the meaning and justification of religious mission in general and Christian mission in particular. A significant number of people are suspicious of mission as a theological term and as a practical task of the church. Christian mission has no place in a religiously plural society, it is said, because it is incompatible with religious pluralism as a mindset and norm of behavior. According to this understanding, mission is equated with religious propaganda, the inducement to change religion, the invasion of privacy, the absolutization of the Christian point of view, and intolerance toward people of other faiths and the irreligious. As a

---

[13]Christine Lienemann-Perrin, "Mission in der Zeitenwende," in *Das Christentum an der Schwelle zum 3. Jahrtausend. Erfahrungsgehalte der jüdisch-christlichen Tradition angesichts von Schwellensituationen und Jahrtausendwechseln*, ed. Albrecht Grözinger and Ekkehard Stegemann (Stuttgart: Verlag W. Kohlhammer, 2002), 151-66.

result, the practice and theory of mission in Europe today are under even more pressure to develop apologetic justifications for the act. To think about the reality and aspiration of mission in the context of *Europe* is one thing, but to notice the peculiarity and particularity of this context and to relate it to other contexts is quite another thing. In other continents, local churches perceive their external contacts themselves and reflect on their contexts missiologically, so that in today's Christianity very different understandings of mission exist beside and sometimes against each other. Putting these into dialogue at both a local and global level will be an urgent task in the coming years.

Among other things, mission has to do with Christianity's outward relations. This leads to a number of questions: How does Christianity regard other religions, how do Christians encounter people of other faiths, and how are Christians themselves changed in this contact? The self-communication of faith toward the outside, that is, toward people of other faiths, is constitutive for Christianity, and how it encounters people of other faiths is crucial for its credibility both inwardly *and* outwardly. . . .

This contribution begins with the thesis that both mission and dialogue belong intimately together. They are understood as two elements of the same issue: mission is primarily the self-explication of faith, and dialogue the attempt to understand the foreign faith. In the tangible encounter with other religions the missionary element and the dialogical element mutually penetrate each other and together embody the apostolic character of the life of the church. With regard to ecclesiology the connection between mission and dialogue belongs to the four features of the church: unity, holiness, catholicity, and apostolicity. In the twofold meaning of depending on the testimony of the apostles *and* an encounter with people of other faiths that aims at understanding, mission and dialogue stand together for the apostolicity of the church.

. . . Under the conditions of religious diversity within modern societies, all religious communities are faced with the task of clarifying the relationship between one's own faith and the stranger, and to set this on a new foundation. Missionary and religious studies that deal with the hermeneutics of the understanding of the stranger should be understood against this background. They are an expression of the attempt to redefine the identity of one's own religion in the coexistence of religions and, at the same time, to represent an openness to other religions using plausible forms of argument. The exchange of ideas concerning the understanding of stranger as it appears within the religions could provide a new focus in the interreligious conversation and, at the same time, stimulate reflection on the theory and practice of mission in the context of religiously pluralistic societies.

1. Mission in different contexts. Mission in the turn of eras: What does that mean in *Africa*? The continent still suffers from the aftereffects of colonial mission, but also stands in the midst of a new process of Christianization, outshining all mission attempts during the time of colonialism. . . .

Alongside this Christianization of Africa and the Africanization of Christianity, mission on the African continent above all means assisting people in the situation of misery and violence. The mission conference in Hammanskraal picked up this missiological theme: *Reflecting Jesus Christ: Crucified and Living in a Broken World.* . . . The participants viewed multiple examples how African Christian mission seeks to be present in a broken world. These ranged from psycho-social advice centers in trauma clinics and church-run facilities for the *healing of memories* to self-help groups for the unemployed, youth, and women.

In *Latin America* too one reflects on Christ as crucified and risen, an emphasis especially visible in the theology of liberation, which is essentially a theology of mission. Of course, time has changed even for the theology of liberation and its carrier groups, the base communities. While they still feel obliged to engage the *option for the poor*, the poor themselves opt for Pentecostal churches to the benefit of the neo-Pentecostal and fundamentalist currents in Latin American Christianity.

To speak of mission in the turn of the era is probably nowhere more appropriate than in today's *Eastern Europe*. The extensive missiological work of South African David J. Bosch was recently translated into Russian. In no time, the forty thousand printed copies were sold out. The need to catch up with missionary theology is immense in Eastern Orthodox churches. . . .

In *Asia* most of the mission efforts of the past have brought about only modest results; about 3 percent of the population in Asia can be claimed to be Christian. But instead of disappearing from the scene, Christianity in Asia shows signs of regeneration and even numerical growth—as this often happens beyond the churches, it is difficult to measure statistically. . . .

If one compares these examples of missionary self-propagation in different continents with *Western Europe*, the contrast could hardly be greater. In general, there can be no talk of the church's self-propagation or of an inflow to them—on the contrary. The statistics concerning the exit from the church demonstrate a yearlong stagnation and decline. In Western Europe, the seasons of mission have changed several times in the last fifty years. One of the reasons for this (not exclusively!) is the religious pluralization of society. It manifests itself partly as diversity within the major popular churches, partly as denominational diversity within Christianity, and partly as a diversity of religions or religious-like groupings. Although this development has given people great freedom in their way of life, religious plurality is not always experienced as a realm of freedom. The population reacts very differently to this religio-cultural pluralization: (1) It can lead to *religious indifference*. In this case, people are increasingly indifferent to the question of how their own religion and other religions relate to each other. (2) Religious freedoms can create a *vacuum of religious orientation* in the population. Disorientation manifests itself in an increased need for religious guidance and in the search for religious identity. (3) Given the diversity of mindsets and norms of behavior, *Christian confessionalism* has received a new impetus. This can be recognized by the fact that Protestant church members occasionally long for an authority with magisterial powers. One wants to use church law to discipline dissenters in their own church. (4) *Religious fundamentalism* flourishes anew in the context of religious diversity. It manifests itself as hatred of all religious and cultural strangers as well as the willingness to use psychological and physical violence.

To where is the era for mission turning? Is Christianity at the beginning of the third millennium, viewed from a global perspective, in a state of dynamic increase or in descent? The answers are very different when asked to different continents, lands, and confessions....

Like a newly emerging system of coordinates, religious plurality in Europe and other parts of the world provides the framework within which future encounters between Christianity and other religions or religious manifestations must be considered. Crucial for this is the question of the relationship between one's own faith and that of the stranger....

2. The foreign and one's own faith in the biblical canon and the Quran.
The foreign and one's own faith: in my estimation, in the coming years this topic will provide a bridge between missiology, the theology of the religions, and the science of religion. New to this question is the attempt to reflect on Christian mission in dialogue with the missiological approaches found in other religions, rather than, on the one hand, omitting mission from interfaith dialogue and, on the other hand, to speak the word of a dialogueless mission. A new faith, a new religion often crystallizes in contest with an existing belief. This is the reason why the hermeneutics of understanding the stranger in the religions is generally less developed than the hermeneutics of othering. For the foreign faith, at least at first glance, there generally seems to be little room in the horizon of one's own faith. In spite of all these tendencies to othering, on closer inspection it turns out that religions also have their zones of contact with other religions, and that these are distinguished through, albeit tense, statements about foreign beliefs and religions. . . .

3. Mission at the edge of the new millennium. Religious pluralization within Western European society and the internal diversity of Christianity amid other religions are two basic conditions under which mission theory and practice must be considered anew. To try this seems to me to be necessary in two respects: in terms of the relationship of Christianity to other religions and—within Christianity—in the relationship between different missiologies.

Christianity and other religions. Without doubt a number of religions tend to perceive the whole in its diversity under one particular perspective. . . . It follows that the missionary claim of religions is at the center of interreligious dialogue and theology of religion. This may also affect the future viability of the theology of religions. The common starting point for such a discussion about religion could be to question various religious sources about the relationship between foreign and personal beliefs. A dialogue between the religions is simple if it is limited to its lowest common denominator. Once limited to this, however, dialogue is certainly boring and over time becomes sterile because it empties religion of its essential content and reduces it to rudimentary fragments. In the future, it will require an exchange of ideas and experiences between different religions about their respective understandings of the encounter with the alien or "mission." For the hermeneutics of difference, there must be just as much room for maneuver as for what religions have in common concerning teachings and ethics. I argue that missiology should be anchored more strongly than before in interreligious dialogue or in a theology of religions, not least because this is the only way for missiology to acquire the necessary capacity for dialogue.

Different missiologies within Christianity. On the one hand, in religiously pluralistic societies, there scope exists for religious self-discovery and there is an increasing sensitivity to religious difference. On the other hand, there is also indifference, disorientation, confessionalism, and fundamentalism in the field of religion. The latter is mirrored in some understandings of mission. Religious indifference is the main standpoint, with each seeking salvation in her or his own way and leaving others alone. Discomfort with the missiological market place of possibilities goes hand in hand with this disorientation. For a time, religious elements from different sources may be combined, but sooner or later, people will experience a profound loss of inner consistency. Confessionalism fits a rigorously oriented missiological course that is incapable of dialogue and intolerant of other currents. Fundamentalism is reflected in religious aggression toward dissidents and a missiological motivated militancy.

In the years to come, one of the central tasks for mission will be to find a balance between plurality and coherence. Paradoxically, the diverse juxtaposition and opposition within pluralistic societies promotes a retreat into one's own religious or ideological garden, and so does not strengthen the understanding of the stranger and the capacity to communicate. This is especially true for the field of mission. In the churches it is obviously difficult to leave space so that different missiologies can communicate with each other. One of the tasks of our time might be to build bridges and seek understanding between different forms of Christianity in secular Europe, in the independent churches of Africa, in Latin American Pentecostals, and in Russian Orthodoxy, to name but a few. However, this is only possible when one examines the common thread which lends coherence to these different traditions. This, in turn, requires anchoring mission and dialogue in the life and teaching of the church. Mission, as a consequence, will be part of theology even in the coming new millennium.

Analysis

In 1973, as part of his work with the Theological Education Fund, Taiwanese theologian **Shoki Coe** (1914–1988) published a ground-breaking article titled "In Search of Renewal in Theological Education."[14] In response to the challenges of theological education within diverse cultural and postcolonial contexts, Coe develops the ideas of "contextually" and "contextualization." This line of thought, he argues, replaces the prior approach of indigenization. This he considered "static" due to its tendency to identify the response to the gospel in terms of "traditional culture" and so was "past-oriented."[15] Such a "return to origins" approach included a twofold danger. First, it seemingly only applied to Africa and Asia and, by extension, was a special type of theology apart from the (Western) norm. Second, and related, it offered no critique against "over-indigenization, an uncritical accommodation such as expressed by the culture faiths, the American Way of Life, etc."[16]

Contextualization, by contrast, retained the idea that the gospel needed to take root in different soils, but added an eschatological component: contextualization is a dynamic process that opens up both the interpretation of the gospel and the local culture to the eschatological future. For Coe, contextualization helps avoid both an over-indigenized "fossilized theology" and a past-oriented and relative "chameleon theology."[17]

> Contextuality ... is that critical assessment of what makes the context really significant in the light of the *missio Dei*. It is the missiological discernment of the signs of the times, seeing where God is at work and calling us to participate in it. Thus, contextuality is more than just taking all contexts seriously but indiscriminately. It is the conscientization of the contexts in the particular, historical moment, assessing the peculiarity of the context in the light of the mission of the church as it is called to participate in the *missio Dei*. Such conscientization can only come through involvement and participation, out of which critical awareness may arise. But it should also engender that capacity to respond and to contextualize. Authentic contextuality leads to contextualization.[18]

---

[14] Shoki Coe, "In Search of Renewal in Theological Education," *Theological Education* 9 (1973): 233-43.
[15] Coe, "In Search of Renewal in Theological Education," 240.
[16] Coe, "In Search of Renewal in Theological Education," 240.
[17] Coe, "In Search of Renewal in Theological Education," 241.
[18] Coe, "In Search of Renewal in Theological Education," 241.

Note the ambiguity in this definition concerning what gospel is, what culture is, and who the agents involved are. The framing reference and unifying factor is the *missio Dei*, the acting God and the constitution of a community in witnessing to something beyond itself. Coe uses three terms to describe the process of contextualization: *conscientization*, *contextuality*, and *contextualization*. Conscientization, the gaining of a critical awareness of the context in light of the *missio Dei*, only occurs through involvement and participation. It occurs not external to the context, only within it, and only in active engagement with this movement to the *missio Dei*. Contextuality is the end result of conscientization. It is the maturity of judgement that instructs the church where and how to participate in the *missio Dei*. Contextualization is the embodiment of this "capacity to respond." This leads Coe not to speak of contextualization alone, but of "contextuality-contextualization." It is an "ongoing process, fitting for the pilgrim people," one which "must be open constantly to the painful process of de-contextualization, for the sake of re-contextualization."[19]

The point of referring to Coe here is twofold. First, to what extent do contemporary theories of contextualization retain the eschatological element that Coe posited as the key difference between contextualization and indigenization? Without question, the idea that the gospel (and the biblical text) criticizes culture remains, but the base dynamic of contextuality-contextualization often fails to appear. For example, Scott Moreau's programmatic definition understands contextualization to be "the process whereby Christians adapt the forms, content, *and* praxis of the Christian faith so as to communicate it to the minds and hearts of people with other cultural backgrounds."[20] Moreau understands this as "*a two-way process in which all sides contribute*," meaning that contextualization occurs "*with* those in the receptor culture(s) rather than *for* them," and that the Christian/missionary learns also "how to be more Christian in our own context."[21] One might ask, however, whether this account of the double agency is sufficient to offset the perpetual temptation of a dominant against a weaker voice in

---

[19]Coe, "In Search of Renewal in Theological Education," 242, 243.
[20]A. Scott Moreau, "Contextualization That Is Comprehensive," *Missiology* 34 (2006): 325.
[21]Moreau, "Contextualization That Is Comprehensive," 327, referring here to Darrell L. Whiteman, "Contextualization: The Theory, the Gap, the Challenge," *International Bulletin of Missionary Research* 21 (1997): 4.

contextualization. For Coe, the eschatology of contextualization is found in the dynamic of cross and resurrection, and in the notion of kenosis. It is a mutual self-emptying for the other that invites participation and seeks the newness of the new creation. As a consequence of this, Coe affirms marginality as part of the contextualization process itself and necessary to the expression of diversified forms of the faith.[22] Whereas Moreau's definition frames it in terms of an us/our and a those/them, seems to suppose Christian/non-Christian contexts, and is hazy on what the individual is and what the community is, Coe formulates the process in terms of response, and as both a location and a beyondness. Basic to this whole process is the type of active involvement and participation that stimulates the capacity to respond and so to contextualize.

The second reason for mentioning Coe is due to the absence of engaged reference to contextualization theory by German missiologists to this point. Lienemann-Perrin certainly adopted and applied the concept of contextualization as developed by Coe from its inception, but here she is in the minority. Coe wrote in 1973 and the material from Sundermeier and Friedli appears two decades later. Contextualization is, by then, part of the basic English language missiological vocabulary. However, as argued above, the English language approaches tend to focus on the "contextuality" side of Coe's dynamic. The German concern, by contrast, better aligned with "conscientization," a trajectory which would lead to the development of a hermeneutics of intercultural engagement.

Sundermeier begins at this point of critique. Traditional mission theology concerned itself with communicating the gospel and with developing strategies to this end. The question was not *what*, but *how* to communicate. This approach assumed that the gospel is a known entity, available for adaption into other forms by the missionary as the actor. Even if one grants some form of mutuality in the process of communication, the direction remains that of someone who knows something (subject) talking to someone who does not know but who must receive this knowledge (object). Sundermeier rejects this position because contextualization is already part of the witness contained in the biblical text. With the issue of culture already present with

---

[22]Coe, "In Search of Renewal in Theological Education," 242.

the speaking of the word, it is not adequate to speak of contextualization—one can only speak of "*re*-contextualization." Furthermore, this process is not one of sender and receiver, because the receiver, the sender, and the message are all changed in the process of communication. Each party is both hearer and speaker (subject and object), meaning that a relationship of understanding, one that encourages the capacity to respond, needs to be in place before communication can occur. This, for Sundermeier, is a question of hermeneutics.

Sundermeier, however, finds the Western approach to hermeneutics insufficient for this missionary concern.[23] The problem is twofold. First, the subject this hermeneutics seeks to understand is not the stranger in his or her otherness, but is the self. The importance of the other lies in what they tell us about ourselves, an approach Sundermeier calls a "hermeneutic of absorption." By contrast, Sundermeier asserts that the other must stand in his or her otherness in any occasion of intercultural understanding. Because each individual is who they are only as they are embedded within a community and a history, so understanding requires a living together. Hermeneutics, so understood, opens the self beyond its own egocentrism, allowing it to meet the other as the other. Second, hermeneutics within the Western tradition focused on text and words. This suffers from the same temptation toward control and the reduction of what is different to something familiar. Because peoples of other cultures and religions express themselves through different media, a hermeneutics of the foreign/foreigner needs to account for a variety of media. Understanding is grounded in language, but this does not mean that the word always has priority. A hermeneutics for understanding the peoples of foreign cultures and religions will focus: first, on the symbols that are used, the myths and rituals; second, on the dimension of the human body and the local medical systems; third, on the arts.

Sundermeier's definition of hermeneutics is participatory and oriented to communal life. Where the temptation to understand the other only in terms of the self turns the other into an abstraction, an intercultural hermeneutic expects a form of exposure that strips away the ego and its controls.

---

[23]For a more detailed development of Sundermeier's hermeneutic of difference, see David W. Congdon, "Emancipatory Intercultural Hermeneutics: Interpreting Theo Sundermeier's Differenzhermeneutik," *Mission Studies* 33 (2016): 127-46.

This requires that each give the other sufficient space to live and grow. The hermeneutical process, in other words, begins by living together in "convivency" or celebration. Such communal life occurs not within an arrangement of helper and receiver. True communion means giving and taking in mutual relation. This is the form mission takes: "an invitation to the eternal feast and may only be regarded as an invitation. It is tied into the framework of the threefold design of convivence, i.e., it is done in the attitude of solidarity, sharing, learning and celebrating within the horizon, and from the perspective, of the poor and those living on the fringe (Lk 14:23)."[24] Should a community of faith gather out of this, it will do so as a community that remains in this mutually defining relationship with the other.

Sundermeier's position is a significant shift from more active definitions of mission based in a dynamic of proclamation and clear response (either accepting or rejecting the gospel). While "understanding" may well be a too passive end, the Friedli reading illustrates something of its significance in the attempt to translate one biblical text. Like Sundermeier, Friedli finds response a necessary element in the process of communication, and this directs attention to cultural anthropology and hermeneutics. Even the initial attempt to understand Exodus 3:14 in the context of Judaism raises not simply linguistic but religious issues. This variety is capable of being expressed through the "polyvalence" of the phrase, the capacity of the language itself to carry multiple meanings. When translating the polyvalent sense into Greek and Latin, the meaning shifts according to the capacity of the receptor language itself and the conceptual range present within that culture. This first change in meaning is important because in addressing the Japanese translation of Exodus 3:14, these translators used the Greek as the basis. Interacting with Greek language for "being" meant that the translators included a range of ideas concerning the nature of being derived from the Buddhist tradition. Friedli's conclusion is that the Japanese Bible inverts the meaning indicated by the Hebrew. This God within the Buddhist imagination would be "impermanent, suffering-prone, and beingless ego."

Friedli's point is not that this translation is simply wrong and requires revision. It is, first, that language has meaning developed within religious

---

[24]Sundermeier, "Convivence: The Concept and Origin," 75.

contexts. To use this language is to continue to think through given religious forms. Second, these religious forms contribute also to our understanding of Jesus Christ and may well reveal neglected parts of the Christian tradition itself. Third, literal translation is no guarantee that communication occurs—it may well hide the meaning of the text and so communicate a partial message. Friedli's criterion of a good translation is whether it produces in the hearer the same type of hope that the original text encouraged. Fourth, Friedli doubts that the best path for encouraging this type of translation lies in approaching the text though the secondary and tertiary layers of the Greek and Latin traditions, that is, through the "tradition." This imposes a filter on the gospel and retards its appropriation within the African, Asian, and Latin American contexts.

Nothing that Friedli argues will be strange to those familiar with the processes of translation. There is no translation without risk because no translation leaves the content of the utterance unaltered. It is impossible to convey the content of a text from one language to another without altering it to some degree. This example illustrates the problem of the relation between mission and culture: the transfer of the gospel from one cultural context to another is only possible if it comes to new expression. But it equally points to using local language and so ideas drawn from the local religious heritage.

The most obvious conclusion to draw from this chapter concerns the shift away from accounts of mission framed by the language of conversion, discipleship, confession, and oriented toward the clear demarcation between one community and another. One might complain that this hermeneutical concentration results in a too passive mission method. In his response to Sundermeier, *Heinrich Balz* (b. 1938) did not question the importance of hermeneutics but did resist its priority over communication. "Communication (by which I mean the transmission of the gospel through which God spoke to me) must be primary, or else mission loses its unique character as mission."[25] Balz took this position, in part, because he did not see the problem raised by Sundermeier as an actual problem. The hearer is no passive object of mission because she can respond by accepting or rejecting

---

[25] Heinrich Balz, *Der Anfang des Glaubens: Theologie der Mission und der jungen Kirchen* (Neuendettelsau: Erlanger Verlag für Mission und Ökumene, 2010), 207.

the message, and the speaker, while remaining the active subject, also receives the message she speaks. However, while true, this observation stands under a lesson from colonial-era missions: no matter how much one sought to prevent imperialism in missions, the theory and accompanying practices followed local (German) accounts of how and where the gospel interacts with culture and so how the body of Christ should take shape. While the intention was for a local embodiment of the gospel, what counted as "local," as "available for redemption," was determined by another cultural experience. A range of expectations governed accepted forms of conversion, discipleship, and the visibility of the community of faith. It is not sufficient, in other words, to affirm that a hearer responds and a speaker also hears. As Coe argued, it is necessary to encourage the capacity of local response, and this occurs only through participation in the context so that both speaker and hearer respond together.

A number of issues follow. First, how does the Christian tradition deal with difference and especially cross-cultural difference? One temptation reads the community of "Jew and Gentile" as having already encompassed all meaningful difference. There will be differences in surface culture (food, dress), but if the church can accommodate within itself such biblical poles as God's-people and not-God's-people, then it can accommodate every form of different between these two poles. So goes the logic, but this suggests that no actual difference exists—we have already encountered and overcome the most significant difference. Should something outside the experience of this community exist, then it does not belong within a community that encompasses all legitimate difference. This encourages an us/them binary. For Sundermeier, this is exactly the problem of hermeneutics within the Western tradition—the purpose of the stranger is to tell us about ourselves and so to confirm us in our established patterns of life. When shaped by these expectations it is possible to exclude voices that do not fit within or reinforce the expected view of the self. We silence voices, silence difference, and in so doing hinder rather than encourage local embodiment and the word of God spoken to us. A hermeneutical approach—attempts to—listen for these voices, recognize them in their difference, and seek new community with them.

Second, the coming into being of a community includes borders, indicators of what is to be excluded. What the community rejects is just as important as what the community affirms. While one may point to a variety of borders (doctrinal, ritual, moral, administrative), the most evident one is the religious border: to be a Christian is not to be a Hindu. But this type of clear line creates a difficulty. What does a local embodiment of the gospel look like when local institutions and social order are framed by a Hindu belief structure and when the language is infused by that belief? This is, by no means, a straightforward question to answer. Religion is not simply divorced from culture. Friedli demonstrates the extent to which even translating the Bible runs in to issues of religious language and thought forms. Nor is it the case that people native to the area all take the same position. It is more the case that a spectrum develops, spanning options from embodying the gospel within certain traditional local religious forms, to a faith parsed through Hindu philosophy, to critiques of these forms as perpetuating unjust social structures (caste). The response is itself pluriform and all in conversation with the religious heritage. With a hermeneutical approach, the community of faith is a place of living together and celebration. It is not for the community to deny, but to point beyond itself and so to become the community of the new creation. The border forms where this community is denied. To cite Sundermeier, "the one who celebrates with me is my neighbour—but the one who denies the celebration refuses to give the community its due respect."[26]

Third, this widens the spectrum of mission. Insofar as it seeks a diverse array of voices, so it listens to the questions posed by those voices. For example, Sundermeier advances the ecological concern, which has become a key focus within more recent non-Western mission theologies. The range of theological ideas expands as the body of Christ works through these questions, and so do the ways in which these ideas find form: dance, art, healing, ritual, myth, liturgy. It also expands the methods available for the study of mission. Friedli defines intercultural theology as "that scientific discipline concerned with God and the offer of salvation which operates in a given culture without absolutizing it."[27] Its methods depend on the social context of a particular local environment, meaning that it does not dispense with

---

[26]Sundermeier, "Convivence," 69.
[27]Richard Friedli, "Intercultural Theology," in *Dictionary of Mission: Theology, History, Perspectives*, ed. Karl Müller et al. (Maryknoll, NY: Orbis Books, 1997), 221.

the methods common within Western culture, but requires that "critical examination be applied also to the total process of intercultural, innerecclesiastic, and interreligious communication in which the West is only one of the participants."[28] Simply stated, the shift away from conversionistic accounts of mission is not due to a lack of interest in conversion. It is due to a shift in the dominant voice. No longer does Western Christianity have the first and last say, even if that voice is shrouded in the language of contextualization. Now the greater concern is with listening and speaking and being converted together toward something new—even while being confirmed in our localness.

This is the key point developed through the Lienemann-Perrin text. The days when mission might be defined simply as the sending of a professional missionary from the Christian West to the non-Christian East are long gone. While echoes of this approach no doubt remain among certain communities, the reality is much more diverse and particular. No single mission theory or practice exists. Rather, the forms and definitions of mission develop in relation to the embodiment of the faith in different political and religious contexts. How one thinks about mission in Europe differs—often to an extreme degree—from how communities in Africa view the same theme. This is because, as Lienemann-Perrin develops, mission is the church in its movement toward that which exists beyond its walls. Nor is this movement secondary to the faith. It is, to cite, "constitutive for Christianity." Dialogue with the other and with difference belongs to the gospel itself, and so to the embodiment of the faith. One big difference between this position and those held in the past lay in the supposed possibility of previous generations to be nonmissionary. Because difference was conceived only in limited cultural terms (as opposed to gender, economic, and religious), it was thought possible not to confront difference and to draw that into the life of the church. Today, no modern society exists without having to account for ranging social, cultural, and religious differences—even if that response is xenophobia and rejection. Every religious community, by extension, needs to entertain these questions as part of its daily life. This need underlies the development of missiology as the hermeneutic of the stranger.

---

[28]Friedli, "Intercultural Theology," 222.

The flesh that Lienemann-Perrin puts on these bones includes identifying how mission takes place in different cultural contexts. This is remarkable for the multiplicity of questions posed to the faith and the corresponding forms of response. It equally speaks to what occurs if local communities fail to respond. With reference to the church in Europe, the development in (Christian) religious indifference, confessionalism, and fundamentalism, all point to a failure of missionary witness and to the variety of contractions that occur when the actual, painful, and joyful encounters with difference fail to inform the life of the community. Alternately stated, no community stands still. Should the Christian community not engage with the changed context, it has fateful consequences for the inward life of the church. Developing a hermeneutic of the stranger underlies missionary engagement in this pluralist world.

As a final point regarding Lienemann-Perrin, she is the first female professor of missiology appointed within the German-language universities. The dating is significant. If the recognition of diversity of voice and its importance was recognized among missiologists in the early 1960s, it still took thirty years before the German language professorial ranks included gender diversity. Moreover, to date, gender diversity remains imbalanced within the university setting. In terms of contextualization, this observation continues a familiar lesson through the text: it is easy to point to difference beyond us, but is much more difficult to accept and promote difference among us. The danger identified by this discussion of mission and culture lies in addressing local concerns only to the point at which they might be controlled and incorporated without demanding change. This is not to suggest all demands which occur in the encounter with difference need be accepted and interoperated. It is to say that the reflection on and embodiment of the gospel makes more significant demands on us than we are often able to accept.

6

Intercultural Theology

INTRODUCTION

Though Hollenweger coined the term *intercultural theology* during the 1970s with his work on Pentecostalism and non-Western Christianity, this did not emerge as a formal missiological method until the early twentieth century. The need for such an approach developed in recognition of the reality of a diverse world Christian communion, along with its significance for redefining mission and for understanding the relationship of the gospel to local cultures. An already-existing World Christianity opened the range of voices to be heard. No longer could the institutional lens of Western missions dominate the discussion, and neither could the ecclesiological and theological categories of the Western tradition as these lacked sufficient cultural and historical sensitivities to identify and describe local embodiments of the faith.[1] Theological identity forms in relation to local questions and the heritage of established answers. Apparent differences in Christian form and expression develop out of the actual cultural, linguistic, religious, political, social, economic, institutional, and historical diversity of each local context. By extension, it is necessary to listen to theological voices on the margins (including women, those on the social and economic peripheries, the colonialized) and to a variety of different texts (including art, dance, song, local liturgies and patterns of worship, sermons and theologies, interreligious relationships, health and healing/exorcism, digital and mass media). As intercultural theology looks to these local voices, so it looks to the geopolitical context and the ways in which changing political and economic power structures (secularization, tourism, religious pluralism, neoliberalism, mass

---

[1] Werner Ustorf, "The Cultural Origins of 'Intercultural Theology,'" *Mission Studies* 25 (2008): 235.

migration, ecological crises, nationalism, fundamentalism, terrorism, and globalization) stimulate different ways in which the faith becomes "visible." Communities perceive and relate to the "world" in a multitude of ways. The key finding within ecumenical missiology of the past fifty years, in other words, is the primacy of culture in relation to the growth and embodiment of the faith, and the seeming inability of established theological methodologies to incorporate this insight.

Within the German context, these developments and the hermeneutical trajectory introduced by Hollenweger, Sundermeier, and Friedli, led to a 2005 position paper that introduced the term *intercultural theology* as a way of giving explanatory shape to "mission studies."[2] Mission studies reflects on both "the relationship between Christianity and non-Christian religions and worldviews," and "between western Christianity and its non-western cultural variations."[3] This definition leads to three specific working areas: (1) the history of Christian faith and its embodiment as found in Africa, Asia, Latin America, and Oceania; (2) intercultural theologies as found in contextual theologies, North-South interactions, migration, and so on; (3) the theology and hermeneutics of interreligious relationship.[4] With this extended range of interactions, intercultural theology is intentional in including a greater variety of methods and interdisciplinary competencies: these now include postcolonial theory, discourse theory, semiotics, peace and reconciliation studies, migration studies, and gender studies, to name but a few.

Intercultural theology as a formal method remains in its early and exploratory stage. **Henning Wrogemann** is one who has attempted to articulate a clear definition. After serving as a pastor of the Evangelical-Lutheran Church of Hanover from 1996 to 2002, he became a lecturer in mission studies and the science of religion at the Missionsseminar Hermannsburg (Hermannsburg Mission Seminary). His doctoral dissertation at the University of Heidelberg (1995) examined the relationship of mission and religion within twentieth-century German systematic theology, and his Habilitation dealt

---

[2] This position paper was produced conjointly by the mission and religious studies section of the Wissenschaftliche Gesellschaft für Theologie (Academic Association for Theology) and the Deutsche Gesellschaft für Missionswissenschaft (German Society for Mission Studies) and later appeared in English as "Mission Studies as Intercultural Theology and Its Relationship to Religious Studies," *Mission Studies* 25 (2008): 103-8.
[3] "Mission Studies as Intercultural Theology," 106.
[4] "Mission Studies as Intercultural Theology," 107.

with the "call to Islam" within international Sunni discourse (2005). In 2007, Wrogemann was appointed professor at the Protestant University Wuppertal–Bethel in the field of the science of religion and intercultural theology.

Wrogemann's text addresses head on the relationship between intercultural theology and mission studies. Intercultural theology developed not simply due to the pressures of secular universities, but as a result of problems internal to mission studies itself. The lessons of colonialization and the role played by Christian missions within this need to be learned. The global growth of the faith is to be celebrated. The bourgeoning diversity of missionary theologies, rationales, forms, and goals need to be understood and engaged with at a critical level. All of this points to an expanding approach to the study of mission.

However, despite this framing of the discipline in terms of understanding the other, a complaint has emerged concerning the ongoing European location of intercultural theology as a method. **Heike Walz**, professor for intercultural theology and science of religion at the Protestant University Augustana, Neuendettelsau, develops this concern. Her doctorate at the University of Basel (2005) examined the role of gender and ecclesiology in ecumenical discussions. From 2005 to 2009 she taught at the Instituto Universitario ISEDET in Buenos Aires, Argentina, and then served as junior professor for feminist theology and gender research at the Protestant University Wuppertal–Bethel (2009–2016). On completion of her Habilitation at the University of Berlin (2016) dealing with human rights in religion and society in Argentina, she became the first woman appointed to a professorial chair in the field of intercultural theology in Germany.

The reading from Walz tests the location of intercultural theology by drawing insights from world Christianity. She questions the extent to which theologies from the Global South might be characterized as "contextual" while those issuing from Europe and North America produce normative metatheories. Do theological reflections beyond Europe contribute also to the theoretical framework of intercultural theology? To so include perspectives out of the Global South as informing intercultural theology means, for example, questioning the global economy. Though this often finds theological supports, it includes evident damaging consequences for indigenous peoples, the poor, and the environment.

The above two readings consider more the methodological issues underlying intercultural theology. **Andreas Feldtkeller's** contribution illustrates the significance of intercultural theology for reframing some of the most difficult missiological questions—in this case religious freedom. Feldtkeller wrote his PhD in New Testament studies and considered the religious background of the gospel within the context of ancient Syria. This study, later published as two separate books, dealt with questions of inculturation, pluralism, and syncretism and resulted in his becoming interested in mission studies.[5] From 1992 to 1995, Feldtkeller served as the pastor of a German congregation in Amman (Jordan), and as a guest professor at the Royal Institute for Inter-Faith Studies in Amman (1994 to 1996). He returned to Germany in 1996 and wrote his Habilitation on the relation between Christians of Arabic background and Muslims in Palestine.[6] In 1999, he was appointed as professor for the science of religion and mission studies at the Humboldt University in Berlin.

As stated, the Feldtkeller text deals with the theme of religious freedom. He begins by identifying three ways religion is often transferred or transmitted within the history of religions. First, within an ethnic group, religion is transferred through the succession of generations. Second, in a political setting, force becomes the main method of religious transference should the leadership seek religious homogenization. Third, religions that make universal truth claims transcend ethnic, cultural, social, and political boundaries through missionary activities. Such missionary transmission is only possible within an environment with a certain measure of freedom, allowing for both the possibility of proclamation and conversion. This leads Feldtkeller to relate mission theology to democratic theory and to make the argument that religious missions contribute to civil society more than threaten it. Mission is necessary to maintain plurality and to prevent a homogenization that would lead to a constricting rule of common sense. Feldtkeller argues for the preservation of the term *mission* and the cause of mission studies.

---

[5] Andreas Feldtkeller, *Im Reich der Syrischen Göttin: Eine religiös plurale Kultur als Umwelt des frühen Christentums* (Gütersloh: Gütersloher Verlagshaus, 1994); Andreas Feldtkeller, *Identitätssuche des syrischen Urchristentums: Mission, Inkulturation und Pluralität im ältesten Heidenchristentum* (Göttingen: Vandenhoeck & Ruprecht, 1993).

[6] Andreas Feldtkeller, *Die "Mutter der Kirchen" im "Haus des Islam": Gegenseitige Wahrnehmungen von arabischen Christen und Muslimen im West- und Ostjordanland* (Erlangen: Erlanger Verlag für Mission und Ökumene, 1998).

The constructive point developed across all three authors is that, yes, mission studies has changed. It has done so, however, due to the diversity of world Christianity itself and the need to include a wider range of voices into the discussion. The faith is being embodied in a myriad of ways, all of which seek to be faithful to the gospel. To better understand this, is to better understand the gospel and how it propagates itself.

....

Henning Wrogemann

"Intercultural Theology—on the Definition and Field of Study of the Sixth Discipline of the Faculty of Theology"
~2015~

IN THE LAST FEW YEARS, the term *intercultural theology* has grown in popularity.[7] ... Whereas the older terms *missiology* or *mission studies* continue to give rise to a great deal of misunderstanding, especially among people not that familiar with missionary issues, it seems that the formulation *intercultural theology* creates less potential for conflict. ...

1. Introduction. Let us briefly recap. Walter Hollenweger used the term *intercultural theology* in three of his essay collections. ... Alongside Hollenweger, two other scholars in mission studies and religious studies, Richard Friedli and Theo Sundermeier, also referred to the term but not in a programmatic way. Afterward, and this was the watershed point in the history of the subject, the term was used in a 2005 position paper drawn up by German scholars in mission studies. It was entitled "Mission Studies as Intercultural Theology and Its Relationship to Religious Studies." ... The combination *intercultural theology/mission studies* was deliberately introduced as a double designation. ...

2. Delimitations: Intercultural theology as a technical term. So what do individual players understand by the term *intercultural theology*? Let us

---

[7] Henning Wrogemann, "Interkulturelle Theologie—Zu Definition und Gegenstandsbereich des sechsten Faches der Theologischen Fakultät," *Berliner Theologische Zeitschrift* 32 (2015): 219-39.

begin by considering the situation in North America. A number of educational institutions appear to have replaced the older subject of *missiology* with *World Christianity*. To be sure, introducing a broader perspective of Christianity as a global and multifaceted religious configuration is to be commended. At the same time, however, this prejudices the discipline toward a historical methodology, which fails to do justice to the broad spectrum of its field of study.

In contrast, when institutions use the term *intercultural theology* or *intercultural studies*, as does the School of Intercultural Studies, located at Fuller Theological Seminary in Pasadena, California, it is legitimate to ask whether this was not merely a change in nomenclature without a material change to the field of study....

In the European debate, at any rate, the term *intercultural theology* is always used to denote shifts in methodological emphasis. A number of proponents see the term as a replacement for the older term *mission studies*....

Here we should critically note that ignoring a problem will not solve it. Missionary movements in both the Christian religious configuration and in other religions are numerically stronger and more widely profiled today than ever before.... Missions [should therefore] be broken down according to their intercultural and religious plurality, and they should also be analyzed as to both their constructive and destructive impact on everyday life and on civil society. These form genuine areas of study of the discipline of mission studies, even following its renaming as intercultural theology. The reason is that if mission studies is to do justice to its own claim to interculturality (and interreligiosity), it will also especially have to take into account the convictions held by players in Africa, Asia, Latin America, Oceania, and elsewhere, as well as the validity claims they raise as a matter of course. This includes the largely positive attitude toward Christian sending as a boundary-crossing event, that is, toward mission. Anyone who views the label *intercultural theology* as a replacement for mission studies and who wants to associate it with the normative agenda of "the age of mission is over" should be honest enough to admit that this view is simply irrelevant to masses of players in the Christianities of other continents.

Second, intercultural theology, when viewed in light of the history of the subject of mission studies from which it developed, focuses on observing and appreciating *the broad spectrum of Christianity as a global religious configuration with cultural-contextual variants.* This implies that respectable scholars must want to recognize and take seriously the missionary intentions that masses of churches and movements all over the world take for granted.

I believe that it also will not do simply to place the term *intercultural theology* alongside the term *mission studies*. This would mean restricting intercultural theology to theologies of inculturation, liberation, or contextuality. This would promote a most unsettling narrowing of horizons....

In my view, none of the possibilities offers a viable solution, neither the *new label-same old subject matter* option, nor the *replacement* option, nor the *outsourcing (parataxical)* option. Instead, I plead for the approach taken in the above-mentioned position paper to be followed: to *interpret* the older term through the lens of the newer combination of words. As it is, the new term conveys a significant shift in emphasis; nevertheless, it should still apply to the history of the subject of mission studies. First, therefore, we need to clarify how the various aspects designated by the terminological components *inter*, *cultural*, and *theology* fit together. Second, we must explain what all of this has to do with the term *mission*....

3. Between cultures—on the term "culture." [Intercultural Theology]: The meaning this combination of words represents or is supposed to represent depends to a large extent on the underlying concept of culture. In this respect, models of intercultural theology intending to be even somewhat constructive cannot get around the task of profiling the operative concept of culture.

The terminological combination *inter-cultural* presupposes that an in-between space exists, that is, a space in between two or more cultural-religious collective *we*'s which would need to be more closely defined. The concept of culture I am taking as a basis here entails three aspects: First, I presume that cultures should be understood as sign systems. A *semiotic concept of culture* alerts us to the fact that everything that exists or holds true in the eyes of a particular culture can potentially be or become a signifier. The aim of intercultural research therefore is to take a hermeneutically sensitive approach in identifying possible significances in another culture or in the—gradually emerging—space between cultures. As far as the discipline of intercultural theology is concerned, this means that its field of studies includes not only *explicit theologies* in the sense of conscious reflective efforts, but also *implicit theologies*—forms of expression determining a course of action communicated by way of a wide range of symbolic, ritual, or generally medial forms.

Now in the age of globalization, some might argue that in terms of what things are taken to mean, cultures will converge more and more. Quite a number of theories in the debate surrounding the issue of hybridization/hybridity essentially amount to this hypothesis. Now such claims operate with a passive concept of culture. I must point out, however, that people are always busy staging and stylizing their own culture in order to maintain, construct, or readjust demarcations between outsiders and their own collective we. From the *perspective of discourse theory*, we therefore need to enquire after role players making cultural-religious validity claims, after the loci of such claims, and after the mechanisms serving as or supplying the warrants for such claims. According to this hypothesis, therefore, interculturality and interreligiosity are never just "there"; they are intentional constructs that meet the purposes of each collective "we." They are stylized to a certain degree and either deliberately or inadvertently become instrumentalized in the process. These collective *we*'s are never about constructing cultural forms for the sake of principle; it always comes down to certain role players making power claims through the medium of culture. This is true in an intrareligious and intracultural sense, and also in an interreligious and intercultural one.

We can understand the semiotic and discourse-theoretical dimensions by the way they interact with one another, and this in turn becomes possible once we recognize, third, that cultures are defined by the tension between communicative and cultural memory. Jan Assmann and Aleida Assmann argue that cultures consist of the two dimensions of lifeworld and monument: the communicative memory and the cultural memory of a collective *we* manifest themselves in these two dimensions. In other words, these two dimensions articulate the synchronous and diachronous forms of expression of a culture, or of what people believe it to be. If this is true, then we can engage in semiotic and discourse-theoretical deliberations about these dimensions. On the one hand, cultures are characterized by that which is proximal, immediate, and taken for granted (such as language and manners), and on the other hand, by that which is distant, that which is directed toward addressees, and that which attracts attention (such as texts, monuments and rituals).

Semiotically, we therefore need to decipher what collective we generally consider to be significant. *Discourse-theoretically*, we also need to analyze how the struggles are fought by which people negotiate the identity of such configurations within the culture of their collective *we*. Such struggles of negotiation have to do with the issue of which subject matter and which symbolical forms should be considered to be of prime importance for the collective *we*. They have to do with where the lines of demarcation between the collective *we* and the outsiders should be drawn, and the same naturally goes for the lines of demarcation between the various subformations competing with one another for preeminence. The struggles also have to do with how stereotyping takes place, with how people defend power relationships that manifested themselves over time, how they call them into question, believe them to be self-evident, or stylize them as foreign. Such a concept of culture makes it possible to describe—even if only approximately—configurations viewing themselves as Christian in terms of their origin, history, and contemporary processes of negotiation.

Instead of primarily cognitive contents, this concerns media; instead of an emphasis on rationality, it concerns performative actions; instead of a postulate about some neutral object of observation, it concerns observing interests and mechanisms of power; instead of the naturalization of conditions or phenomena, it concerns raising critical awareness of what has already come into being and of the contingent character of religious, cultural, and social configurations in general; instead of the fiction of authentic identities, it concerns observing concurrencies and disruptions; instead of monolinear patterns, it concerns the complex interplay of various role players and factors.

In this sense, the expression *intercultural theology* conveys several new accents that are extremely significant methodologically, even though they still basically fall into the same trajectory as the older history of the subject of mission studies. Its important and basic ideas include the following: implicit and explicit theology; a semiotic and discourse-theoretical concept of culture; culture as communicative memory and as cultural memory; stylizations of one's own paradigm and of that of outsiders, as well as naturalizations of hierarchical patterns; and theology both as an object of investigation and as a perspective.

4. A suggested definition for intercultural theology. After these preliminary remarks, let us now proceed to define the term intercultural theology. I propose the following definition: (1) *Intercultural theology reflects on the missionary/boundary-crossing interactions of Christian faith witness motivated by the claim that its salvific message has universal validity.* (2) *These interactions interrelate with the respective cultural, religious, social, and other contexts and players to give rise to a wide range of local variants of Christianity.* (3) *The awareness of being affiliated with each other challenges these variants of Christianity* (4) *to keep on renegotiating normative contents of Christian doctrine and praxis with each other in the tension between universality and particularity.*

This definition systematically links together elements associated with the terms *mission, culture, society, religions,* and *intercultural ecumenism.* Let us turn our attention to the individual segments of the definition.

1. Intercultural theology reflects on the missionary/boundary-crossing interactions of Christian faith witness motivated by the claim its salvific message raises to universal validity. The discipline of intercultural theology carries on the tradition of mission studies, albeit in a new guise. The crux of the matter is that the Christian message as attested by the New Testament is indisputably intended to be a salvific message that claims to be valid everywhere. This message testifies to a fundamental deficiency in the humanity of all people. It also extends an offer of salvation that can address this deficiency. This offer is addressed to all people. It extends across all boundaries drawn between different communities of descent, cultures, social classes, and sexes, and whatever other boundaries there may be.

This message serves as the motivation behind missionary interactions, whatever form they may take. In these interactions, people witness to the Christian faith, regardless of the specific shape this faith may have taken in the local context. I intentionally use the term *interactions* so as to be able to denote the wide range of Christian configurations in churches, congregations, movements, organizations, initiatives, or individual forms of expression. The term *faith witness* makes it possible to subsume both well-reasoned forms and less well-reasoned ones.

Methodologically, the circumstance that *intercultural theology* reflects on these validity claims and interactions may be understood in two ways. It is necessary to distinguish between *theology* as a term describing a *field of study*, and *theology* as a term describing an *academic perspective*. Intercultural theology applies methodology derived from disciplines such as religious studies, cultural studies, ethnology, and media studies in order to reflect on the field of study of boundary-crossing interactions of Christian faith witness. Its purpose in doing so is to describe the observable phenomena as multifariously as possible. In this sense, the field of intercultural theology is closely related to religious studies and to various disciplines of cultural studies. The older term *mission studies* covered these aspects very well.

This must be clearly distinguished from the academic approach to intercultural theology in the sense of a *theologically normative perspectivity*: in this second step, the aim is to reflect on the phenomena described in the first step and to interpret them theologically against the backdrop of various reference systems. The intercultural theologian is called to take a stance on the phenomena on the basis of a well-reasoned positionality. It soon becomes evident that this is a challenging task when we consider that it is well possible to refer to very diverse reference systems. Examples may include the history of Christian dogma and theology in its entirety, or, conversely, the specific profile of a particular denominational tradition, an insistence on the exclusive validity of biblical references, or a focus on intercultural processes of negotiation.

In the phraseology used in the first segment of our definition, the term *intercultural theology* undergirds the missionary dynamic of the discipline. At the same time, the term *intercultural* indicates that this missionary dynamic is not prefigured by any geographical paradigms. Today, boundary-crossing interactions take place in every direction: missionary initiatives of South American origin are found in African and Asian contexts just as much as the reverse is true; African initiatives are to be found in their thousands in Europe, North America, Latin America, and Asia. Missionary movements take place in every geographical direction and in every social-societal-cultural direction.

2. These interactions interrelate with the respective cultural, religious, societal, and other contexts and role players to give rise to a wide range of local variants of Christianity. Intercultural theology does not just reflect on missionary/ boundary-crossing initiatives, but also on those forms of expression that come about as a result of the interaction between these initiatives and various contexts and role players. Accordingly, the discipline of intercultural theology is tasked with deciphering the increasing variety of local variants of Christianity according to their cultural, religious, and societal conditionality.

Of course, these three "areas" (culture, religion, society) can only be distinguished from one another in an ideal-typical fashion, since the boundaries between them are often fluid. Intercultural theology will need to apply the methodology of religious studies and cultural studies (theology as a field of study) in order to ascertain the precise nature of the relationship between these entities. Semiotically speaking, it will need to ascertain which allocations of meaning are made possible by the distinctions between these areas. From a discourse-theoretical perspective, it will need to ascertain who alleges that certain phenomena belong to one or the other of these entities, who stands to benefit, and on the basis of which discursive locus such allegations are made.

Intercultural theology (theology as a perspective) will then go on to take a positional-normative approach in order to determine how certain forms of expression of Christian content should be interpreted. More about that below.

Compared to the older discussion, what is new about intercultural theology is that methodologically speaking, it selects a more critical approach. Cultures, religions, and societies emerge as contested entities: on the basis of findings arrived at in the development of postcolonial theory, local variants of Christianity must be considered, first, in terms of their own internal pluriformity. This raises the question: On the basis of which criteria it is even permissible to maintain that such configurations are delimitable phenomena? Second, the aim is to appreciate the imponderabilities, disruptions, and interests that contributed to the process in which such Christian variants (no matter how large or small these configurations may be numerically) took shape. Finally, the idea is to pay attention to the attempt to justify certain phenomena—this has to do with things like invented traditions, mnemotechnical strategies, processes of rewriting, paraphrasing, and overwriting traditions, and the assertions of identity associated with them.

What is also new is that, semiotically speaking, intercultural theology pays much more attention to the implicit theologies manifesting themselves in certain media like symbolic and ritual performances. This research concern closely aligns intercultural theology with cultural studies, religious studies, and anthropology.

In comparison to the older history of the discipline, intercultural theology thereby achieves a much greater appreciation of the complexity of the research area. It is much more difficult to do justice to this complexity under the heading of mission studies and its associated connotations (no matter how justified or unjustified they may be). The term *intercultural theology* is better able to reduce to a single concept the new emphases mentioned above than is the older term *mission studies*. Therein lies its advantage. That being said, this advantage may not come at the cost of a loss of memory as to its area of expertise.

3. *The awareness of being affiliated with each other challenges these variants of Christianity.* . . . Intercultural theology deals with Christianity as a global religious configuration with many local variants. It goes without saying that the talk about *the one* Christianity—as if we were dealing with an even approximately delimitable entity—amounts to a discourse in itself. From a global perspective, the question always is: who belongs to this configuration and who does not, who has the right to assert membership, and, conversely, who denies whom this right, on what basis, and with which intention? Undoubtedly, the driving force behind this discourse in all its global, regional, and local manifestations is an awareness of being affiliated with each other: it is precisely because all the different confessional allegiances, denominations, and cultural configurations of the Christian essence consider themselves to be affiliated with each other that questions of affiliation are the subject of such intense debate.

In many countries, national Christian councils or national associations of individual configurations such as the Pentecostal churches (who in places like West Africa often distance themselves from other configurations self-identifying as Christian) serve as the platforms for such discourses. . . . Confessional, denominational, theological, ritual, and medial differences in general must be contextualized in various respects in order for us even to come close to understanding them in terms of their origin, their praxis, and their validity claims. In addition, it is necessary to pay attention to the many new forms that are emerging, such as the movement of the so-called orthodox evangelicals, or charismatic streams within various church bodies. Another example is the many different forms of what we may designate "Spirit piety," a praxis contingent on the respective local religio-cultural contexts, such as that which is espoused by the so-called revivalist churches in central Africa.

4. ... *To keep on renegotiating normative contents of Christian doctrine and praxis with each other in the tension between universality and particularity.* On the one hand, intercultural theology has to do with analyzing and describing the above-mentioned phenomena; on the other hand, it also reflects on the tension-filled discourses in which the identity of the Christian faith, Christian doctrine, and Christian praxis are negotiated. The validity claims arise from both the Christian tradition (whatever certain role players may invoke in that regard) and from the aspect of cultural-contextual relevance. When people claim certain Christian forms of expression to be relevant in one context may serve as an enhancement or as source of distress for role players in a different context. Descriptively speaking, intercultural theology is tasked in this regard with explaining any validity claims which may be raised in terms of their *semiotic* and *discourse-theoretical* dimensions.

Above and beyond that, however, it is also necessary to inquire into the respective associations with streams of Christian tradition. We may label this the *connective dimension*: Which elements are considered to be relevant? Which confessional, denominational, or other preferences are brought to bear? In what way do these paradigms act as a catalyst for certain processes, or as religio-cultural or possibly even political filters? Which specific authorities are invoked, and how? Which forms of communitization and hierarchization are presupposed as a matter of course? Which media receive special attention? This has to do with invocations of or references to Christian traditions.

An approach such as this can only be *intercultural* if, while engaging in the academic study of diverging theological validity claims, it takes into consideration the authority of the biblical tradition. This is because the biblical tradition is the *only corrective* at our disposal in the *intra*-Christian but *inter*cultural process of negotiation, unless controversial issues are to be decided by an ecclesiastical magisterium (as is the case in the Roman Catholic Church) or on the basis of the preeminence of certain confessional documents (as is the case in Lutheran churches, for example). It is also conceivable to operate on the basis of the preeminence of a contextual understanding of the "good life," or of visions, dreams, or prophetic inspirations by the Spirit.

Basically, the point is, first, to appreciate the cultural-contextual variants, second, to aid them in their perception of each other, and, third, to bear in mind *the interrelatedness between these variants as parts of a multifaceted construct of religious traditions.* There are more than enough hot topics around, such as how to deal with HIV/AIDS, the issue of interreligious relations, the role and the rights of men and women in society and in the church, questions surrounding the issue of spirituality, exorcisms and belief in the supernatural, issues of poverty and wealth, the question of political engagement, the understanding of justice, and many others, combined with conceptions of God's sovereignty, various conceptions of the Christ, conceptions of how the power of the Holy Spirit is to be experienced, questions about the weight dreams, visions, and prophecies carry, conceptions of church, or the concept behind worship.

In addition, it is necessary to analyze how role players from various contexts and traditions treat each other: what the intrareligious but intercultural processes of exchange and demarcation look like exactly. In this regard, issues regarding the respective embeddedness in societal, political, and social factors play a role. We may label this the *communicative dimension*: it concerns the issue of how the processes of exchange take place despite or perhaps precisely because of the tensions alluded to above. . . .

Intercultural theology can also contribute toward ecumenical understanding by analyzing how cultural configurations typically represent *foreign* brothers and sisters in the faith, and by counteracting stereotyping through a differentiated view. On closer consideration, *the* Pentecostals, *the* ecumenists, *the* Orthodox, *the* evangelicals, or even *the* Indian Christians turn out to be fictive constructs. In this way, conventional classifications become fluid, which may in turn open up communicative spaces for mutual appreciation.

That which is considered to be normative is subject to constant renegotiation. The ongoing dynamic may be described as the *missionary dimension*:

validity claims always point beyond a given context, which creates new tension and evokes corresponding processes of negotiation.

To begin with, the task of intercultural theology is therefore an analytical-descriptive one: to observe phenomena within their complex sets of conditions and in as many of their different facets as possible. This however does not absolve intercultural theology of its responsibility in a second step methodically to think through the phenomena and to take a normative position on them. If the intercultural theologian were never to be anything but an observer, then she would take her own position out of the equation with respect to the discussion at issue. This would not only be intellectually unsatisfactory, but it would also mean that she arrogates a hegemonic status for herself in that she regards all the other players as objects of study while treating her own position as exempt. She needs to do theology in the sense of making an academic defense of her own faith so as to introduce herself into the discourse.

Heike Walz
"A Critique of European Reason? Challenges for Intercultural Theology from Latin America and Africa"
~2015~

1. Intercultural theology between the worlds—reduced to Europe? In the 1970s, mission theologians Hans Jochen Margull, Walter Hollenweger and Richard Friedli programmatically introduced the concept of intercultural theology.[8] They called for theology to overcome its Eurocentric perspectives and to open up to the contextual theologies from Africa, Asia, Latin America, and the Pacific. To what extent over the intervening forty years has this call been heard? ... Do people in the South still develop contextual theologies for their own contexts, while people in the transatlantic North develop theoretical

---

[8]Heike Walz, "Kritik der europäischen Vernunft? Herausforderungen für die Interkulturelle Theologie aus Lateinamerika und Afrika," *Interkulturelle Theologie* 42 (2015): 261-83.

metareflections on what *intercultural theology* and *interculturality* mean? ... [Andreas] Feldtkeller raises the question as to "whether intercultural theology remains a science of intermediation that is confined to Europe."[9]

Two observations support this thesis. *First*, the developments within and considerations of intercultural theology have, to this point, infrequently examined what kind of "intercultural theology" exists in regions beyond the West and which concepts are used there to reflect on these same issues.

Second, theoretical concepts developed in Africa, Asia, Latin America, or the Pacific are rarely used. Seldom is the question raised as to how other contexts understand "culture" or "interculturality." ... Despite this, however, one can say that a shift in perspectives away from Eurocentrism is now underway. ...

For the Roman Catholic communion, one can interpret the election of Pope Francis from Argentina as a change in perspective toward Southern Christianity. An awareness has grown within the realm of the German-speaking science of religion that the traditional understanding of religion over against secularity is a Eurocentric idea that cannot be applied to contexts beyond the West. ...

Studies in World Christianity have, in a threefold way, encouraged this turn away from a Eurocentric understanding of non-European expressions of Christianity. *First,* these studies describe different expressions of Christianity in the six continents of Africa, Asia, Latin America, Pacific, North America, and Europe in a balanced relationship to one another. Europe is decentralized because European Christianity is now understood as a contextual variant of global Christianity. *Second,* female and male missiologists and theologians from different continents work together in North-South cooperations. *Third,* studies in the field of world Christianity try to open spaces for understanding the immense diversity of Pentecostal and charismatic Christianity in Africa and Asia. Even unfamiliar, awkward and, in Western and European eyes, obnoxious phenomena should be understood as independent forms of Christianity, and these should not too swiftly be evaluated according to the normative standards of Occidental and dogmatic theology.

These three aspects of the concept of *world Christianity* shape my reflections on intercultural theology. ... In what follows, I focus on three main

---

[9]Andreas Feldtkeller, "Missionswissenschaft und Interkulturelle Theologie: Eine Verhältnisbestimmung," *Theologische Literaturzeitung* 138 (2013): 242.

questions, and in so doing I intend to reflect on the concept of intercultural theology in relation to two key areas of concern. One key concern is that of the *theological area*: What theological challenges does the Global South pose for northern discourse concerning intercultural theology? The second key concern is the *methodological area*. To what extend does intercultural theology engage in a "critique of European reason"? How do contextual theologies of the Global South relate to their own and to other contexts, such as the European context? What contribution do they make in mediating between different forms of Christianity, of cultures and religions? To what extent do they contribute to the development of a theory of theology's interculturality?

I will apply these questions to two examples: The first example from Latin America concerns the challenges of contextual *Andean theologies* in Bolivia and Peru. Harmony is the main feature in these. The second example, taken from Africa, concerns the challenge posed by *postcolonial* theory as exemplified by Musa W. Dube from Botswana. This concept is takes more of a confrontative-provocative direction.

2. Interculturality within Andean theology. It is first necessary to say something about the term *Andean theology* itself. The Andean languages *Quechua* and *Aymara* do not have abstract words like *indigenous, religion, god, spirit,* or *soul*. As a consequence, terms like *Andean theology* and *Andean philosophy* constitute an "intercultural deconstruction" and an extension of what is understood as theology and philosophy in the Greek-Occidental sense....

2.2. Intercultural theology as planetary theology: To drink out of multiple religious rivers. The *challenge* of Andean thinking lies in its holistic, ecological, and cosmic nature: to be human means to be a part of nature and the cosmos. As a consequence, for intercultural theology this indicates a change of perspective from an anthropocentric focus toward a "planetary" theology, as it is called in Latin America. Andean theology thinks not using the category of "grace," but that of "ethical balance." Land cannot be thought of as property. And this position is diametrically opposed to the global economical and capitalist principle of profit.

Here we encounter the above-mentioned "critique of European reason." As early as 1994 the economist and theologian Franz Hinkelammert from

Germany/Costa Rica published his *Kritik der utopischen Vernunft* [Critique of utopian reason].[10] He criticized the claim implicit within the neoliberal economic model that it is without alternative and the only way to utopia. Yet, across Latin America, the indigenous form of life, the *buen vivir* (good life) has emerged as a clear alternative. This is a biocentric model of economy, one that aims at living together in various ways and in harmony with nature. With regards to models of economy, there exists a clash between the "Andean" and the "Western-European" ways of thinking. The church's participation in development involves it in this conflict, in the form, for example, of the phenomenon of *land grabbing*: transnational and foreign companies buy large amounts of land. For the indigenous and rural populations, this often means that they are driven away from their land and end up paupers. . . .

3. Interculturality in African postcolonial theology. Musa W. Dube is the most important postcolonial biblical female theologian in Africa. . . . Like many postcolonial male and female thinkers and theologians she is a cosmopolitan migrant and completed her PhD in New Testament studies in the United States.

3.1. The postcolonial African biblical theology of Musa W. Dube. Dube combines postcolonial critique with expressions of traditional African heritage. Her provocative thesis is that biblical texts were used for the colonization of thinking and knowledge. She addresses the following hermeneutical questions to the text: What kind of influence does the reading of the Bible have for international relations? How do other cultures, religions, continents, and countries deal with the text? Dube formulates questions of central importance for intercultural theology. Accompanying Dube's postcolonial critique is her methodological approach. She uses the African tradition of *storytelling* in an innovative way, and interprets biblical texts using myths from Botswana, popular sayings, songs, and symbols. . . .

3.2. Intercultural theology as the healing of international relations of power. Postcolonial critique provokes an epistemological questioning of theology in its entirety: To what extent does theology engage in a decolonialization of its nomenclature and modes of thinking? The German context does not fancy a radical epistemological critique of European theologies. To do intercultural theology in the way of Dube would mean starting with a reflection on "colonial

---

[10]Franz J. Hinkelammert, *Kritik der utopischen Vernunft: Eine Auseinandersetzung mit den Hauptströmungen der modernen Gesellschaftstheorie* (Mainz: Matthias-Grünewald, 1994).

wounds," even those wounds caused by current imperialism and globalization. As Dube suggests, intercultural relations always occur within the historical and actual "entanglements" . . . between Europe and the former colonial countries. Postcolonial sociologist Shalini Randeria coined the term *entanglement*. Europe cannot think of interculturality as one-sided and self-referential— rather this was *always* part of entangled relations with the Global South.

Postcolonial studies frame a *theoretical proposal* for interculturality that links together Asia, Latin America, and Africa. The recently published volume *Postcoloniality—Decoloniality—Black Critique* demonstrates the convergences and divergences.[11] Though contextual variants have developed in every continent, these overlap with each other and "turn in the same direction," epistemically criticizing coloniality and structures of enslavement (*enslavism*). This can be demonstrated by the example of male and female thinkers that utter a "critique of European reason."

The literary scholar Gayatri Spivak from India/United States of America is one of the most important English-language representatives of the theory of *postcoloniality*. Her *Critique of Postcolonial Reason* deals with the topic of *Othering*. . . : the "civilized" European subject constituted itself through a negative distinction from "non-Western figures."[12] In terms of Latin American theories of *decoloniality* one has to mention Walter Mignolo from Argentina/United States of America. In his book *Epistemischer Ungehorsam* [*Epistemic Disobedience*], he pleads for a disentanglement from "Western thinking" by renouncing the "coloniality of power, thinking and being."[13] Mignolo understands coloniality as the "dark side" of European modernity, the one that is most hidden. The political scientist Achille Mbembe from Cameroon/South Africa coined the term *black critique*. In her *Critique of Black Reason*, she forwarded the thesis that global capitalism developed out of the slave trade.[14] The figure of the "negro" as human commodity is now spreading out globally toward subaltern humanity, a phenomenon she calls "*the world becoming Black*."

---

[11]Sabine Broeck and Carsten Junker, eds., *Postcoloniality–Decoloniality–Black Critique: Joints and Fissures* (Frankfurt: Campus Verlag, 2015).
[12]Gayatri Chakravorty Spivak, *A Critique of Postcolonial Reason: Toward a History of the Vanishing Present* (Cambridge, MA: Harvard University Press, 1999).
[13]Walter D. Mignolo, *Epistemischer Ungehorsam: Rhetorik der Moderne, Logik der Kolonialität und Grammatik der Dekolonialität* (Wien: Turia + Kant, 2016).
[14]Achille Mbembe, *Critique of Black Reason* (Durham, NC: Duke University Press, 2017).

In each case and with its own accent, postcolonial, decolonial, or black critique has been formulated over against "European reason." Postcolonial theologies are informed by these intercultural metareflections from the Global South in entanglement with the global North.

This exemplary debate of potential contributions to an intercultural theology helps nuance the often characterized image of liberation theologies from Latin America and the reconciling theologies of inculturation in Africa. In our examples the harmonic and integrative contribution stems from Latin America while the confrontative and provocative, liberating approach stems from Africa. . . .

4. Intercultural theology "between corn beer and lemonade." Intercultural theology "between the worlds" could be further developed by using the following impulses from the Global South:

- Intercultural theology in a planetary perspective would take as its starting point human existence as part of nature and cosmos.

- Intercultural theology cannot be a one-sided development from within Europe, but it is always part of the often-overlooked *entangled* relations with the Global South.

- In Andean and African postcolonial perspective, the search for harmony and healing of international power relations is an important element of intercultural relations.

- These relations demand that intercultural theology exposes itself to postcolonial, decolonial, or black critique theoretically and theologically.

- One has to reflect on the extent to which interculturality is constituent for theology as a whole and in what way German speaking theology could be called a theology "drinking from various religious rivers."

- The term *culture* would have to remain open to non-European understandings that often do not differentiate between the profane and the religious, between nature and culture.

For further reflections two steps are important: first, one has to raise questions concerning the "critique of European concepts" as developed, and second, I want to propose a contextualization of these impulses for German speaking contexts.

The examples of contextual theologies helps bring about "alternative ways of thinking." . . . But I would like to discuss with male and female theologians and thinkers from the Global South whether the "critique of European reason" . . . actually hits the mark given that "the West" or "European thinking" appears as an homogenized whole. Dominant as well as opposing discourses exist within "Western European" traditions. Furthermore, the confrontation between "Western European" and "non–Western European" thinking ignores the reality of entanglement and succumbs to Stuart Hall's postcolonial critique of the European dichotomy "the West and the rest." Andean theology as well as African postcolonial theology drink out of various rivers, and among them is the river of European reason and its critique.

Given that postcolonial and Andean challenges comprise methods of critique that are not accepted by Western academic discourses . . . a contextualization to the German-speaking context is necessary.

Indeed the *cultural turn* within cultural sciences correlates intensively with the *postcolonial turn,* but a German speaking independent postcolonial theology is only of recent invention. . . . I am repeatedly told that postcolonial theologies appear "foreign." This opinion goes together with the suppression of the history of German colonialism. . . .

In short, it is clear that intercultural theology is not a project that can be reduced to Europe, but rather can be further developed interculturally. As the myth of Anansi and the calabash teaches us about wisdom, knowledge and wisdom is distributed throughout the whole world.

....

Andreas Feldtkeller
"Mission and Religious Freedom"
~2002~

2. Mission is only mission when it respects the freedom of religion. Even before the nineteenth century, some considered freedom of religion to be a necessary prerequisite for the possibility of mission.[15] For instance, in a letter written in 1697, Gottfried Wilhelm von Leibniz established a link between

---

[15]Andreas Feldtkeller, "Mission und Religionsfreiheit," *Zeitschrift für Mission* 28 (2002): 261-75.

the freedom of religion that had just been accorded to Christianity in China, and the proposal to engage in Protestant mission there.

But there is more in this text that we are using here as our case study: missionaries portrayed themselves as public heralds of a principle of religious freedom without any specific orientation, without any distinction as to the people groups or religion to which it allegedly applies, a principle that basically declares the matter of religious affiliation to be an issue for which people answer only to themselves and to God.

Flowing from the pen of Americans and presented for an American public, this of course refers to the principle of the freedom of religion in its form as an integral part of the self-understanding of contemporary American society. It builds on the heritage of the many dissenters who emigrated from Europe to America in order to practice their religion freely. According to this self-understanding, freedom of religion may not be one-sided, it may not be an attempt to secure freedoms for one's own group that do not apply to others.

This must be seen against the backdrop of the experience that, in the long run, religious freedom can only be maintained if it is based on reciprocity, if it accords the same freedom to all people to follow their own consciences and to pursue whatever course they please.

With respect to the hypothesis we proposed in the beginning, the real question is whether mission and the freedom of religion are like two sides of the same coin only if we are talking about our *own* religious freedom, or whether mission also substantially relates to the religious freedom of *others*, and in particular the freedom to reject or decline the message brought by the missionary religion.

This hypothesis would be trite and inconsequential if it only applied to religious freedom for ourselves. In that case, the hypothesis would only appear to contradict the widespread preconception that mission and religious freedom are mutually exclusive, since this preconception concerns religious freedom for those who object to mission. Behind it lies the suspicion that mission generally does not respect such freedom of religion.

The hypothesis would only be groundbreaking and only dispel this suspicion if it concerned religious freedom in both directions. And that is what I intend it to mean: that mission betrays itself if it restricts or manipulates in any way the freedom of others to decide against what is being offered by way of mission. This hypothesis rests on the conviction that mission undermines its own basis of life when it employs any form of pressure or any means of coercion in order to disadvantage competing beliefs in favor of its own cause.

On the level of generally accepted Christian doctrine, there is certainly a great deal of support for the contention that mission should fully respect the freedom of others: according to the testimony of New Testament texts, Jesus always respected the freedom of those whom he addressed, and he also showed respect to people who did not receive him and his teaching (such as the so-called rich young man). At the threshold of the Middle Ages, Augustine impressed on the church that conversion to Christianity must be voluntary and that it should be inwardly confirmed even before outward baptism is performed. Charlemagne's wide-scale violations of this principle—he was the first in the history of Christianity forcibly to baptize masses of people—incurred the condemnation of individual church officials and of an ecclesiastical synod. The violent dissemination of Christianity in Latin America flouted a clearly formulated doctrinal decree issued by Pope Paul III to the effect that mission should proceed by way of proclamation and good example. It is not as if Paul said anything new in this decree; he simply summarized the existing doctrinal tradition of the church. Even the grand mission-theory models from the New Imperialism period did not sanction any mission methods fundamentally deviating from this tradition.

It cannot be denied, however, that in practice, the dissemination efforts of Christianity often took on a completely different format—we should not and may not sugarcoat that aspect in any way, shape, or form. But it is important to remember that violations of religious freedom committed in the course of mission always contradicted accepted Christian doctrine.

This assigns a critical potential to the hypothesis of the link between mission and the freedom of religion over against the factual history of Christian expansion. It calls attention to the often great disparity between the course mission should have pursued simply on the basis of its own teaching, and what actually happened. In particular, it sensitizes us to an overly close association between mission and power, to the abuse of power which restricts the freedom of religion of others.

This raises the question as to what is meant in this hypothesis by *mission*: How should the term be defined in order for the hypothesis to be declared valid? Is this just an empty ideal of mission, or does it correspond to an actual reality?

My point of departure in these deliberations is neither a purely descriptive nor a purely normative definition of mission, but rather an analytical one. I see mission as a phenomenon occurring in a number of different religions, and I believe that we can only grasp its significance for the history of humanity when we pay attention to its plurality: the concurrence of a range of missions often competing for the same people. Key for such an analytical definition of mission is the description of certain structural characteristics of mission that distinguish it from other forms of the transmission of religion with different structural characteristics.

I have already proposed such an analytical definition of mission elsewhere, and so I cite that definition in an abbreviated format only: the term *mission* takes shape by distinction from two other basic types of the transmission of religion, namely (1) the transmission of religion within the framework of a community of descent, and (2) the transmission of religion within the framework of expanding political rule.

In contrast to the two other basic types, mission is chiefly defined as the transmission of religion with no consideration for people's affiliation to communities of descent, motivated by the conviction that all people share a common existence as human beings and that what they have in common outweighs their affiliation to separate communities of descent. In this process, it regularly becomes evident that the basic anthropological constitution shared by all people is flawed, that it is marked by a deficiency. The goal of the message passed on in mission is to address this deficiency: since all people have this deficiency in common, they should also all be informed as to how they can be liberated from it. Mission addresses and invites people to make a decision to accept this message. For this reason, the transmission of religion in mission typically has a different social form to the other two basic types: since mission calls on people to make a decision as individuals, it follows that mission in the actual sense only wins individuals for the religion in question. It is only possible to win whole communities of descent or other existing social groups when mission is linked with one of the other two basic types of the transmission of religion: when the conversion of one family member leads to the conversion of the entire family, or when the conversion of a political ruler prompts the entire population to accept the religion in question.

The advantage of such a definition of mission is that it makes it possible clearly to distinguish between three different intentions behind the transmission of religion, each of which consequently gives rise to a certain manner of transmission: the intention to preserve within the community of descent the traditions that sustain the life of the community of descent; the intention to bring to bear within the political domain those religious principles that also serve to legitimize the political power; and of course the intention to make known to all people the solution to the deficiency that is common to all people.

Other forms of the transmission of religion will be seen to be combinations of the basic types discussed above. These combinations occur whenever different intentions intersect, for instance when the original intention of mission intersects with the desire to expand political power. The history of religion demonstrates very clearly that this particular form is a hybrid form in that the two forms on which it is based first manifested themselves independently of one another in the history of religion, and only interconnected with one another in a secondary process.

The purpose of this kind of analysis is not to interrogate the extremely problematic impact of the hybrid form we just discussed with regard to the history of Christian expansion. The history of Christian mission has been and continues to be affected by this problem, since people often pursued very different interests under the pretense of mission. But the distinction helps us to recognize that the concept of mission does not inherently contradict the principle of the freedom of religion—in other words, it does not suffer from a "birth defect," so to speak; according to its original intention, mission actually opens up space for the freedom of religion.

3. Freedom of religion could not have come into being without mission. If we proceed on the basis of the three basic types of the transmission of religion described above, then we can demonstrate that the basic type we have designated "mission" is the only one among them with a positive relationship to religious freedom. This observation serves as the basis for the statement we made in our hypothesis: freedom of religion originated at the same time as mission and is inconceivable without it.

When religion is passed on within the framework of a community of descent, it is taken for granted that children are incorporated into the same religion as their parents and that they adhere to it for life. In traditional societies, it is considered extremely important for the cohesion of society that all members remain faithful to the community's religious foundations, and that no one breaks rank. This does not allow for freedom of religion. On the contrary, there is strong societal pressure for people to adhere to their traditional affiliation.

When religion is transmitted in connection with the expansion of political rule, it is obvious at first glance that this leaves no room for religious freedom either. Whereas the religion of the community of descent compels people to remain as they were, the imperial religion forces them to change: it compels people to adopt the religious views and practices of the political rulers, or at least to acquiesce to their outward implementation.

The freedom of religion could not come into being in a world with only these two older basic types of the transmission of religion, or a combination of them. It was only when the missionary religions came along that the idea and practice of the freedom of religion became possible. They created a climate in which external factors no longer determined people's religious affiliation at the outset, but where people were able to decide for themselves whether they found a certain view of human existence, its deficiencies, and the possibilities it offered for salvation convincing or not.

But how could missionary religions originate in societies where there was no freedom of religion, and how could the freedom of religion originate at the same time? One important factor in this regard seems to have been the lifestyle of solitary ascetic seclusion that presumably became popular in India in the sixth century BC. To a society where religious traditions are passed down within the family as a binding legacy, it must have come across as a considerable break with tradition for people to seclude themselves in the forest as individuals or as groups under the guidance of teachers, and to practice an ascetic lifestyle radically different from the religion that had been handed down until then. But by secluding themselves in the forest, the ascetics also evaded any possible sanctions against their break with tradition. In this way, they created the space to be able to make religious decisions of their own, or rather to pursue their own inspirations as to which religious praxis best addressed the deficiency they perceived in their human existence. Apparently, the ascetic movements managed within a relatively short time to elicit a certain amount of admiration from sedentary people in the area (though perhaps not necessarily from the family associations they had left, or at least not right away). It seems that this made it possible for asceticism with a religious motivation to become a socially accepted form of behavior, and that a semiotic interrelatedness between the two lifestyles came into being. Wandering ascetics roamed from one human settlement to the next, subsisting on the donations of food and clothing they received, and sharing in return the basic principles of the religious doctrines that had prompted their asceticism. The extent to which this kind of behavior was socially accepted also determined the potential and the freedom of the sedentary sponsors of the wandering ascetics to adopt some of the teachings they disseminated. From the perspective of the history of religion, this is the *Sitz im Leben* for the *simultaneous* emergence of mission and religious freedom.

It is against the background of the wide range of such ascetic movements (among which Jainism also played an important role) that Buddhism developed over time as the most successful stream. Buddhism significantly contributed to the establishment of the missionary form of the transmission of religion in India, thereby creating societal freedom for religious decisions. In addition, Buddhism generated the key impulse to disseminate beyond the borders of India the principle of wandering ascetics passing on a religion. This impulse had a both direct and indirect impact in places as far away as the Mediterranean, where Christianity in particular picked up on this praxis. What ensued was a centuries-long struggle for the freedom for people to abandon the traditional religions of their families and to adopt Christianity.

It is only when the praxis of the missionary religions has established freedom of religion that religious freedom also becomes possible in contexts where religion is transmitted within the framework of communities of descent, or rather where missionary transmission overlaps with transmission within communities of descent (which holds true for practically all missionary religions). By encountering the missionary form of transmission, people become aware that religion calls for a decision, that is, that religion always allows for the possibility that people might decide against it.

That being said, it is often difficult for people to concede this freedom to others in practice: in places where the framework of the state essentially guarantees religious freedom, it is usually the family that puts up the strongest resistance when its members individually try to make use of their religious freedom to decide for a religion other than the traditional religion and denomination of their family.

4. Freedom of religion continues to depend on mission. The basic prerequisite for freedom to decide against the religion of one's own community of descent is for people to be aware of alternative religions and to be able freely to choose from among them. Such alternatives are given in contexts where they are made available by way of missionary transmission—after all, mission simply means making religious teachings available to people who are not already committed to these teachings by way of descent, so that they can decide their affiliation for themselves. If only the other two forms of the transmission of religion exist, then there is no such thing as free choice—then the only option people have is to stick with the religion into which they were inducted at birth, or, in the other scenario, with the religion which was forced on them by political fiat.

When Christians in Western societies decide to remain in the church and denomination to which their parents belonged (i.e., the religion of their "community of descent"), then this is a free decision, since they live in an environment that would also allow them the freedom to adopt a different religion, such as Buddhism, and since they would also be able to join a Buddhist community within their own society. They would be able to join for the very reason that Buddhism is present in Western societies as a missionary religion, that it is open to receive people who were not born into Buddhist families, and that it is prepared to disseminate Buddhist teachings so freely that Western people are able to become familiar with them and to decide whether they find them convincing or not.

People living in modern pluralistic societies might consider it superfluous for the availability of alternative religions first to need to be established by way of mission. They might assume that it is sufficient for religious alternatives to be available and for people to be able to make use of them as they please.

But it is important to realize that a society in which religious alternatives "are available" does not simply create itself, but that such a society is the result of mission, or, more precisely, the result of mission in the plural, the result of a wide range of missionary religions making their teachings available. There is no option in between mission and the transmission of religion within the community of descent—no kind of neutral space where religion is just there for the taking. This apparently neutral space itself is a result of mission, since it can only be established under two prerequisites that are characteristic particularly for missionary religions and not for religions in the context of communities of descent: (1) a religious community becomes willing to make its religious orientation accessible also to people outside of its own community of descent, and (2) information about this religious orientation is made available in the public domain—not just in the sense of factual knowledge, but in the sense of extending an invitation for people to participate in the praxis of a religious community.

It follows that the attitude many Germans have toward mission and religious freedom is self-contradictory: on the one side, they cherish the value of religious freedom, while on the other side, they consider anything even remotely associated with mission to be politically incorrect and detrimental to the freedom of religion. But if in accordance with this view the transmission of religion were to be restricted to transmission within the community of descent, then this would most certainly sound the death knell for religious freedom. Practically speaking, there would no longer be any alternative religious orientations available, and yet these alternatives in and of themselves create the freedom to choose one's religion; in addition, it would soon no longer be even partially acceptable for people to change their religion (which is an important aspect of the practice of religious freedom).

5. The concepts of mission and religious freedom comprise each other. Reviewing our above deliberations, it becomes clear that "mission" and "religious freedom" were conceptually formulated so as to relate to one another.

We defined mission such that its structural characteristics include a decision taken by the addressees either to accept or decline a message. But a decision of this nature means implementing religious freedom as it was defined above.

We defined religious freedom such that whereas it is seen to be threatened by outward compulsion or by outward impediments, the same does not hold true for inner ties. Defining religious freedom in this way makes it highly compatible with the missionary transmission of religion, but it conflicts with claims raised by religions of communities of descent, or by religions sanctioned by political rulers.

In both cases, it would have been possible to define the terms differently, to define them in such a way that there would have been no internal coherence between mission and religious freedom.

We could also define mission in the sense of the hybrid form of the transmission of religion described above, in which the intention of passing on teachings relevant for all of humankind overlaps with the intention to expand political rule. If we defined mission in this way, then there would be no positive association between it and religious freedom at all. On the contrary, mission would then designate a form of behavior that in the history of humanity has suppressed the freedom of religion like no other.

We could also define religious freedom very differently.

It is conceivable to define religious freedom as the absence of outward and inner religious ties, perhaps in the sense of modern Western individualism, which is at best willing to consider religion only when presented without any strings attached.

It would also be conceivable to define religious freedom in such a way that being free from any inner ties becomes more important than being free from outward restrictions. Such a definition would view freedom of religion as the freedom to meet the religious expectations of the social context, without being troubled by the knowledge of any religious teachings that might lead to inner commitments.

In neither case would mission take the form of the transmission of religion that best coincides with religious freedom; instead, it would refer to other forms of the transmission of religion or even to the renouncement of the transmission of religion altogether.

We need therefore to direct a critical question at the hypothesis proposed here: Was this hypothesis not perhaps formulated in a manipulative way by selecting certain compatible definitions of mission and religious freedom, and by rejecting other incompatible definitions?

The answer to this is that while the definition of the selected terms might be subject to a certain degree of subjectivity since alternative definitions are available, this does not hold true for the issues they describe. Whoever thinks that it would be better to use different labels for the issues we have designated as *mission* and *religious freedom* is perfectly free to do so. A suggestion that seems to me to be worthy of discussion, if somewhat unwieldy, would be to use the label *offering an alternative religious orientation* (instead of mission) and *leeway to consider alternative religious orientations* (instead of religious freedom). Such descriptive designations might make the internal coherency between the two even more obvious.

It is certainly legitimate to consider the interrelatedness between mission and religious freedom to be one created by an artificial meaning construct. However, the locus of this construct is not the arbitrariness of the deliberations presented here, but rather the recent European and North American history of religion.

We have defined religious freedom with an emphasis on its development as a result of the conflicts of modern-day Europe. It developed as a result of the war of liberation against the dictates to the religious individual by the power of the state. This war of liberation led to the partial overthrow of the old structures in Europe. It also led by way of immigration and a fresh start to the development of an understanding of religious freedom in North America that has subsequently been enshrined in constitutions on both sides of the Atlantic. This understanding of religious freedom aims at safeguarding inner convictions and their implications for religious praxis, particularly including possible dictates of conscience beyond the individual's control.

We have treated mission here as it has come to be viewed as a result of three factors: first, the decolonization process and its associated "purification of motives for mission" (which did not only begin in the twentieth century, but has paralleled in the form of a conflict the entire contemporary history of mission and colonialism); second, the drive to return to the mission praxis of the New Testament era; and third, the observation that Christianity has never been the only missionary religion on the planet, and that it is being confronted even in its heartland by a wide variety of rival missionary religions.

In other words, the coherency between the terms *mission* and *religious freedom* came about as a result of the way the two terms developed following modern-day European experiences. Nevertheless, what these terms refer to was not and is not restricted to Europe or to modern times. As a result, the correlation between the terms was not and is not restricted to Europe or to modern times either. On the contrary, the modern European and North American terminology simply allows us to define this correlation. We are justified in describing this—in keeping with our hypothesis—as a fundamentally intrinsic correlation that applies wherever mission and religious freedom (as they were defined here) occur.

ANALYSIS

Much has changed since Gustav Warneck's initial axiomatic definition of mission: mission is a task external to the church conducted by professional missionaries sent from the Christian West to the non-Christian East. The turn of the twentieth century was a period confident in the successes of Western civilization and the Christian faith over against the "pagan" nations. As this century progressed, however, through conflict and pain, but also through growth and an emerging diversity of voice, this confidence and ambition has proven to be misplaced. The 2011 statement from the Lausanne Movement, "The Cape Town Commitment," for example, presents a sharp departure from that vision of the exotic missionary.[16] Mission is located first in God and so in love, a love that finds expression for the whole world. This definition results in a number of forms of missionary witness, including critical accounts of the church's failure to live according to its own message with regard to the poor and marginalized.

Two points are worthy of note. First, though clear differences exist, the expansion in the definition of mission is wrongly interpreted through a simple binary framework of a liberal rejection against an evangelical preservation of mission. The framing definition of mission through the colonial period points to a range of problems, and it is necessary to admit and confront the problems. Second, this expanded and positive account demands different methodological approaches to the study of mission in theory and practice. As one consequence of this, the discussion of the gospel and of

---

[16]"The Cape Town Commitment: A Confession of Faith and a Call to Action," *International Bulletin of Missionary Research* 35 (2011): 59-80.

culture and of their interaction can become rather complicated with the obvious potential danger of further distancing mission theory from its practice.

Nor, as the above reference to Lausanne makes clear, is this expansion confined to German language missiology. Within English-language missiology the favored term has become *world Christianity*, and while one might point to certain methodological differences between this approach and intercultural theology, it is concerned with identical questions concerning the embodiment of the faith in different locations, languages, and cultural mindsets.[17] And, like the discussion amongst theorists of intercultural theology, this shift within English-language missiology prompts Peter Phan to ask after the compatibility of world Christianity and Christian mission.[18] Phan begins with the observation that Christianity begins in Africa and West Asia, meaning that the faith follows no simple course from Jerusalem, through Rome to Germany, then on to the United Kingdom and finally to America before expanding to become a global religion. The best image to explain the historical expansion of the faith is not a tree with a single trunk holding up the branches, but as a rhizome, a plant with "a subterranean, horizontal root systems, growing below and above ground and moving crablike in all directions."[19] Applying this history to mission, criticism is made of approaches that view missions through the single lens of the "sending" churches and their administration (individual missionaries, missionary societies, mission boards), and to the definitions of success shaped by this institutional approach (conversions, baptisms, establishment of ecclesial structures). Attention should instead fall on those who receive the gospel and the manner in which this reception is expressed through local culture, custom, tradition, and idiom. In this history, Christianity is not monoform but pluriform; there is no Christianity but Christianit*ies*. It is this plurality that reaffirms the necessity of mission theology and activity. Each locality hears, sees, and responds to the gospel in plural ways and so it must be spoken and embodied in ways hearable and seeable within each locality.[20]

---

[17] For a comparison of the differences of the world Christianity and intercultural theology approaches, see John G. Flett, "Method in Mission Studies: Comparing World Christianity and Intercultural Theology," *Theologische Literaturzeitung* 143 (2018): 717-31.

[18] Peter C. Phan, "World Christianity and Christian Mission: Are They Compatible? Insights from the Asian Churches," *Asian Christian Review* 1 (2007): 14-31.

[19] Phan, "World Christianity and Christian Mission," 18.

[20] Phan, "World Christianity and Christian Mission," 31.

In other words, while intercultural theology points to a more general shift in our understanding of mission studies and so also to our understanding of mission practice, it is itself part of a wider realignment. Of course, given the negative appreciation of Western missions through the twentieth century, some see an opportunity within this methodological concern to eliminate mission as a legacy of the colonial period. Andreas Feldtkeller addresses this exact concern.[21] For him, the attention paid to Christianity's interculturality is not a new idea related to the diversity of a now global communion—it is itself located within the faith's own missionary self-understanding. This is evident in the shape and content of the New Testament and in establishing "the connection between Christianity's present, historical, and original interculturality, you also establish the connection between interculturality and mission."[22] Mission is not the consequence of a theological conservatism, but of an intercultural openness, a moving toward those who see differently and who pose different questions. Theories and practices of mission belong in multiple and diverse forms to all the different Christian communions. Should one ignore these, one fails to attend to the shape of the faith as it actually exists in different contexts. In other words, based on the premises of intercultural theology itself, mission remains central to this field of study.

This is the main point made in Wrogemann's contribution. Missions is and will remain a live question because the church is a living community witnessing to the gospel within the complexity of histories, societies, languages, values, and cultures. This complexity means that mission, of necessity, will be an ongoing concern, and points to the inadequacy of singular normative theological definitions of mission. The question becomes one of how best to conceive and study mission within this complexity. Intercultural theology emerges as a key option because it is able to set missions within a wider context of Christian interactions and resulting tensions. One benefit of this approach rests in its refusal to flatten the difference that properly constitutes the global Christian communions. Note here the complex approach to cultures. No longer can theories of contextualization trade on a static definition of culture that fails to attend to the different levels at which each culture works, the power relations within each culture, the self-image

---

[21]Feldtkeller, "Missionswissenschaft und Interkulturelle Theologie," 3-12.
[22]Feldtkeller, "Missionswissenschaft und Interkulturelle Theologie," 11.

of that culture constructed through time, or the various motivators and shapers of action implicit within that culture, to name but a few of the dynamics constantly in play. Nor should one rely on claims to the "universality" of the gospel as a way of smoothing out that complexity. The gospel is universal only to the extent that it addresses our full human complexity. If it fails to do that, it fails to speak to the human, it becomes a construct imposed from without—theology takes the form of colonization. While complex, however, tools exist to assist with the processes of understanding.

The danger lies in producing only descriptive accounts of mission and failing to develop any evaluative insight that might inform and direct these practices and accompanying theories. Wrogemann suggests that "the task of intercultural theology is . . . an analytical-descriptive one." But if this is the case, if one only observes different theologies and how they become embodied in a community and its institutions, liturgies, and mores, is not intercultural theology simply now a form of social science with a special interest in the Christian faith and its social interactions? What is the relationship of intercultural theology to the wider theological tradition? Wrogemann notes this danger, suggesting that the intercultural theologian must become more than an observer, and must attempt some, albeit provisional, evaluative judgment on what is occurring. The question remains as to how this might occur in a way that opens rather than closes the range of discussion, given that the authorities and methods that provide the evaluative standards for normative judgments often remain submerged.

One way of moving beyond this impasse, as developed by Walz, lies in drawing other cultural narratives into the theory itself. Already with the original publication of the 2005 position paper, some expressed concern that intercultural theology reflected more a European approach than one engaged with world Christianity. This critique has strengthened over time—but has done so in constructive ways. As part of this caution, Walz introduces non-European accounts of culture and their critical significance into the theoretical framework of intercultural theology itself.

Walz gives two illustrations: First, Andean theology frames the world in terms of humanity being itself part of the cosmos. While this may, at first, appear to be a benign theological observation (human beings are part of God's good creation), its significance becomes apparent on the issue of property ownership.

In agreement with many other Indigenous cultures, no one "owns" the land. If property ownership is the basis of the modern Western economic system, then this theological position stands in contrast to fundamental ideas underlying Western capitalism. To what extent might this observation inform local Western theologies precisely as a concern of the *world* Christian communion and its missionary movement across boundaries?

The second illustration of Musa Dube looks at differences in theological method itself. Can Christian theology be formulated through local stories and myths? This question, of course, raises a number of related questions concerning the interpretation of the biblical text, the relations of a community to its religious heritage, where and how cultures identify value, and the differing forms of aesthetic and the embodiment of authority, to name a few. If one might name harmony as the end to which Andean theology points, what values are enshrined in Western theological models? The type of theologizing associated with Western academic method, in other words, more reflects a particular culture and its associated values and forms of authority, than is the necessary form of theological reflection and construction itself.

Much of this discussion of "coloniality" and of the criticisms applying to Western Christianity from outside may well appear new and even confronting. What do these have to do with mission? First, it uncovers the claims to power often hidden underneath theological positions. For example, how often is reference to the "gospel" used to legitimate the Western economic system and so to silence Christian communities in other parts of the world? Second, it indicates the potential degree of difference when the gospel is embodied in different localities. Difference does not mean simply difference in clothing or food. It can mean very different ways of reading the world and the place of human beings in it. And these different readings will teach us also something about the gospel and the nature of our own obedience to it. In this way, intercultural theology assists missionary engagement because it helps reveal where we ourselves have accommodated the gospel to particular cultural narratives and have participated in historic evils such as slavery and colonization.[23] Acknowledging this is often a painful process, but is necessary

---

[23] As an example, see the links between the ideas of "manifest destiny," white superiority, and the missionary enterprise found in: Wendy J. Deichmann Edwards, "Forging an Ideology for American Missions: Josiah Strong and Manifest Destiny," in *North American Foreign Missions, 1810-1914: Theology, Theory, and Policy*, ed. Wilbert R. Shenk (Grand Rapids, MI: Eerdmans, 2004), 163-91.

as part of Christian discipleship. As intercultural theology narrates this interaction of gospel and cultures, so its basic commitment is that no culture is allowed to absolutize itself over the gospel and so against other cultures.

Within this methodological discussion, and its introduction of a range of new terms, perspectives, and voices, it is often the case that its significance is clouded by abstract concepts. Where does the rubber meet the road? Feldtkeller illustrates the potential significance of this approach by examining the question of religious freedom. Religious freedom is only possible where it is religious freedom for all. This, at once, means that mission and the possibility of conversion and the grounding of religious communities is necessary in every society seeking religious freedom, and that same freedom means that mission cannot engage in coercive behaviors. The suspicion is that mission does not respect religious freedom, that it constructs an uneven playing field. Jesus Christ modeled religious freedom and the tradition of the church followed this witness. Yet especially in the missionary practice of the colonial era, coercive approaches dominated, and this against the church's own doctrinal stance: Christian missions, often using theological justifications (the eschatological urgency of saving souls), violated religious freedoms.

Feldtkeller's realignment of mission and religious freedom begins not with a narrow focus on Christian missions, nor with a theology of freedom—it begins with a comparative discussion of religious transmission and with an account of missionary practices in history. This serves, on the one hand, to critique approaches labeled *mission* within Christian communities but which occur with theologically deficient processes of religious transmission. On the other, it highlights that mission does not inherently oppose religious freedom. More than this, a positive account of mission itself propels religious freedom. It also serves to critique versions of mission and claims to religious freedom weaponized against religious and social difference. Religious freedoms only develop within and are maintained in societies that permit plural religious missionary activities and allow space for these even within family structures (communities of dissent). This is not to suggest that religious freedom requires some form of secular individuality that abstracts religious commitment from those communities embodying and giving value to those commitments. It is precisely as a missionary community that opens itself to the other and invites the sharing of religious life that religious freedom is a freedom and not cypher for oppression.

Conclusion

The Proper Complexity of Context

If one thing is evident from this survey of one hundred years of German missiology, it is the seamless relationship between theories of culture and associated evaluative measures, theological assertions regarding the nature and embodiment of the church, theories and practices of missionary transmission—and the extent to which these all embodied key markers of German self-identity. Theories of contextualization are themselves part descriptions of the community out of which they develop: how this community embodies the gospel, the values it promotes, the rituals it accepts as necessary, those it is willing to forego, the authorities it draws on, and how it orders these authorities. Applying this understanding of "context" in a place other than our own holds obvious dangers: it can confirm our own constructs, cultivate a deafness to the Word being spoken in a different tongue, and blind us to our own potentially destructive accommodation of the gospel. As one clear example, German missions' strong account of contextualization supported German culture's own self-narrative and resulted in a problematic affinity with the ideology of National Socialism.

These liaisons between mission theory and National Socialism seem obvious in hindsight. Concepts such as *Volk* color an entire way of seeing the world. Reference to *Volk* framed the understanding of culture, assumptions concerning normative social institutions, gave priority to village life as bearing an essentialized identity, and provided evaluative means for the relative merits or faults of all cultures. It included, by way of example, expectations concerning the shape and purpose of education, health, economics, religion, governance, and the nature of their interaction. All of this found support in strong biblical warrants and sophisticated theological argument for the being of a people, a *Volk*, and for how God works in and through creation and culture.

While the temptation may be to limit this observation to the particular German experience during an extraordinary geopolitical moment, it must be recognized as a more general problem. Certain ideas (e.g., freedom, democracy, individual choice, law, sacrifice) can come to hold fundamental cultural significance. To call them into question is to call into question an entire belief system or "way of life," with the associated accounts of how communities come into being and are structured. No doubt such accounts include important internal criticisms, but these tend to reinforce the overall narrative because they assume that narrative to be basic. The vision is a totalizing one: to deny *this* account of being a people is to deny the *possibility* of becoming and being this people and so of the *generation* of this people through time and across cultures. The key concern through the discussion centered on the nature of "embodiment," on how the church takes shape as a living community. It is difficult for us to envision a world beyond our own, because other worlds appear "insubstantial" in relation to our own material experiences.

On simple theological grounds, no pure, disembodied gospel exists. To argue for a "kernel" detached from every cultural and historical location speaks only to a range of culturally located assumptions that prioritize a certain form of rationality and intellectual ascent. It is to ignore the very form the gospel has taken in that context, and results in a missionary approach that advocates first for that located form. None of this is to deny the reality of an "objective" gospel. It is to say that the objectivity of the gospel is always its embodiment in communities. In this way, it is possible also for Christian communities to be a countersign to the gospel—to take an objective form which proves the gospel's claims false.

The gospel remains a Word from outside, but only ever comes to us embodied. These are, of course, theological assertions—which goes to the point. What counts as "good news" is itself tied to local social, cultural, and religious questions. If the gospel fails to answer the most pressing questions in any context, it is not good news for that people. For example, Mercy Amba Oduyoye observes how—in their account of salvation—Western missionaries failed to take seriously the African approach to spiritual realms. Simply affirming that witchcraft did not exist and so maintaining a "superficial assessment of the indigenous culture and its hold on the people who belong to it led to the Africans' superficial acceptance of Christianity."[1] To answer these questions requires a complex, lived (conscious/intentional) affinity with that context, its range of questions, the traditional answers, and how these answers have taken form in various institutions, rituals, and social structures.

One might develop this complexity of context and of theology yet further. Susan Abraham observes how, when the idea of culture entered theological thought, contextualization was itself a first attempt to address the "limitations of universalizing modes of theological thought."[2] Yet this very attempt demonstrated the dominance of the concepts of place and time as defined within a Western account of reality. Time and place are ideas, and ideas with a context—they are themselves part of a view of the world and its organization. Kosuke Koyama notes that the Christian faith affirms the "purposefulness of history." He denies, however, that this equates to "purposeful linear history."[3] The latter, in Koyama's opinion, underlies imperialism and "notions of manifest destiny." He concludes that "the image of straight line, the image of efficiency, and that of the Biblical *hesed*, steadfast love, cannot go together."[4] In other words, to identify God's love with one singular history is to replace the gospel with a singular culture. By contrast, God's love awakens people to the truth of history and includes all histories and so all ways of understanding history.

Too much contextualization theory assumes the "hegemony of modern western sociocultural theory."[5] Some might read this strong statement as reflecting a left-leaning ideology. Such an interpretation, however, would be wrong. It develops out of an evangelical missionary experience in Papua New Guinea. The heart of the problem, Michael Rynkiewich argues, lies in an underlying account of communication, one which assumes that

---

[1] Mercy Amba Oduyoye, *Hearing and Knowing: Theological Reflections on Christianity in Africa* (Maryknoll, NY: Orbis Books, 1986), 14.
[2] Susan Abraham, "What Does Mumbai Have to Do with Rome? Postcolonial Perspectives on Globalization and Theology," *Theological Studies* 69 (2008): 377.
[3] Kosuke Koyama, "New World—New Creation: Mission in Power and Faith," *Mission Studies* 10 (1993): 73.
[4] Koyama, "New World—New Creation," 73.
[5] Michael A. Rynkiewich, "The World in My Parish: Rethinking the Standard Missiological Model," *Missiology* 30 (2002): 303.

communication occurs between two cultures: the missionary from one context and language, speaking to a person from another context and language.[6] The problem with this account is threefold.

First, it draws on an understanding of culture as sui generis and unique, and so one ideational and static. We construct big-picture ideas of cultures and this flattens out the realities of power relations, cultural change, and the various forms of relationship cultures have to their own histories, religious heritages, and movements such as globalization. Culture, in this sense, reflects more Western approaches to knowledge and its ordering, than the messy realities of living cultures and their different forms of interaction.

Second, it permits a clean division of the world. This is, in one respect, a classic missionary problem. To cite Keith Bridston regarding a central assumption of the colonial era: "One of the concomitants of thinking of the mission frontier as identical with the geographical limits of Western imperial expansion was the idea that this line also divided the world between Christianity and paganism."[7] Though it has undergone change, this twofold characterization of the world remains in place. The common terminology within contemporary missiology is that of North/South. Though it intends to be a positive designation, speaking to the shifting center of the faith from Europe and North America to Latin America, Africa, and Asia, it fails to address the complex political and economic history behind this characterization.[8] So described, it remains bound to the division of the West from the non-West. When this occurs, the West retains the focus, providing the norm against which other "younger" churches are measured. In terms of contextualization, the ongoing binary reinforces an assumption both of the fundamental Christianness of Western cultures and the non-Christianness (perhaps even anti-Christianness) of the non-West.

It, third, permits a clean demarcation of agent. To return to Scott Moreau's definition of contextualization as "the process whereby Christians adapt the forms, content, and praxis of the Christian faith so as to communicate it to

---

[6]Rynkiewich, "The World in My Parish," 303.
[7]Keith R. Bridston, *Mission, Myth and Reality* (New York: Friendship Press, 1965), 41.
[8]See S. D. Muni, "The Third World: Concept and Controversy," *Third World Quarterly* 1 (1979): 119-28; Klauspeter Blaser, "Multicultural Christianity: A Project for Liberation; The Meaning of the Conflict North-South for Theology and Our Churches," *International Review of Mission* 82 (1993): 203-16.

the minds and hearts of people with other cultural backgrounds."[9] The purpose is missionary: it is the Christian who *adapts* the faith in order to communicate it, and the expectation is that this event of communication is between two different particular locations (the Christian/the other). Rynkiewich describes this account of communication where there is a binary pair of sender/receiver as "mechanical."[10] This encourages a question: To what extent is contextualization a technique to be learned?

Robert Schreiter's positive account of the spiritual and social reconciliation between God and the human begins with a range of warnings concerning what reconciliation is not. One warning cautions against reducing reconciliation to "a technical rationality," to "a skill that can be taught to deal with a problem that can be managed."[11] To take this approach is to confuse reconciliation with one set of cultural values, that is, to shape the process according to the norms found within technology-rich cultures. By extension, with this approach the assumed norm, cultures that fail to value and work within this technical rationality become devalued and no longer equal partners in the process. The question to be asked here concerns whether and the extent to which theories of contextualization assume Western forms of technical rationality as basic. This is one potential danger with the above ideational account of culture and the related binary set of agents. Among other things, it frames the gospel becoming local as a "problem to be solved," and so follows classic Western values developed during the Enlightenment era—including the priority of Western forms of expression and the need to "help" non-Western cultures attain these forms.

The point being made here is simple: the failings evident in the German account of context are observable also in other contemporary theories of contextualization. This is not to reject the range of available typologies that describe general ways in which the gospel enters and interacts with cultures.[12] The challenge outlined here lies prior to the typologies and within

---

[9] A. Scott Moreau, *Contextualization in World Missions: Mapping and Assessing Evangelical Models* (Grand Rapids, MI: Kregel Publications, 2012), 36.

[10] Rynkiewich, "The World in My Parish," 303.

[11] Robert J. Schreiter, *Reconciliation: Mission and Ministry in a Changing Social Order* (Maryknoll, NY: Orbis Books, 1992), 26.

[12] As a classic example, see Stephen B. Bevans, *Models of Contextual Theology* (Maryknoll, NY: Orbis Books, 2002).

the many basic framing assumptions that might be exposed as embodying values associated with Western history and culture—even if the theory itself develops in reference to a context outside the West. In other words, no matter the range of theological supports, something is not "contextual" if the processes, agents, and ends all conform to Western standards, and develop as a normative account available for application in every context and without reference to any particular context. It is not contextualization if the process is not something to be discovered. Nor, as the German example makes clear, is this concern benign: profound consequences can follow for those at "home." Missionary claims are often used to legitimate theological self-narratives, and once legitimated communities become blind to their own forms of cultural accommodation, the violence of conformity to a type, and the political domestication of the faith which results.

In terms of formal theological approaches, this discussion challenges established methodologies for the study of the faith and of mission. The basis of this challenge lies not in an abstract account of context, but in the visible, living, reality of world Christianity and in the nature of its theological discourse using all manner of sign, symbol, ritual, institution, politics, liturgy, mission, poetry, art, dance, dress, governance, financing, cultural artifact, language, public discourse, speech, preaching, architecture, health, education, history, and story. The faith itself calls received methods into question insofar as these methods reflect a certain set of assumptions and values derived from one culture.

The shift detailed through this book, from an account of context located within the German experience to the approach of intercultural hermeneutics, is this question of method. On the one hand, the shift developed during the 1960s as Western academics began hearing these methodological concerns articulated by non-Western voices. The move to hermeneutics reflects an attempt to understand each context in its own terms, and to let other voices drive the discussion. The methodological challenge lies in rejecting singular approaches in general, and the way this continues to affirm the dominance of Western voices and values, while also seeking to name what coinheres across these communities of the gospel.

On the other hand, this is easier said than done. Though a methodological shift, it is nonetheless located within the *German* context and so this understanding of the nature of knowledge and its production continues to be driven by that history and framing structures. Inviting difference into *this* discussion still suggests a particular location and set of rules. First, though the theme has been one of finding diversity of voice, the dominant majority of authors in this text are white and male. The reason for this is historical, and is, as such, illustrative. Not until the 1990s does a German-language university gain its first female missiology professor, and the current record is not much better. Though one might acknowledge proper diversity as a theoretical commitment, does such diversity come to occupy a central position in the conversation, or does it remain marginal? Related to this, second, is the complaint that the hermeneutical approach itself remains wedded to the Western value system. Werner Ustorf notes the Western cultural origins of intercultural theology, and Heike Walz observed how infrequently metatheoretical contributions from those outside Europe are incorporated within the field.[13] Even in the attempt to widen the discourse and to avoid the type of normative claims that often suppress and control this discussion, significant questions remain as to whether the hermeneutical approach develops the sought-after bridges between the West and the non-West.[14]

These concerns alert us to a significant problem, but it is not one without hints at another direction. Already in his original statement of contextualization Shoki Coe pointed to the need for mutuality in the process. This begins not simply with "taking context seriously," nor does it cling to that tired opposition of arguing whether it is the church or the world that "sets the agenda." In each case, the categories of context, church, and world are far too static, becoming abstractions into which we project our own values. Coe, by contrast, sets the whole within the eschatological ferment of the resurrection and the coming kingdom.[15] Contextualization as a process is located in relation to something beyond, which comes to us and to which we are called to respond. It means both a valuing of contexts as the location of God's acting and our own embodiment, and a moving beyond our own contexts in

---

[13]Werner Ustorf, "The Cultural Origins of 'Intercultural Theology,'" *Mission Studies* 25 (2008): 229-51.
[14]Francis Anekwe Oborji, "Missiology in Its Relation to Intercultural Theology and Religious Studies," *Mission Studies* 25 (2008): 113-14.
[15]Shoki Coe, "In Search of Renewal in Theological Education," *Theological Education* 9 (1973): 243.

the mutuality of becoming the people of God. This "moving beyond," however, is not out of context, for this is again to render context an abstraction and to become susceptible to confusing the faith with our particular embodiment of it. "Moving beyond" is, instead, the movement in which contextualization occurs, the movement in which the people of God become local, responding both to the Word of God and to the need of the world.

This is the point taken up by Theo Sundermeier and his treatment of intercultural hermeneutics. Our calling as the people of God is not to subsume all difference. We are not called to egocentrism and solipsism. We are not called to "turn in on ourselves," to cite Luther's definition of sin. Instead, living in the context of celebration, we are called to be opened out of our own egocentrism and to participate in the history of Jesus Christ. This mutuality means the embodiment of the gospel in a community that retains difference as proper to the gospel itself. Or, to again draw from Schreiter, this process "is not a skill to be mastered, but rather, something discovered—the power of God's grace welling up in one's life."[16] Contextualization is the spiritual attitude of the body of Christ before the world as it moves toward the convivence of God.

Because contextualization is itself an embodied process in which the eschatological ferment of the resurrection draws participants beyond themselves and so into context as the realm of God's own acting, it can be experienced as a movement of crisis and trauma. Moving, for the sake of the other, from complex and established historical accounts into this mutually anew discovery of the Word of God is often depicted as a movement of loss. This is, in an important sense, true. It means disestablishing identities and self-narratives based both on an internal self-criticism that illustrates a disconnect between the ideals and the lived reality, and on an encounter with difference that calls those identities into question. The coordinated temptation is to smooth over any potential trauma of theological difference by identifying "local theologies" as variations of a normative and overarching "theology." In reality, context properly shapes the whole of theology. The temptation lies in denying our own location and, in this, to (re)assert the dominance of a particular contextual reading. The feeling of loss comes not

---

[16]Schreiter, *Reconciliation*, 26.

from the oft-stated defensive claim of a supposed degradation of the gospel, of a placing context above the biblical Word. There is, of course, a possibility that such might occur. However, the most recent examples (colonization, National Socialism, apartheid) demonstrate that such accommodation has been foremost a problem of the Western tradition. It is also apparent that the charge of syncretism developed with the form of the gospel as it appeared in the "home" churches providing the standard, and against which all other developing theologies became "contextual."[17] The experience of trauma, in other words, results from the relativizing of improper claims concerning the normative status of one (our) particular contextual embodiment of the gospel, and so from reasserting the primacy of God's Word in relation to every embodiment of the gospel. As one missionary adage holds: the first to be converted is always the Christian and the Christian church. The feeling of trauma stems from thinking that we already are converted, that we already possess the gospel, and so from the refusal to be converted. A theological account of context must be one that assumes some loss of identity, an opening of our histories to the history of Jesus Christ, a commitment to being converted to Jesus Christ as he is embodied in other languages and ways of life.

This points to a significant shift in agent. Part of the concern regarding the potential missionary passivity of the hermeneutical approach stems from an overly activistic missionary mandate. This approach suited cultures steeped in pragmatism, which regarded themselves as "chosen" by God, and was reinforced by locating mission in the command "to go" as defined by triumphalist readings of Matthew and the "Great Commission." Again, the concern results not in the rejection of the biblical language of "to go" and "being sent." It is, as William Carey makes clear, that this reading of the Great Commission developed in terms of the opportunity afforded by the Western colonial endeavor. This historical circumstance as informed by the culture of the period established a particular interpretive framing associated with geographical expansion and a division of the world into Christian/pagan.[18]

---

[17]On the concept of "critical syncretism," see John Roxborogh, "Loyalty to Christ: Conversion, Contextualization, and Religious Syncretism," *Point Series* 40 (2016): 318-30.

[18]William Carey, *An Enquiry into the Obligations of Christians, to Use Means for the Conversion of the Heathens, in Which the Religious State of the Different Nations of the World, the Success of Former Undertakings, and the Practicability of Further Undertakings, Are Considered* (Leicester: Ann Ireland, 1792).

"To go" is not a "command" given to individual missionaries from a Christian West to a pagan world; it is a call to the community accompanying Emmanuel (God with us) in his eschatological mission as revealed through all four Gospels and the wider biblical narrative. Our charge is to read the whole of the Bible as a missionary text, because it is the Word of a missionary God.

The priority falls on the community itself as the witness to the gospel, to its possibility as an embodied social reality. Mission is the participation of a community of joy in the ferment of the resurrection, which draws that community beyond itself and so into history and context as the realm of God's own acting. The Word remains a word from outside, meaning that the community is called to encounter its identity as a matter of continual surprise. If we understand the embodiment of the gospel as something that can only come out of the local culture, then mission is itself the process of discovering local expression. The gospel is not something an individual or community can "bring"—it is only something that a community seeks to embody (or is embodied by). The two questions are related: the legitimacy of missions and the local embodiment of a Christian community.

This missionary attitude helps protect against an undue "domestication" of the message. Such domestication takes two forms. The first, and most well-known, identifies the gospel with a particular wider cultural and political identity (manifest destiny). But there is a second form. This abstracts the gospel from the context in the pretense that it can exist apart from its embodiment. Such abstraction succeeds only in reifying the form of the gospel existent within the local context. In both cases, the problem of domestication reduces the proper "corporality" of the church, its coming into being as a body, to a possession, to a given and known entity. This will always be a temptation for the church, the temptation to propagate a particular lived form as the gospel itself. As a missionary community, however, the corporality of the gospel is an ongoing event—it belongs to the church to be continually coming into being and receiving its identity in Christ, and this occurs insofar as this body moves toward the "world." The Christian community is obliged to be always opening up its own life in the expectation that the promises of God concerning the reconciliation of the world are true. Mission as the body following its head, Jesus Christ, as it is impelled to do so by the Spirit, directs the local community beyond its own closed history and into the history of Jesus Christ: it participates in his mission to the world.

None of this is to relativize truth to the point that each embodiment of the faith becomes incommensurable, isolated from one another. Quite the opposite: the process of contextualization in which difference is discovered and affirmed, in which we move beyond ourselves, is contingent on the mutuality of living together in joy. To quote Andrew Walls, "Christ's completion . . . comes from all humanity, from the translation of the life of Jesus into the lifeways of all the world's cultures and subcultures through history. None of us can reach Christ's completeness on our own. We need each other's vision to correct, enlarge and focus our own; only together we are complete in Christ."[19] Difference and so plurality does not oppose or dilute truth; it is necessary to the fullness of our being in Christ.

The problem is not the relativity of truth because our being in Christ means the conversion of our local histories. The problem rests, instead, in an account of the universal that understands difference only as partial or even in opposition to truth. A certain embodied form of truth is assumed and this provides the normative standard against which "conversion" is evaluated. This was a key problem during the colonial period where, as Hans Jochen Margull indicated, theological ideas such as the christological title of "lord" merged with and justified the actions of Western colonial authorities. It became a symbol of power and not of the lord as servant. The danger of this approach lies in the blindness to (or even sanctification of) violence that is done to local Christian communities, and especially in the disassociation that often occurs between this new community, their history and heritage, and their wider community. To lose one's history is not to change one's identity—it is to be set adrift without an identity. This results in the local community becoming dependent on the identity of another community foreign to the context, surviving only in a relationship of dependence. It is the very opposite of the notion of conversion and of the reconciliation of one's own history and identity to God in Christ.

---

[19] Andrew F. Walls, "The Ephesian Moment: At a Crossroads in Christian History," in *The Cross-Cultural Process in Christian History: Studies in the Transmission and Appropriation of Faith* (Maryknoll, NY: Orbis Books, 2002), 79.

The proper universality of the gospel is not one of a normative cultural and so social-political language that takes on different accents in different places. It is universal in the sense that every tribe, tongue, and nation can confess Jesus Christ as lord. He is the lord of *these* tribes, tongues and nations, and so their servant in such a way that they remain these tribes, tongues, and nations in all their difference from one another. The gospel becomes local and takes on local form, and is universal due to its very plurality of form. Legitimate diversity exists within the church, and this means contest concerning such things as doctrine, liturgy, structure, biblical authority, and leadership. Recognizing this impels us evermore toward meeting and engagement, to that spiritual and missionary attitude of seeking the faces of the other, inviting the other to see our faces, and celebrating in worship together.

Bibliography

Abraham, Susan. "What Does Mumbai Have to Do With Rome? Postcolonial Perspectives on Globalization and Theology." *Theological Studies* 69, no. 2 (2008): 376-93.
Arbuckle, Gerald A. *Culture, Inculturation, and Theologians: A Postmodern Critique.* Collegeville, MN: Liturgical Press, 2010.
Archbishop's Council on Mission and Public Affairs. *Mission-Shaped Church: Church Planting and Fresh Expressions of Church in a Changing Context.* London: Church House Publishing, 2004.
Arroyo, Jossianna. "Transculturation, Syncretism, and Hybridity Critical Terms." In *Caribbean and Latin American Thought: Historical and Institutional Trajectories*, edited by Yolanda Martínez-San Miguel, Ben Sifuentes-Jáuregui, and Marisa Belausteguigoitia, 133-44. New York: Palgrave Macmillan US, 2016.
Arrupe, Pedro. "Letter to the Whole Society on Inculturation." *Studies in the International Apostolate of Jesuits* 7 (1978): 1-9.
Asad, Talal. *Genealogies of Religion: Discipline and Reasons of Power in Christianity and Islam.* Baltimore: The Johns Hopkins University Press, 1993.
Balz, Heinrich. *Der Anfang des Glaubens: Theologie der Mission und der jungen Kirchen.* Neuendettelsau: Erlanger Verlag für Mission und Ökumene, 2010.
Begbie, Jeremy. "The Confessing Church and the Nazis: A Struggle for Theological Truth." *Anvil* 2 (1985): 117-30.
Bevans, Stephen B. *Models of Contextual Theology.* Maryknoll, NY: Orbis Books, 2002.
Blaser, Klauspeter. "Multicultural Christianity: A Project for Liberation; The Meaning of the Conflict North-South for Theology and Our Churches." *International Review of Mission* 82 (1993): 203-16.
Bonhoeffer, Dietrich. *Letters and Papers from Prison.* Minneapolis: Fortress Press, 2010.
Bridston, Keith R. *Mission, Myth and Reality.* New York: Friendship Press, 1965.
Broeck, Sabine, and Carsten Junker, eds. *Postcoloniality—Decoloniality—Black Critique: Joints and Fissures.* Frankfurt: Campus Verlag, 2015.
"The Calling of the Church to Mission and Unity." *The Ecumenical Review* 4 (1951): 66-71.
"The Cape Town Commitment: A Confession of Faith and a Call to Action." *International Bulletin of Missionary Research* 35 (2011): 59-80.

Carey, William. *An Enquiry into the Obligations of Christians, to Use Means for the Conversion of the Heathens, in Which the Religious State of the Different Nations of the World, the Success of Former Undertakings, and the Practicability of Further Undertakings, Are Considered.* Leicester: Ann Ireland, 1792.

Carvalhaes, Claudio. "Communitas: Liturgy and Identity." *International Review of Mission* 100 (2011): 37-47.

Castro, Emilio. "Bangkok, the New Opportunity." *International Review of Mission* 62 (1973): 136-43.

The Church for Others, and the Church for the World: A Quest for Structures for Missionary Congregations. Geneva: World Council of Churches, 1967.

Coe, Shoki. "In Search of Renewal in Theological Education." *Theological Education* 9 (1973): 233-43.

Congdon, David W. "Emancipatory Intercultural Hermeneutics: Interpreting Theo Sundermeier's Differenzhermeneutik." *Mission Studies* 33 (2016): 127-46.

Cullmann, Oscar. *Christ and Time: The Primitive Christian Conception of Time and History.* Philadelphia: Westminster Press, 1950.

Drescher, Hans-Georg. *Ernst Troeltsch: His Life and Work.* Minneapolis: Fortress Press, 1993.

Edwards, Wendy J. Deichmann. "Forging an Ideology for American Missions: Josiah Strong and Manifest Destiny." In *North American Foreign Missions, 1810-1914: Theology, Theory, and Policy*, edited by Wilbert R. Shenk, 163-91. Grand Rapids, MI: Eerdmans, 2004.

Feldtkeller, Andreas. *Die "Mutter der Kirchen" im "Haus des Islam": Gegenseitige Wahrnehmungen von arabischen Christen und Muslimen im West- und Ostjordanland.* Erlangen: Erlanger Verlag für Mission und Ökumene, 1998.

———. *Identitätssuche des syrischen Urchristentums: Mission, Inkulturation und Pluralität im ältesten Heidenchristentum.* Göttingen: Vandenhoeck & Ruprecht, 1993.

———. *Im Reich der Syrischen Göttin: Eine religiös plurale Kultur als Umwelt des frühen Christentums.* Gütersloh: Gütersloher Verlagshaus, 1994.

———. "Mission und Religionsfreiheit." *Zeitschrift für Mission* 28 (2002): 261-75.

———. "Missionswissenschaft und Interkulturelle Theologie: Eine Verhältnisbestimmung." *Theologische Literaturzeitung* 138 (2013): 3-12.

Flett, John G. *Apostolicity: The Ecumenical Question in World Christian Perspective.* Downers Grove, IL: IVP Academic, 2016.

———. "Method in Mission Studies: Comparing World Christianity and Intercultural Theology." *Theologische Literaturzeitung* 143 (2018): 717-31.

Freytag, Walter. "Changes in the Patterns of Western Missions." In *The Ghana Assembly of the International Missionary Council, 28th December, 1957 to 8th January, 1958: Selected papers, with an Essay on the Role of the I.M.C*, edited by Ronald Kenneth Orchard, 138-47. London: Edinburgh House Press, 1958.

———. "The Meaning and Purpose of the Christian Mission." *International Review of Missions* 39 (1950): 153-61.

———. "Mission im Blick aufs Ende." *Evangelische Missions Zeitschrift* 3 (1942): 321-33.

———. "Vom Sinn der Weltmission." In *Reden und Aufsätze*, edited by J. Hermelink and Hans Jochen Margull, 201-17. Munich: Chr. Kaiser Verlag, 1961.

Friedli, Richard. *Fremdheit als Heimat: Auf der Suche nach einem theologischen Kriterium für den Dialogue zwischen den Religionen*. Zurich: Theologischer Verlag, 1974.

———. "Intercultural Theology." In *Dictionary of Mission: Theology, History, Perspectives*, edited by Karl Müller, Theo Sundermeier, Stephen B. Bevans, and Richard H. Bliese, 219-22. Maryknoll, NY: Orbis Books, 1997.

———. "Kultur und kulturelle Vielfalt: Bemerkungen zur interkulturellen Übersetzung von Ex 3,14." In *Die Begnung mit dem Anderen: Plädozers für eine interkulturelle Hermeneutik*, edited by Theo Sundermeier, 29-38. Gütersloh: Gütersloher Verlagshaus Gerd Mohn, 1991.

Gensichen, Hans-Werner. "German Protestant Missions." In *Missionary Ideologies in the Imperialist Era, 1880-1920*, edited by Torben Christensen and William R. Hutchison, 181-90. Århus, Denmark: Aros, 1982.

———. "Grundfragen der Kirchwerdung in der Mission: Zur Gespräch mit J. C. Hoekendijk." *Evangelische Missions Zeitschrift* 8 (1951): 33-46.

———. "Knak, Siegfried." In *Biographical Dictionary of Christian Missions*, edited by Gerald H. Anderson, 371. Grand Rapids, MI: Eerdmans, 1998.

———. "My Pilgrimage in Mission." *International Bulletin of Missionary Research* 13 (1989): 167-69.

———. "Walter Freytag 1899-1959: The Miracle of the Church Among the Nations." In *Mission Legacies: Biographical Studies of Leaders of the Modern Missionary Movement*, edited by Gerald H. Anderson, Robert T. Coote, Norman A. Horner, and James M. Philips, 435-44. Maryknoll, NY: Orbis Books, 1994.

The Growing Church. London: International Missionary Council, 1938.

Gutmann, Bruno. *Freies Menschentum aus ewigen Bindungen*. Kassel: Bärenreiter-Verlag, 1928.

———. "Urtümliche Bindungen und Sünde." *Neue Allgemeine Missions-Zeitschrift* (1934): 20-31.

Hartenstein, Karl. "Adaptation or Revolution." *The Student World* 28 (1935): 308-27.

———. *Die Mission als theologisches Problem: Beiträge zum grundsätzlichen Verständnis der Mission*. Berlin: Furche Verlag, 1932.

———. "Was hat die Theologie Karl Barths der Mission zu Sagen?" *Zwischen den Zeiten* 6 (1928): 59-83.

———. "Wozu nötigt die Finanzlage der Mission." *Evangelisches Missions-Magazin* 79 (1934): 217-29.

Hassing, P. "Bruno Gutmann of Kilimanjaro: Setting the Record Straight." *Missiology* 7 (1979): 423-33.

Herskovits, Melville J. *Man and His Works: The Science of Cultural Anthropology*. New York: Knopf, 1948.
Hinkelammert, Franz J. *Kritik der utopischen Vernunft: Eine Auseinandersetzung mit den Hauptströmungen der modernen Gesellschaftstheorie*. Mainz: Matthias-Grünewald, 1994.
Hockenos, Matthew. "The Church Struggle and the Confessing Church: An Introduction to Bonhoeffer's Context." *Studies in Christian-Jewish Relations* 2 (2007): 1-20.
Hocking, William Ernest. *Re-thinking Missions: A Laymen's Inquiry After One Hundred Years*. New York: Harper and Brothers, 1932.
Hoedemaker, L. A. "The Legacy of J. C. Hoekendijk." *International Bulletin of Missionary Research* 19 (1995): 166-70.
Hoekendijk, J. C. "Zur Frage einer missionarischen Existenz." In *Kirche und Volk in der deutschen Missionswissenschaft*, 297-354. Munich: Chr. Kaiser Verlag, 1967.
Hollenweger, Walter J. "Die Kirche für andere—ein Mythos." *Evangelische Theologie* 37 (1977): 425-43.
Hutchison, William R. "American Missionary Ideologies: 'Activism' as Theory, Practice and Stereotype." In *Continuity and Discontinuity in Church History*, edited by F. Forrester Church and Timothy George, 351-62. Leiden: Brill, 1979.
———. *Errand to the World: American Protestant Thought and Foreign Missions*. Chicago: University of Chicago, 1987.
Jäschke, Ernst. "Bruno Gutmann 1876–1966: Building on Clan, Neighborhood and Age Groups." In *Mission Legacies: Biographical Studies of Leaders of the Modern Missionary Movement*, edited by Gerald H. Anderson, Robert T. Coote, Norman A. Horner, and James M. Philips, 173-80. Maryknoll, NY: Orbis Books, 1994.
John Paul II. *Redemptoris Missio: On the Permanent Validity of the Church's Missionary Mandate*. Washington, DC: United States Catholic Conference, 1990.
Kasdorf, Hans. "The Legacy of Gustav Warneck." *International Bulletin of Mission Research* 4 (1980): 102-7.
Keysser, Christian. *A People Reborn*. Pasadena, CA: William Carey Library, 1980.
Knak, Siegfried. "The Characteristics of German Evangelical Missions in Theory and Practice." In *Evangelism*, edited by John Merle Davis and Kenneth G. Grubb, 289-356. New York: International Missionary Council, 1939.
———. "Mission und Kirche im Dritten Reich." In *Das Buch der deutschen Weltmission*, edited by Julius Richter, 240-44. Gotha: Leopold Klotz Verlag, 1935.
———. "Totalitätsanspruch des Staates und der Totalitätsanspruch Gottes an die Völker." *Neue Allgemeine Missions-Zeitschrift* 10 (1933): 401-21.
Koyama, Kosuke. "New World—New Creation: Mission in Power and Faith." *Mission Studies* 10 (1993): 59-77.
Krusche, Werner. "Parish Structure—A Hindrance to Mission? A Survey and Evaluation of the Ecumenical Discussion on the Structures of the Missionary Congregation." In

Sources for Change: Searching for Flexible Church Structures, edited by Herbert T. Neve, 51-100. Geneva: World Council of Churches, 1968.

Latourette, Kenneth Scott. *A History of Christianity*. New York: Harper & Brothers, 1953.

Leuenberger, R. "Zum Problem der Volkskirche." *Reformatio* 26 (1977): 10-33.

Lienemann-Perrin, Christine. "Mission in der Zeitenwende." In *Das Christentum an der Schwelle zum 3. Jahrtausend. Erfahrungsgehalte der jüdisch-christlichen Tradition angesichts von Schwellensituationen und Jahrtausendwechseln*, edited by Albrecht Grözinger and Ekkehard Stegemann, 151-66. Stuttgart: Verlag W. Kohlhammer, 2002.

———. *Training for a Relevant Ministry: A Study of the Contribution of the Theological Education Fund*. Geneva: Christian Literature Society, World Council of Churches, 1981.

Lienemann-Perrin, Christine, and James R. Cochrane, eds. *The Church and the Public Sphere in Societies in Transition*. Pietermaritzburg: Cluster, 2013.

Lienemann-Perrin, Christine, and Wolfgang Lienemann, eds. *Religiöse Grenzüberschreitungen: Studien zu Bekehrung, Konfessions- und Religionswechsel*. Wiesbaden: Harrassowitz, 2012.

Lienemann-Perrin, Christine, Atola Longkumer, and Afrie S. Joye, eds. *Putting Names with Faces: Women's Impact in Mission History*. Nashville: Abingdon Press, 2012.

Linz, Manfred. *Anwalt der Welt: Zur Theologie der Mission*. Stuttgart: Kreuz-Verlag, 1964.

Maluleke, Tinyiko Sam. "Christ in Africa: The Influence of Multi-culturity on the Experience of Christ." *Journal of Black Theology in South Africa* 8 (1994): 49-64.

Margull, Hans J. *Hope in Action: The Church's Task in the World*. Translated by Eugene Peters. Philadelphia: Muhlenberg Press, 1962.

———. *Theologie der missionarischen Verkündigung: Evangelisation als ökumenisches Problem*. Stuttgart: Evangelisches Verlagswerk, 1959.

———. "Verwundbarkeit." *Evangelische Theologie* 34 (1974): 410-20.

———. *Zeugnis und Dialog: Ausgewählte Schriften*. Ammersbek bei Hamburg: Verlag an der Lottbek, 1992.

Marhold, Wolfgang. *Fragende Kirche: Über Methode und Funktion kirchlicher Meinungsumfragen*. Munich: Chr. Kaiser Verlag, 1971.

Mbembe, Achille. *Critique of Black Reason*. Durham, NC: Duke University Press, 2017.

McGavran, Donald A. *The Bridges of God: A Study in the Strategy of Missions*. London: World Dominion Press, 1955.

———. Foreword to *A People Reborn*, by Christian Keysser, viii-xxiii. Pasadena, CA: William Carey Library, 1980.

———. "Will Uppsala Betray the Two Billion?" In *The Conciliar-Evangelical Debate: The Crucial Documents, 1964–1976*, edited by Donald A. McGavran, 233-41. Pasadena, CA: William Carey Library, 1977.

Mead, Margaret. "Socialization and Enculturation." *Current Anthropology* 4 (1963): 184-88.

Mignolo, Walter D. *Epistemischer Ungehorsam: Rhetorik der Moderne, Logik der Kolonialität und Grammatik der Dekolonialität*. Wien: Turia + Kant, 2016.

"Mission Studies as Intercultural Theology and Its Relationship to Religious Studies." *Mission Studies* 25 (2008): 103-8.

Moreau, A. Scott. *Contextualization in World Missions: Mapping and Assessing Evangelical Models*. Grand Rapids, MI: Kregel Publications, 2012.

———. "Contextualization That Is Comprehensive." *Missiology* 34 (2006): 325-35.

Mott, John R. "Closing Address." In *World Missionary Conference, 1910: The History and Records of the Conference, Together with Addresses Delivered at the Evening Meetings*, edited by Robert E. Speer, 347-51. Edinburgh: Oliphant, Anderson and Ferrier, 1910.

Muni, S. D. "The Third World: Concept and Controversy." *Third World Quarterly* 1 (1979): 119-28.

Neill, Stephen. *Colonialism and Christian Missions*. New York: McGraw-Hill, 1966.

———. *The Unfinished Task*. London: Edinburgh House Press, 1957.

Newbigin, J. E. Lesslie. "Integration—Some Personal Reflections 1981." *International Review of Mission* 70 (1981): 247-55.

Ntombana, Luvuyo. "The Trajectories of Christianity and African Ritual Practices: The Public Silence and the Dilemma of Mainline or Mission Churches." *Acta Theologica* 35 (2015): 104-19.

Oborji, Francis Anekwe. "Missiology in Its Relation to Intercultural Theology and Religious Studies." *Mission Studies* 25 (2008): 113-14.

Oduyoye, Mercy Amba. *Hearing and Knowing: Theological Reflections on Christianity in Africa*. Maryknoll, NY: Orbis Books, 1986.

Ortiz, Fernando. *Cuban Counterpoint: Tobacco and Sugar*. Durham, NC: Duke University Press, 1995.

The Pasadena Consultation: Homogeneous Unit Principle. Wheaton, IL: Lausanne Committee for World Evangelization, 1978.

Phan, Peter C. "World Christianity and Christian Mission: Are They Compatible? Insights from the Asian Churches." *Asian Christian Review* 1 (2007): 14-31.

Pierard, Richard V. "Völkisch Thought and Christian Missions in Early Twentieth Century Germany." In *Essays in Religious Studies for Andrew Walls*, edited by James Thrower, 138-49. Aberdeen: Department of Religious Studies, University of Aberdeen, 1986.

Ratzinger, Joseph. "In the Encounter of Christianity and Religions, Syncretism Is Not the Goal." *L'Osservatore Romano (weekly edition)*, April 26, 1995.

Redfield, Robert, Ralph Linton, and Melville J. Herskovits. "Memorandum for the Study of Acculturation." *American Anthropologist* 38 (1936): 149-52.

Richter, Julius. *In der Krisis der Weltmission*. Gütersloh: Bertelsmann, 1934.

———. "Mission: Evangelische Mission." In *Die Religion in Geschichte und Gegenwart: Handwörterbuch im gemeinverständlicher Darstellung*, edited by Hermann Gunkel and Leopold Zscharnack, 41-47. Tübingen: J. C. B. Mohr, 1930.

"Richtlinien der Glaubensbewegung 'Deutsche Christen' 1932/1933." In *Kirchen- und Theologiegeschichte in Quellen*, vol. 4, *Neuzeit*, edited by Heiko Augustinus Oberman, Adolf Martin Ritter, and HansWalter Krumwiede, 117-21. Neukirchen-Vluyn: Neukirchener Verlag, 1977.

Roxborogh, John. "Loyalty to Christ: Conversion, Contextualization, and Religious Syncretism." *Point Series* 40 (2016): 318-30.

Rynkiewich, Michael A. "The World in My Parish: Rethinking the Standard Missiological Model." *Missiology* 30 (2002): 301-22.

Schmidt, Norbert. "Kontextualisierung und Ethnotheologie: Gedanken aus der Perspektive eines missionierten Landes." *Theologische Beiträge* 28 (1997): 103-14.

Schomerus, Hilko Wiardo. "Die Mission und das Volkstum." In *Missionswissenschaft*, 136-49. Leipzig: Verlag Quelle und Meyer, 1935.

Schreiter, Robert J. "Contextualization from a World Perspective." *Journal of Theology (United Theological Seminary)* 97 (1993): 97.

———. *Reconciliation: Mission and Ministry in a Changing Social Order*. Maryknoll, NY: Orbis Books, 1992.

Schuster, Jürgen. "Karl Hartenstein: Mission with a Focus on the End." *Mission Studies* 19 (2002): 53-79.

Schwarz, Gerold. "Karl Hartenstein 1894-1954: Missions with a Focus on 'The End.'" In *Mission Legacies: Biographical Studies of Leaders of the Modern Missionary Movement*, edited by Gerald H. Anderson, Robert T. Coote, Norman A. Horner, and James M. Philips, 591-601. Maryknoll, NY: Orbis Books, 1994.

Schweyer, Stefan. *Kontextuelle Kirchentheorie: Eine kritisch konstruktive Auseinandersetzung mit dem Kirchenverständnis neuerer praktisch-theologischer Entwürfe*. Zurich: TVZ Theologischer Verlag, 2007.

Shorter, Aylward. *Jesus and the Witchdoctor: Approach to Healing and Wholeness*. Maryknoll, NY: Orbis Books, 1985.

———. *Towards a Theology of Inculturation*. Maryknoll, NY: Orbis Books, 1988.

Slenczka, Notger. "Kontext und Theologie: Ein kritischer Versuch zum Programm einer 'kontextuellen Theologie.'" *Neue Zeitschrift für systematische Theologie und Religionsphilosophie* 35 (1993): 303-31.

Spivak, Gayatri Chakravorty. *A Critique of Postcolonial Reason: Toward a History of the Vanishing Present*. Cambridge MA: Harvard University Press, 1999.

"A Statement by Some Members of the Meeting: Presented by the Chairman of the German Delegation." In *The Authority of the Faith*, edited by John Merle Davis and Kenneth G. Grubb, 183-85. London: Oxford University Press, 1939.

Sundermeier, Theo. "Convivence: The Concept and Origin." *Scriptura* 10 (1992): 68-80.

———. "Erwägungen zu einer Hermeneutik interkulturellen Verstehens." In *Begegnung mit dem Anderen: Plädoyers für eine interkulturelle Hermeneutik*, 13-28. Gütersloher Verlag: Gütersloh, 1991.

―――. "Gensichen, Hans-Werner." In *Biographical Dictionary of Christian Missions*, edited by Gerald H. Anderson, 238. Grand Rapids, MI: Eerdmans, 1998.

―――. "Konvivenz als Grundstruktur ökumenischer Existenz heute." In *Ökumenische Existenz heute*, edited by W. Huber, D. Ritschl, and Theo Sundermeier, 49-100. München: Chr. Kaiser Verlag, 1986.

―――. "My Pilgrimage in Mission." *International Bulletin of Missionary Research* 31 (2007): 200-202.

Tofaeono, Ama'amalele. "Behold the Pig of God: Mystery of Christ's Sacrifice in the Context of Melanesia–Oceania." *Pacific Journal of Theology* 33 (2005): 82-101.

Troeltsch, Ernst. "Die Mission in der modernen Welt." *Die christliche Welt* 20 (1906): 8-12.

―――. "Missionsmotiv, Missionsaufgabe und neuzeitliches Humanitätschristentum." *Zeitschrift für Missions und Religionswissenschaft* 22 (1907): 129-39, 161.

Tylor, Edward Burnett. *Primitive Culture: Researches into the Development of Mythology, Philosophy, Religion, Art, and Custom*. J. Murray, 1871.

Ukwuegbu, Bernard. "'Neither Jew nor Greek': The Church in Africa and the Quest for Self-Understanding in the Light of the Pauline Vision and Today's Context of Cultural Pluralism." *International Journal for the Study of the Christian Church* 8 (2008): 305-18.

Ustorf, Werner. "The Cultural Origins of 'Intercultural Theology.'" *Mission Studies* 25, no. 2 (2008): 229-51.

―――. *Sailing on the Next Tide: Missions, Missiology, and the Third Reich*. Frankfurt am Main: Peter Lang, 2000.

―――. "'Survival of the Fittest': German Protestant Missions, Nazism and Neocolonialism, 1933–1945." *Journal of Religion in Africa* 28 (1998): 93-114.

Visser 't Hooft, W. A. "Accommodation—True and False." *South East Asia Journal of Theology* 8 (1967): 5-18.

Walls, Andrew F. "The Ephesian Moment: At a Crossroads in Christian History." In *The Cross-Cultural Process in Christian History: Studies in the Transmission and Appropriation of Faith*, 72-81. Maryknoll, NY: Orbis Books, 2002.

Walz, Heike. "Kritik der europäischen Vernunft? Herausforderungen für die Interkulturelle Theologie aus Lateinamerika und Afrika." *Interkulturelle Theologie* 42 (2015): 261-83.

Warneck, Gustav. "Die cur hie? Unser Programm." *Allgemeine Missions-Zeitschrift* 1 (1874): 3-10.

―――. *Evangelische Missionslehre: Ein missionstheoretischer Versuch*. Gotha: Friedrich Andreas Perthes, 1897, 1905.

―――. "Der Missionsbefehl als Missionsinstruction." *Allgemeine Missions-Zeitschrift* 1 (1897): 41-49, 89.

―――. "Missionsmotiv und Missionsaufgabe nach der modernen religionsgeschichtlichen Schule." *Allgemeine Missions-Zeitschrift* 34 (1907): 3-15, 49.

―――. "Die moderne Weltevangelismus-theorie." *Allgemeine Missions-Zeitschrift* 24 (1897): 305-25.

———. *Outline of a History of Protestant Missions from the Reformation to the Present Time.* New York: Fleming H. Revell, 1906.

———. "Thoughts on the Missionary Century." *Missionary Review of the World* 23 (1900): 413-17.

Warren, Max A. "The Christian Mission and the Cross." In *Missions Under the Cross*, edited by Norman Goodall, 24-45. London: Edinburgh House Press, 1953.

———. "Why Missionary Societies and Not Missionary Churches?" *Student World* 53 (1960): 149-56.

Whiteman, Darrell L. "Contextualization: The Theory, the Gap, the Challenge." *International Bulletin of Missionary Research* 21 (1997): 2-7.

Wrogemann, Henning. "Interkulturelle Theologie—Zu Definition und Gegenstandsbereich des sechsten Faches der Theologischen Fakultät." *Berliner Theologische Zeitschrift* 32 (2015): 219-39.

Yates, Timothy. *Christian Mission in the Twentieth Century.* Cambridge: Cambridge University Press, 1994.

Finding the Textbook You Need

The IVP Academic Textbook Selector
is an online tool for instantly finding the IVP books
suitable for over 250 courses across 24 disciplines.

ivpacademic.com

www.ingramcontent.com/pod-product-compliance
Lightning Source LLC
Chambersburg PA
CBHW030439300426
44112CB00009B/1075